Mother of Invention

How Good Ideas Get Ignored
in a World Built for Men

KATRINE MARÇAL

Translated By Alex Fleming

WILLIAM
COLLINS

William Collins
An imprint of HarperCollins*Publishers*
1 London Bridge Street
London SE1 9GF

WilliamCollinsBooks.com

HarperCollins*Publishers*
1st Floor, Watermarque Building, Ringsend Road
Dublin 4, Ireland

First published in Great Britain in 2021 by William Collins

This William Collins paperback edition published in 2022

1

Typeset by Palimpsest Book Production Ltd, Falkirk, Stirlingshire

Printed and bound in the UK using 100% renewable electricity
at CPI Group (UK) Ltd

MIX
Paper from
responsible sources
FSC™ C007454

This book is produced from independently certified FSC™ paper
to ensure responsible forest management.

For more information visit: www.harpercollins.co.uk/green

To Guy

Contents

INVENTIONS

TECHNOLOGY

FEMININITY

INVENTIONS

1

In which we invent the wheel and, after 5,000 years, manage to attach it to a suitcase

Bernard Sadow was a Massachusetts family man employed in the luggage industry – someone paid to sit at his desk, day in day out, and think about the business of suitcases. In his forties, he was now vice president at US Luggage, and not bad at his job.

It was 1970, and Sadow was on his way back home after a holiday with his wife and children in Aruba. In the winter months, this Dutch island in the Caribbean was favoured by affluent Americans searching for a warmer climate.

Sadow stepped out of the car outside the small airport and grabbed hold of his family's suitcases. A 70 centimetre suitcase could hold around 200 litres of luggage and weigh up to 25 kilos, so with one in each hand he could just about balance the weight and waddle his way over to check-in.

This was back in the day when it was possible to show up at the terminal 20 minutes before take-off. The 30-odd hijackings that took place in the USA each year hadn't yet led to the introduction of metal detectors, or staff hired to prevent you from boarding the plane with a gun in your back pocket.

By contrast, the problem that Sadow faced on this homeward journey was one that many of the world's major airports had appointed dedicated task forces to solve. Passengers would get sweaty and irritated at having to lug their suitcases in and out of departure lounges and through ever-expanding terminals.

But there was help at hand: for a small fee, porters would take care of your bags, the only alternative being a complex network of trolleys. Porters, however, were far from ubiquitous, and in order to access the trolley system, you first had to find it, so Sadow did what most people tended to do: he picked up his family's suitcases and started to carry them.

But why?

That was the question Sadow would come to ask himself that day, and it would change his industry for ever.

While queuing at customs, Sadow noticed a man who presumably worked at the airport. He was moving a heavy machine on a wheeled pallet. As the man quickly manoeuvred around him, the businessman spotted the four wheels rolling across the airport floor. Sadow looked down at his own hands, white-knuckled from their grip on the suitcases, and suddenly said to his wife: 'I know what luggage needs: wheels!'

When he got home to Massachusetts, he unscrewed four castors from a wardrobe and fixed them to a suitcase. Then he put a strap on his contraption and trotted it gleefully around the house. This was the future. And he had invented it.

All of this happened barely one year after NASA had launched three astronauts into space in the biggest rocket ever built. With millions of litres of kerosene, liquid oxygen and liquid hydrogen as fuel, Apollo 11 had blasted itself free of the earth's gravitational pull. Hurtling through space at a speed of 20,000 miles per hour, the astronauts had entered the weaker orbit of the moon, cruised through the windless darkness and taken humankind's first steps on a powdery moondust that smelled of used fireworks.

Yet when Neil Armstrong, Buzz Aldrin and Michael Collins returned to earth, they picked up their suitcases by their handles, carrying their luggage as it had been carried since the birth of the modern suitcase in the mid-nineteenth century. The question, then, is not why it occurred to Bernard Sadow that suitcases should have wheels. The question is: why it had never occurred to us before?

———————

The wheel is considered one of humanity's most fundamental inventions. Without the wheel there are no carts, cars or trains, no waterwheels for water power, and no potter's wheels on which to make jugs to carry said water in. Without the wheel we have no cogwheels, jet engines or centrifuges, no pushchairs, bicycles or conveyor belts. But before the wheel there was the circle.

The world's first circle was probably drawn in the sand with a stick. Perhaps someone might have seen the moon, or the sun, and decided to replicate their shapes. Cut the stalk from a flower and you have a circle. Chop a tree and you're met by its annual rings. Throw a stone into a lake and you see its ripples expand on the water. The circle is a shape that comes up time and again in nature – from cells to bacteria, pupils to celestial bodies. And outside of every circle you can always draw another. This, in itself, is the primary mystery of space.

For the human body, however, the circle is not natural. Your dental hygienist tells you to brush your teeth in small circular motions, but you don't: you scrub them back and forth. The human arm prefers straight lines. This is because of the way our muscles are positioned, and the system of tendons and muscular attachments that connects them to our bones. No part of the human body can rotate 360 degrees: not your wrist, nor your ankle, nor your arm. We invented the wheel to accomplish that which our physical form cannot.

Historians long considered the world's first wheel to have been made in Mesopotamia. It was a round potter's wheel, which is to say it was not used for transport. But today some scholars believe that miners were carting copper ores through tunnels in the Carpathian Mountains long before the Mesopotamians started throwing pots on circular discs. The world's oldest wheel still in existence is 5,000 years old. It was unearthed in Slovenia, about 20 kilometres south of Ljubljana. In other words, the technology that Bernard Sadow realised he could apply to his suitcase problem was at least five millennia old.

The patent for his invention came two years later, in 1972. In his application, he wrote: 'The luggage actually glides . . . any person, regardless of size, strength or age, can easily pull the luggage along without effort or strain.'

Similar patents for suitcases on wheels did in fact already exist, but Bernard Sadow wasn't aware of this when the idea first occurred to him. He was the first person to turn the idea into a commercially successful product, and is therefore considered the father of the wheeled suitcase; but why it took a whole 5,000 years to reach this point is more difficult to explain.

The wheeled suitcase has become an archetypal example

of how innovation can be a very slow-footed thing. The 'blindingly obvious' can stare us expectantly in the face for an eternity before it actually occurs to us to make something of it.

Robert Shiller, a winner of the Nobel Prize for Economics, has suggested that many inventions take time to catch on precisely because a good idea alone won't cut it. Society at large must also recognise the usefulness of the idea. The market doesn't always know what's best for itself, and in this particular case, people just didn't see the point of wheels on suitcases. Sadow presented his product to buyers from almost all of the USA's major department stores, and initially all of them rejected it.

It wasn't that they thought the idea of a suitcase on wheels was a bad one. They just didn't think anyone would want to buy the product. A suitcase was for carrying, not for trailing around on wheels.

'Everybody I took it to threw me out,' he would later recount. 'They thought I was crazy.'

Eventually the new product came to the attention of Jerry Levy, vice president at department-store chain Macy's. He towed it around in his office, then called in the buyer who had originally rejected it and gave him the order to buy it. This proved a wise move. Soon Macy's were marketing the new suitcase using the very wording from Sadow's patent application: 'The Luggage That Glides'. And nowadays it is of course impossible to imagine a world in which suitcases on wheels are anything but standard.

Robert Shiller argues that this is easy to say in hindsight. He notes that inventor John Allan May had in fact attempted to sell a suitcase on wheels some four decades before Sadow. May had noticed that over the course of human history, humanity had put wheels on increasingly diverse objects: cannons, carts, wheelbarrows – essentially anything that could be classed as heavy. A suitcase on wheels was just a natural continuation of that logic. 'Why not make *full* use of the wheel?' he asked, when he presented his idea to over 100 different groups of people. But no one took him seriously. In fact, they laughed in his face. Make full use of the wheel? Why not just fit people with wheels? Then *we* could roll! Practical, no?

John Allan May never did sell any suitcases.

Economists tend to work from an assumption that humans act rationally. But in reality we overestimate ourselves, often taking it as given that all the good inventions have already been made. By extension, we tend to reject new ideas that we perceive as being too 'simple' or 'obvious'. We imagine that the technology we have at our fingertips is the best currently possible, which is a reasonable assumption in our everyday lives. If refrigerators open from the front and cars are manoeuvred by a steering wheel, there must be a good reason for it, we think. This, however, is the very thinking that makes us miss obvious things like putting wheels on suitcases.

Robert Shiller clearly can't let the matter go; it comes up time and again in his writing. In his book *Narrative Economics* the famous economist suggests that our resistance to rolling suitcases can be explained by group pressure, which often plays a role in the scepticism surrounding newfangled ideas. We will happily assume that if no one else – especially no one we perceive as successful – is doing something, there must be a deep-rooted, rational reason why we shouldn't, either. What if it's harmful – or even dangerous? In short, better the devil you know. If no one else is rolling their suitcases then there's no point even going there. This way of thinking can hold us back. Shiller, however, wasn't entirely satisfied with this explanation. The issue of the wheeled suitcase is a thorny one: why would we insist on lugging our suitcases, when wheeling them is so much easier?

Nassim Taleb is another world-renowned thinker who has pondered the mystery of the rolling suitcase. Having lugged heavy suitcases through airports and railway stations for years, he was astonished by his own unquestioning acceptance of the status quo. He went on to investigate this phenomenon in his book *Antifragile*.

Taleb sees our incapacity to put wheels on suitcases as a parable of how we often tend to ignore the simplest solutions. As humans, we strive for the difficult, grandiose and complex. Technology like wheels on suitcases may appear obvious in hindsight, but that doesn't mean it was obvious before.

Similarly, there is no guarantee that a new technology will be utilised, just because it has been invented. After all, it took 5,000 years for us to put wheels on a suitcase – an unusually long time in context, perhaps. But in medicine, for example, it isn't at all uncommon for decades to pass between a discovery being made and the resulting product reaching the market. Among many other factors, seeing a new technology's potential requires the right person to be in the right place at the right time. In many cases, not even the inventor is fully aware of the implications of what they have invented. It often takes someone else coming in and having a look to see how it could be applied, someone with an instinctive grasp of how the new technology can be turned into a product.

And if no one with that type of competence appears, more often than not nothing will come of the invention. A great many things can remain 'half-invented' for centuries, Taleb suggests. We may have the idea, but we don't know what to do with it.

'Why aren't you doing anything with this? This is the greatest thing!' cried a 24-year-old Steve Jobs after seeing a pointer move across a computer screen for the first time. This was at Xerox Parc, a commercial research centre in California that was home to some of the world's best data engineers and programmers in the 1970s. Jobs had managed to talk himself into a tour of the legendary centre in exchange for offering Xerox the chance to buy 100,000 shares in Apple for $1 million. This turned out to be a bad deal. For Xerox.

The cause of Jobs' delight was a plastic gadget called a 'mouse', which one of the engineers on the tour had used to move a pointer across a computer screen. On that screen 'icons' appeared that opened and closed 'windows'. Crucially, the engineer wasn't operating the computer with written commands, but with clicks. In other words, Xerox had invented both the mouse and the modern graphical user interface. The only problem was that they didn't see what they had stumbled across.

Jobs, however, did.

Jobs took the idea of the mouse and the graphical user interface back to Apple, and on 24 January 1984 the company launched its Macintosh, the machine that would come to define what we mean by a 'personal computer'.

With the simple click of a mouse, you could put things into 'files' that you saw on the screen in the form of icons. Apple's Macintoshes cost $2,495 apiece, and they would come to change the world. Jobs' insight was to realise that the mouse Xerox had shown him was more than just a button and a wire: it was the device that would get normal people to start using computers. Had Jobs never visited Xerox that day, who knows, we might have had to wait 5,000 years for the modern PC. This is precisely Taleb's point: innovations aren't nearly as obvious as they appear in hindsight. Steve Jobs was a pretty exceptional person, after all: not many people have his talent for seeing how new technology can be transformed into products.

In a similar way, we tend to think that the invention of the wheel immediately revolutionised the world. For the wheel is, of course, a work of genius. With it, people could reduce friction, create leverage, and transport the previously immovable.

We imagine that someone, all those thousands of years ago, had a sudden eureka moment, then ran back to her village and gleefully told her peers about the brainwave she had had when seeing tree trunks rolling in the forest. Her fellow villagers would have looked on in shock and awe as she described her idea, knowing that from that moment on, nothing in their lives would ever be the same. Everything would be on wheels.

Spoiler: that's not how things went. In fact, for a long time the wheel was one of those brilliant ideas that was great on paper, less great in practice.

A bit like ladder-proof tights.

In the Roman Empire's heyday, Roman legionaries with shields and plumed helmets marched all the way from Rome to Brindisi and from Albania to Istanbul, traversing an empire bound together by its roads of stone. The Roman roads were ideal for men parading around in sandals. Less so, however, for transportation on wheels.

That's because, when building their roads, the Romans

laid large, flat stone slabs onto layers of concrete that in turn rested on small, loose stones. When horse-drawn carriages trundled along them, their iron-rimmed wheels drove ruts into the emperor's expensively laid slabs, much to his chagrin. So the powers that be did what they often do in such situations: they regulated. The emperor set load limits for wheeled carriages, and they weren't generous.

Over the centuries, the Roman system was gradually turned upside down, with big stone slabs supporting the smaller round stones on top. This meant that wheeled vehicles could suddenly weigh much more without destroying the very fabric of the roads they were travelling on. But this system wasn't without its own problems. When carriage wheels rolled over the surface, the small stones would be pushed out towards the sides of roads. This left them in need of constant maintenance, which was both expensive and problematic. All of a sudden, new processes like road-maintenance systems were urgently needed just to make it all work – but who would ensure that maintenance was done?

It was only in the eighteenth century, when Scottish inventor John McAdam realised that the small stones should instead be angular, that the wheel had its breakthrough in Europe. Unlike round stones, which were jostled outwards by the cartwheels, angular stones were pressed together, meaning that McAdam's roads remained flat.

But there was a but. You see, the small stones in his system had to be exactly the right size in order for this to happen. As a result, labourers were positioned along the sides of the roads and tasked with breaking the stones into exactly the right sort of pieces. Many of these workers were women and children. For the wheel to revolutionise the world, the world had to first adapt to the wheel. And that took time. Not to mention some very labour-intensive work.

Sometimes it wasn't even worth trying. In the Middle East, camels were long favoured over wheels as a means of transportation. This was an economic decision: camels were significantly cheaper to run, trudging on day by day with 250 kilos on their backs, fuelled by just a handful of prickly twigs and dry leaves that they chewed for hours on end. Their routes didn't have to be laid with small stones of just the right angularity, because the camels moved freely across the sand. This is often how it goes with innovation: the new technology might well be *the greatest thing*, but it isn't always economical. Still, it's hard to imagine any such economic explanation as to why the wheel only made it onto our suitcases in 1972.

For a long time leisure travel was a pursuit reserved largely for the wealthy. Young nobles would have their belongings packed up in trunks big as wardrobes and set out on formative tours to Paris, Vienna and Venice. Naturally, when you had servants to lug around your every possession, you had little need for a suitcase on wheels.

The journeys themselves were also of quite a different ilk. In *The Emigrants*, Vilhelm Moberg's classic series of novels about a hard-up Swedish family who set out for America in search of a better life, the protagonists stuff their worldly possessions, clothes and carpentry tools into hulking great cases made of metal, wood and leather. These 'America trunks', as they came to be known in Sweden, were built to withstand long boat journeys, not for ease of transportation. Besides, wheels had little use when a return to Sweden was never on the cards.

In fact, what we would now call a suitcase only came into

being at the end of the nineteenth century, with the dawn of modern mass tourism. It was to the whistle of trains and the honk of steamboats that people first started travelling for pleasure, and they did so with a new type of bag. This bag's innovation sat atop it for all to see: the handle. This is what distinguished the modern suitcase from its predecessors – the fact that it could be carried in just one hand.

When travel first started to take off, Europe's major railway stations were inundated with a swell of porters, who would help passengers with their bags. But by the middle of the twentieth century the porters were dwindling in number, and so passengers increasingly carried their own luggage, or used luggage trolleys.

In 1961, British society magazine *Tatler* published a feature on the problem. As they saw it, the products on the market were simply not fit for purpose in this new age, and the luggage industry had to come up with something new. This was, after all, an era and economy in which people (yes, even *Tatler* readers) increasingly had to haul their own luggage. You would be sweating like a pig before you even got to customs in Madrid, the magazine declared. Something had to be done.

Many suitcases on the market were fitted with handles made of high-quality leather, but these still cut 'tramlines' into your hands, according to *Tatler*. After walking the 200 metres to change trains at the Spanish border, you would have half a mind to give up. This was a huge problem for the new generation of globetrotters. So *Tatler* rolled up its sleeves and did its bit, testing out new suitcase models to see how comfortable they were to carry.

Naturally you could buy your suitcase at Harrods, they wrote. That would simplify your travel. The illustrious British department store stocked a luxury suitcase that *Tatler* said had one of the most comfortable handles on the market. But, as we know, good taste doesn't come cheap. *Tatler* therefore urged the industry to focus on innovation in terms of design. New handles in cutting-edge materials were the great hope – though surely it wasn't too much to ask that the 'cutting edge' be of the less literal variety?

Wheels, however, were not on *Tatler*'s radar. That same year – 1961 – Soviet cosmonaut Yuri Gagarin became the first human in space. We could launch people up into orbit, yet apparently we couldn't conceive of wheels on suitcases. This is when things start to get really puzzling.

In fact, advertisements for products applying the technology of the wheel to the suitcase can be found in British newspapers as early as the 1940s. These aren't suitcases on wheels, exactly, but a gadget known as 'the portable porter': a wheeled device that could be strapped onto your suitcase so that you could roll it. In other words, a commercial product existed that made it possible to build your own wheeled suitcase. So why didn't this idea catch on?

The new wheel-strap device had its first sighting at a railway station in Coventry in 1948. It was reported by the local newspaper as a sensation. According to the article, a porter hurried down the platform to aid a 'pretty, slightly built brunette' with her big, heavy suitcase. 'No thanks – I'll carry it myself,' she replied. Then she bent down, took the khaki-coloured strap and triumphantly trundled her newly wheeled suitcase towards the waiting train. People were peering out of the train windows to catch a glimpse, the article reported, alongside a suspiciously well-composed image of the woman in question on the platform.

To a modern reader this bears all the hallmarks of some

sort of PR coup. The company that had patented the product also just happened to hail from Coventry, and both inventors were quoted in the newspaper. They saw a bright future for their innovative idea, especially 'in these days of man-power shortage'.

But now we come to our mystery's first clue. You see, that news story about the woman gliding her suitcase along the railway platform is actually found in a section of *The Coventry Evening Telegraph* entitled 'Women and the Home', next to some impeccably English cooking tips ('Margarine mixed with finely grated or chopped raw vegetables . . . makes an excellent sandwich spread'). The implication here is that only women needed to roll their suitcases. Men, on the other hand, could just as well carry them. Men have, on average, 40 to 60 per cent more upper-body strength than women, and when carrying a suitcase it's your arms, back and shoulders that take the brunt of the weight. Generally – though not always – this makes it harder for women.

For both of the Coventry inventors, it went without saying that their new product was primarily intended for the ladies. The inventors even went on to produce an actual suitcase on wheels, drawing the not-too-outlandish conclusion that if wheels could be strapped onto a suitcase by a customer, they could also be fitted there by the company from the start. In doing so, they actually manufactured a wheeled suitcase long before Bernard Sadow even thought to. But this was a niche, inexpensive product for English women, and it didn't catch on. That a product for women could make life easier for men and transform the global luggage market was not an idea that the world of the 1960s was ready to entertain.

In 1967, a Leicestershire woman wrote a sharply worded

letter to the editor of her local newspaper. She owned a bag with strapped-on wheels, of the type that had been introduced two decades earlier by the Coventry inventors. But when she took it aboard her local bus in 1967, the conductor forced her to buy an additional ticket for the bag, his argument being that 'anything on wheels was classed as a pushchair'. His passenger, however, was unconvinced, asking: 'If I boarded a bus wearing roller-skates, would I be charged as a passenger or a pram?'

———————

One man who had good reason to ponder the question of women and loads was Sylvan Goldman, who owned an American grocery-store chain in the 1930s.

Like any good businessman, Sylvan Goldman was interested in maximising the financial profit of his businesses. He had noticed that most of the people who bought food in his stores were women, but also that they never bought more than what they could carry in one of the store's shopping baskets. Now, generally speaking, there are two ways to grow as a company: either you get more customers, or you sell more to your existing ones. Sylvan Goldman's problem was that the latter strategy appeared to be limited to what the women could carry.

So Goldman started thinking about what might help women to get more food to the checkout, preferably leaving them with one hand free to pluck even more goods from the shelves. That was when he – 40 years before Bernard Sadow – came back to the wheel. He invented the world's first shopping trolley and introduced it in his stores.

And what happened next?

No one wanted to use them. They refused. In the end, Goldman had to hire trolley-driving models to stroll around the store just to normalise the concept. Many men saw the trolley as a personal affront: 'You mean with my big strong arms I can't carry a darn little basket like that?' they cried. In other words, before Sylvan Goldman's invention could make him a multimillionaire, he first had to confront the notion that it was unmanly to wheel a trolley. This was a notion with a certain weight to it.

And, above all, a long history.

Back in the twelfth century, poet Chrétien de Troyes told the story of Lancelot, the tragic knight who falls in love with Queen Guinevere, betrays his best friend, King Arthur, and fails to find the Holy Grail. In Chrétien de Troyes' poem, Guinevere is abducted, forcing Lancelot to search far and wide for his beloved queen. Having lost his horse, he is clinking and clonking his way down the side of a country road in full armour, when a dwarf pulls up to him in a small cart.

'Dwarf! Have you seen the queen pass?' he cries.

The dwarf answers neither yes nor no. Instead, he makes an offer to the ill-fated knight.

'If you ride in my cart then tomorrow I'll tell you what happened to the queen,' he says.

Now, this may seem like a win-win: not only will Lancelot get a lift, he will also get the information he's looking for. But in actual fact the dwarf has just asked him to perform one of the most demeaning acts known to a knight: to ride in a vehicle on wheels. This would have been implicit to the twelfth-century reader, but it isn't at all apparent today. For why would the wheel ever be considered unmanly?

In antiquity, warriors and kings had ridden chariots across

battlefields and had crossed the Tiber in thundering horse-drawn carriages with barbarian prisoners in tow. These chariots obviously had wheels. But as the cavalry grew in military and strategic importance, the carriage – and with it the wheel – fell out of favour. Allowing oneself to be pulled along on wheels was no longer compatible with any form of masculine chivalry. This is the crux of Lancelot's dilemma, and what makes the dwarf's offer so diabolical.

The very point of the poem is to show how low noble Lancelot is prepared to stoop in the name of Queen Guinevere and love. As low as it takes, as it turns out. He boards the cart. And with that the wheels start turning towards the saga's tragic end.

But let's return to Bernard Sadow and his groundbreaking invention, the wheeled suitcase. In one of the few interviews the inventor gave, he discussed how difficult it was to get any American department-store chain to bite at his idea.

'At this time, there was this macho feeling. Men used to carry luggage for their wives. It was . . . the natural thing to do, I guess.'

In other words, the resistance the suitcase faced from the market had everything to do with gender. This one little factor is something that economists, who have long pondered why it took so long to attach wheels to suitcases, have missed.

We couldn't see the genius of the wheeled suitcase because it didn't align with our prevailing views on masculinity. In hindsight we obviously find this bizarre. How could this pretty arbitrary notion that 'a real man carries his own bag' prove robust enough to stymie what we now see to be a blindingly obvious innovation? How could the predominant view on masculinity turn out to be more stubborn than the market's desire to make money? And how could the crude idea that men must carry heavy things prevent us from seeing the potential in a product that would come to transform an entire global industry?

These questions lie at the very heart of this book. Because, as it happens, the world is full of people who would rather die than let go of certain notions of masculinity. Doctrines like 'real men don't eat vegetables', 'real men don't get check-ups for minor things' and 'real men don't have sex with condoms' literally kill very real men of flesh and blood every single day. Our society's ideas on masculinity are some of the most unyielding ideas we have, and our culture often values the preservation of certain concepts of masculinity over death itself. In this context, such ideas are certainly powerful enough to hold back technological innovation for five millennia or so. But we just aren't used to thinking about gender in relation to innovation in this way.

In a 1972 advertisement for a wheeled suitcase, a woman in a miniskirt and high heels is struggling to lug a big, pale suitcase. The woman is shot in black and white; she symbolises the past. The future, meanwhile, sashays straight past her, in the shape of a woman wearing an androgynous brown suit and a scarf around her neck like a tie. This woman – the very image of modernity – is *wheeling* her suitcase. There's a smile on her face, and her gaze is lifted towards freedom.

The wheeled suitcase took off when society changed. In the 1980s more women started to travel alone, without a man to carry their luggage, or to be expected to carry their luggage, or to be deemed insufficiently manly if he didn't. The wheeled suitcase carried with it a dream of greater mobility for women: a society in which it was both normal and accepted that women could travel without a male escort.

In the 1984 Hollywood film *Romancing the Stone*, starring

Michael Douglas and Kathleen Turner, Turner's character takes a wheeled suitcase with her into the jungle. The suitcase is of the type that Bernard Sadow invented: the wheels are on the long side, and she tows it behind her with a strap. It is endlessly toppling over in the dense tropical vegetation, much to Michael Douglas's exasperation. He, meanwhile, is trying to save them from villains, swinging from vines and tracking down a legendary gigantic emerald. In this context, Kathleen Turner's suitcase is a joke – one that is constantly falling flat.

This was a genuine problem with the suitcases based on Bernard Sadow's original model. Because their wheels were on the long and not the short side, the first wheeled suitcases weren't particularly stable. You had to drag them slowly and carefully behind you on a leather leash, preferably along a smooth surface.

By the early 1980s Danish luggage company Cavalet had already realised that you could get around this problem by placing the wheels on the short side instead. But as industry giant Samsonite decided to stick to its original wheel position, this remained the standard until 1987. That was when US pilot Robert Plath created modern cabin baggage. He turned Sadow's suitcase on its side and made it smaller. This was when the wheel finally revolutionised the luggage industry.

The new product was soon all the rage. They were initially marketed to airline cabin crews, who started wheeling their bags across smooth terminal floors in their glamorous uniforms as the passengers stared wide-eyed. They wanted one, too.

Soon every luggage company had to follow suit, and the suitcase was transformed – from something carried by the handle to something wheeled behind you. This in turn started to influence the design of both aeroplanes and airports. All of a sudden, much of the industry had to be rebuilt and rethought. The entire market changed.

Robert Plath's cabin bag became a constant feature of the modern businessman's arsenal, alongside the discreet swish of wheels against anonymous airport floors in a time zone far from home. It became a symbol of globalisation. Today men don't appear threatened by a set of 3 centimetre wheels, but as recently as the 1970s they were.

It was only after we had taken ourselves to the moon and back that we were ready to challenge our notions of masculinity enough to start putting wheels on suitcases. The department stores and buyers who had initially refused to invest in the product realised that gender roles were changing: that the modern woman wanted to be able to travel alone, and that man no longer had the same need to prove himself through raw physical strength.

The very ability to think these thoughts was the missing ingredient needed to make the wheeled suitcase possible. You had to be able to envision male consumers prioritising comfort over carrying. And you had to be able to envision women travelling alone. Only then could you really see the wheeled suitcase for what it came to be: an entirely obvious innovation.

It isn't hard to see why cabin crews became the wheeled suitcase's real trailblazers. The first to adopt the product on a large scale, they served as free, living, breathing advertisements as they paraded the airport floors. Not to mention that they were largely women who – you guessed it – travelled alone. The wheeled suitcase made its breakthrough when these women grew in number.

In sum, the suitcase began to roll when we changed our perspective on gender: that men must carry, and that women's mobility must be limited. Gender answers the riddle of why it took some 5,000 years for us to put wheels on our bags.

This answer may come as a surprise. After all, we don't imagine the 'soft' (notions of femininity and masculinity) as being capable of holding back the 'hard' (constant technological advancement).

But that was precisely what happened with the suitcase. And if it could happen with the suitcase, then our notions of gender must really be quite robust.

2

In which we start the car without breaking our jaw

She wrote that she was taking the boys to see her mother. She just didn't say how. Her husband assumed they had taken the train. This was August 1888, and the summer holidays had just started in the Grand Duchy of Baden, a southwestern state in the newly unified German Empire.

That morning, Bertha Benz carefully manoeuvred the horseless carriage out of the factory in which her husband had constructed it. Her two teenage sons, Eugen and Richard, helped. Day was breaking, and they didn't want to wake anyone, least of all their father, Karl Benz. Only once they were far enough away from the house did they start the engine, before taking it in turns to drive the 90 kilometres to Pforzheim, a town on the edge of the Black Forest. No one had ever made a trip like this before, which was why Bertha had had to steal the vehicle.

Karl Benz had been adamant that his invention should be called 'the horseless carriage'. For years the vehicle had been something of a local sensation in Mannheim, the neat and orderly town that the Benzes called home. The first time Karl Benz had driven his horseless carriage in front of a specially invited audience, he was so taken by his own invention that he had steered straight into the garden wall. Both he and Bertha, who sat beside him, were thrown headlong when the brickwork made mincemeat of the three-wheeled carriage's front wheel. There was nothing for it but to carry the scrap metal back to the factory and start again.

We should bear in mind that Bertha had invested almost all of her money into this invention. First she had put her entire dowry into the company. Then she had persuaded her parents to give her an advance on her inheritance. The 4,244 *gulden* that she had then sunk into her husband's business would have been enough to buy them a luxurious house in Mannheim. Instead, Bertha Benz flung it all at this dream of a four-stroke engine capable of powering a carriage without horses. After years of trials, the world's first automobile did, in fact, drive. It reached a speed of 16 kilometres per hour, and had a four-stroke petrol engine and a single cylinder. The Benz Patent-Motorwagen, as the vehicle was called, produced 0.75 horsepower, but what mattered most was that it worked.

In the early days Karl Benz had test-driven his horseless three-wheeler at night, so as not to cause a stir. At the sight of the car, children would often shriek, old folks would drop to their knees and make the sign of the Cross, and labourers on the highways would turn tail and run, leaving tools strewn behind them. The more superstitious among them thought the devil himself had landed, in a snarling carriage on three hellish wheels drawn by some invisible force. But, more importantly, the market doubted its utility. What was this machine really good for?

To make matters worse, Karl Benz, whose name would eventually go down in history as one half of Mercedes-Benz, was in all honesty no great businessman. Although he had started selling his vehicle in early 1888 – some two years after being granted his patents – the horseless carriage had proven more popular in France than in Germany. On the home front, Benz had been tied up in long discussions with the local authorities and police regarding the speed at which he would be allowed to drive. Should he even be allowed to drive it within the city limits? Eventually the regulators relented, and at long last Karl Benz's invention made a splash as a quasi-futuristic spectacle at the German Empire's technology fair in Munich.

Karl Benz had finally been noticed and had finally won his medal. But what was his commercial concept, really? While almost no one doubted that the engine Benz had constructed would find many uses, they were less convinced by the carriage itself. What use did it have? This was why Bertha Benz got up at five on the morning of 5 August 1888.

Pforzheim, where Bertha's mother lived, lay 90 kilometres from Mannheim. Bertha and her sons hatched a plan to drive there without Karl's knowledge – for fun, yes, but also to prove that this invention was not just a new engine but an entirely new means of transport.

The journey to Pforzheim – where they arrived triumphantly some 15 hours later, only to find Grandma out of town – was eventful. Bertha had anticipated that the horseless carriage would break down more than once, and on this front it hadn't disappointed.

First came a blockage in a fuel pipe, which Bertha used one of her hatpins to clear. Then, later, they had to insulate an exposed ignition wire, for which one of her garters came in handy. Bertha, Eugen and Richard took turns at the wheel, but whenever they came to a hill the boys would have to get out and push: the engine couldn't cope well with inclines. Bertha would sit in the driver's seat and try to rope the locals into lending a hand. If the uphill stretches were arduous, the downhill ones were downright hair-raising: the 360 kilo car could only brake on a wing and a prayer, using a lever to the right of the seat. No one had ever driven a horseless carriage this far, nor on so many hills, and the brake blocks on the Benz Patent-Motorwagen 3 soon wore out. When they stopped in the little village of Bauschlott, Bertha asked a shoemaker to cover them with leather.

With this, she and her sons invented the world's first brake linings.

Water was a constant issue. The engine needed regular cooling to prevent it from exploding. Bertha and her entourage took water from wherever they could: inns, rivers and – at a push – the odd ditch that they passed. In the small town of Wiesloch, south of Heidelberg, they stopped to buy Ligroin, a petroleum fraction commonly used as a laboratory solvent, to refuel. Local pharmacist Willi Ockel sold them the bottle, blissfully ignorant that in so doing he became the world's first filling station.

When Bertha Benz reached Pforzheim that evening she sent a telegram to Karl. Her husband wasn't angry, just shocked, and when Bertha and her sons returned to Mannheim the next day, Karl decided to furnish the horseless carriage with a lower gear. To cope better with those Black Forest hills. Not to mention the rest of the world. By the end of that year, an updated model of the Benz Patent-Motorwagen 3 was being commercially produced, and by 1900 Karl Benz was the world's biggest car manufacturer.

It was a woman who undertook the world's first long-distance car journey. In spite of this, the world soon came to the conclusion that women were less suited to driving than men. A woman was not a creature you could let loose willy-nilly in a motorised vessel. No: she was a fragile thing, fashioned by God to be laced up in corsets and to move through the world in 15 kilos of petticoats, wide-brimmed hats and long gloves. Science claimed that she was weak, timid and easily scared, and that any stimulation to her brain might have an adverse effect on her womb. None of these ideas about women's suitability for the road were in any way new.

In its day, the Roman Empire had once attempted to solve Rome's traffic problems by prohibiting women from riding in carriages. Getting around on Rome's streets was no simple matter: its narrow roads wound through an intricate mesh of alleys, and you also had sweaty throngs of garlic sellers, feather merchants and olive-oil producers to contend with. In many spots only one cart could pass at a time, so slaves would be sent up ahead to stop any oncoming vehicles, like fleshy, privately owned traffic lights on legs.

Rome was at war with Carthage at the time, and this had led to a politically motivated ban on various forms of luxury consumption: no one wanted to go to Africa to die while seeing their own upper classes wallowing in luxury. The aim was to cleanse Rome's streets of anything that could be considered a provocation by the local population and thus dent the fighting spirit. And was there anything more decadent than a woman on wheels? A female carriage ban was introduced, much to the fury of Rome's rich matrons. But more than that, the poet Ovid claimed that until the ban was revoked, women were even aborting foetuses from their own wombs in protest.

At the dawn of the twentieth century, the issue wasn't so

much the perceived decadence of a woman on wheels as the notion that they simply weren't up to it. A woman was far too emotionally unstable, physically weak and intellectually inferior for the driving seat, it was thought. This was the very same argument that was used against her when it came to her right to vote, and her right to pursue a higher education – two other things women were trying to negotiate access to during these years. Women were getting into cars at a time when their role in public life was being discussed as never before. And all of these debates on who they were and what they were capable of gradually worked their way into, and informed, technological development.

Back then, cars were custom-built for the consumer. You would order what you wanted and the car would be built bespoke. Most car manufacturers didn't have time to put a great deal of thought into the market as a whole; rather, they improvised.

People of the time used a wide range of transport types somewhat arbitrarily, from their own two feet, to horses, donkeys, trains, trams and even cars. And the cars themselves could be powered in a variety of ways: by petrol, electricity or steam. At the turn of the century, one third of all of Europe's cars were electric. In the USA there were even more.

It would be easy to picture the petrol- and electric-car manufacturers of the day endlessly bickering over which technology was best. However, in the early years of the automobile it was in fact their product's superiority over horses and carts that the manufacturers were most eager to promote. Which was logical, given that the horse-driven transport market was the one they wanted to tap.

The petrol-powered cars of the day – the successors to the Benz Patent-Motorwagen 3 that Bertha Benz had driven to

Pforzheim – were pretty unreliable. Both difficult to start and loud, they were not so much a vehicle as a pressure-pistoned, machine-oil-spattered way of life. This was a macho machine for high-speed travel, cars that could take you far from home and (hopefully) bring you back again. It was the adventurer's car, and adventure, as we know, is for men. Not women.

As a result, an idea soon emerged of the electric car as more 'feminine'. It was seen as a more natural successor to the horse-drawn cab than the petrol car, something that would simply take you where you needed to go. The petrol car, on the other hand, was in many ways less a means of transport than a sport for young (male) daredevils who liked to flash the cash. American car columnist Carl H Claudy wrote: 'Has there ever been an invention of more solid comfort to the feminine half of humanity than the electric carriage?' How convenient it was for a woman to be spared all the washing of manes, hooves and tails that came with a horse-drawn cab! Instead she could simply call the garage for a car. That this applied to only the most affluent of women goes without saying.

The petrol car, on the other hand, had to be cranked into life to even start. This was a sweaty and often dangerous operation. First you had to stand by the engine and pull a little wire that stuck out through the radiator, then take the crank and give it a few upward pulls, then go back to the driver's seat and turn on the ignition, return to the engine, catch the crank in the right position and, finally, give it a few decisive cranks to start it up.

By contrast, electric cars could be started from the driver's seat. They were also quiet and easy to maintain. The first car to ever go over 100 kilometres per hour was in fact an electric. Over time, however, the petrol cars caught up, and the electric car became the slower, more reliable option.

'Electrics . . . will appeal to anyone interested in an absolutely noiseless, odourless, clean and stylish rig that is always ready,' read the advertising copy of 1903. The accompanying image depicts two women wearing hats, gloves and big smiles. One woman is driving, while the other sits merrily beside her. The electric car's curves were smooth.

A 1909 advertisement takes a similar approach, encouraging the male consumer to buy an electric car for 'Your bride to be or your bride of many Junes past'. The message: this is the car for those who value comfort. No petrol, no oil, no cranking, no risk of explosion or your dress catching fire. Come and buy without worry.

In *Taking the Wheel*, historian Virginia Scharff cites American commentators of the time who argued that 'No license should be granted to anyone under eighteen . . . and never to a woman, unless, possibly, for a car driven by electric power'. Around 1900, electric cars accelerated faster and had safer brakes than petrol cars. In many ways they were the ideal choice for city travel, but due to their battery issues, they couldn't go particularly far. The battery needed charging roughly every 60 kilometres, and the cars struggled on the poor roads outside of the big cities. This, however, only seemed to make this type of vehicle *more* suitable for women in the eyes of the market: after all, women needn't travel particularly far. In fact, it was a good thing if they couldn't.

Why would a woman even need a car? Other than for visiting her friends, going to the shops, or taking a turn with the kids, of course? The woman's car was simply a different vehicle to the man's. Was it even a car? Perhaps it could be seen as more of a pram – one that allowed the woman to tuck herself in alongside her kids? Indeed, one car columnist wrote: 'In no way can a child get so much air in so little time as by the use of the automobile . . . It would not be amiss to call the electric the modern baby carriage.' At the time the car was seen as a 'clean' mode of transport: unlike horses, it didn't drop manure on the street.

Whether powered by electricity or petrol, the first generations of cars were expensive things. Henry Ford was the American to change all that. In 1908 he created his petrol-powered Model T, which sought to open up the car world to everyday Americans. The Model T, which cost $850 when it rolled off its production line in Detroit, Michigan, was intended as a vehicle for everyone. Ford's very business concept was to create a car so affordable that even the workers who built it would be able to drive. The now-legendary Model T came to be known as the car 'that put the world on wheels'. The only question is, whose world was it really?

The same year that Henry Ford launched his revolutionary Model T, he bought an electric car for his wife, Clara. This was thought to be more suitable for her. Clara Ford's electric was a world away from the rattling Model T. It was a luxurious drawing room on wheels, a motorised lounge in which she could receive her female friends while taking a leisurely spin around the city. Clara Ford had no steering wheel, but instead steered the carriage from the back, using two different tillers: one for going forward, the other for reversing. The car had built-in crystal vases for flowers, and space for three ladies to cruise in comfort.

Charging stations for electric cars soon started to crop up in the retail districts of large American cities, all so that rich women could charge their cars as they shopped. The archetypal female motorist of the early 1900s was a far cry from Bertha Benz unclogging a fuel pipe with her hatpin near the Black Forest in Germany. In fact, many had started to view the car as the most intolerable type of luxury consumption. Automobiles were shiny vehicles for transporting women wearing large ropes of pearls between the home and the opera box. Woodrow Wilson, 28th President of the United States, worried they would incite the masses to revolution. In other words, we find ourselves right back with Rome's matrons driving their carriages through slave-lined streets.

Increasingly, electric cars were being developed with women in particular in mind. These were the first cars to be fitted with roofs, for example, as women (unlike men) were supposed to want shelter from the rain, to 'preserve her toilet immaculate, her coiffure intact', to be precise. Similarly, it was the electric-car manufacturers who thought to position levers and controls so as not to catch on a woman's clothing. The electric became the car that could be driven in a skirt, not because of its 'feminine' associations, but because this was a firm demand of the market it was being aimed at.

However, the electric industry was not always happy about being associated with the 'fairer sex'. These were high-tech, reliable city cars, and the industry believed that they should have been of interest to anyone who wanted to get to work on time without an oil-spattered suit. E P Chalfant, a member of the board for Detroit Electric, wrote rather resentfully: 'The gasoline car dealers have branded the electric as a car for the aged and infirm and for the women.' Another man made a similar complaint about how his friends had warned him against buying an electric car: 'It was called a lady's car,' he testified.

Its feminine associations had positioned the electric car entirely wrongly on the market, Chalfant believed. After all, who was it that made the decisions on what car a family should buy? The man, of course. Which meant it was to him that the electric cars needed to adapt, not to woman. In

1910, Detroit Electric tried to counteract the electric car's feminine image by introducing a new man's model, the aptly named Gentlemen's Underslung Roadster.

It didn't catch on.

In 1916, American industry magazine *Electric Vehicles* ran a series of articles analysing the electric car's commercially unfortunate associations with femininity. 'The thing that is effeminate, or that has that reputation, does not find favor with the American man.' And, later: 'Whether or not he is "red-blooded" and "virile" in the ordinary physical sense, at least his ideals are.' In other words, if women liked something, be that a car or a colour, the American man would almost always distance himself from it as a matter of principle. This was, sadly, what had happened with the electric car, the magazine concluded.

Of course, this was as illogical as it was absurd. In reality, electric cars were just as suitable for men as they were for women. But, as the magazine pointed out, a car buyer cannot be expected to use logic or reasoning in such a way. 'Having imagined effeminacy into the electric, he dismisses it from his mind and buys a gas car without a struggle.' In other words, if it wanted to survive, the electric-car industry would have to get better at building macho cars: enough with the crystal vases and the downy seats.

What transpired, however, was the exact opposite. Electric cars didn't become 'more manly', or at least not until Elon Musk revved them up a century or so later. Instead, the petrol car took over almost completely. Not just by becoming even cheaper, thanks to Henry Ford, but also by becoming more 'feminine'.

Henry Leland was CEO of the Cadillac Motor Company in the early 1900s. Born on a farm in Vermont, he served alongside Abraham Lincoln in the American Civil War, and later went on to buy one of Henry Ford's ailing car businesses to found Cadillac. 'When you buy a Cadillac, you buy a round trip,' was the company's slogan. This was the luxury petrol car, and in these years, luxury consisted in just that: having a car that didn't need to be towed home.

In many ways it was in fact Henry Leland who dealt the death blow to the electric car, and funnily enough, it all began with an incident that had a lot to do with gender. Leland often retold it as the tragic tale of Byron Carter.

Byron Carter was one of Leland's friends. The now-legendary origin story has it that one day Carter stopped on a bridge near Detroit to help out a female driver. Her car had stalled, and she couldn't crank it back up again. Note that she didn't have an electric car: if she had, she could have started it from the driving seat, no cranking required. But by this point the car industry had started to market petrol cars to women, too. There were even options with wider doors that accommodated skirts. And, perhaps more importantly, most households only had one car, which the woman would also have access to. Many women also preferred petrol cars because of the speed. And so here we have a woman stranded on a Detroit bridge, in a petrol Cadillac that she couldn't start.

Cranking a petrol car had always been tough. But as the technology had developed, it had only become trickier and more dangerous, given the increasing engine power. When Byron Carter stopped on the bridge that fateful day, close combat with some heavy machinery lay in wait.

Naturally, being the gentleman that he was, Carter rolled

up his shirtsleeves and stepped out to help the woman. This would turn out to be the wrong decision. You see, as she sat there in her car, the woman had forgotten to adjust the spark. The crank kicked back out of Carter's hand and hit him square in the jaw. The bone was crushed, and a few days later he died of complications relating to his injury.

For Henry Leland, enough was enough. Carter had been his friend, and to make matters worse, the car that had killed him had been a Cadillac. Leland felt responsible, and so he made the decision that the crank had to go. Surely it must be possible to use electricity to turn on a petrol car, thereby starting it from the driver's seat without a crank, he thought. It was worth a proper shot – if just to prevent another friend from dying while helping out an incapable woman on the side of the road.

Within a relatively short space of time, Cadillac managed to construct an electric starter for petrol cars. The only problem was that it was far too big to fit in any car. Leland needed help. And that's when he found Charles F Kettering. In an Ohio barn.

Charles F Kettering was a gifted engineer who had previously constructed the world's first electric cash register. The first time he had even seen a car had been on his honeymoon, when he had chanced upon a doctor whose newfangled vehicle had broken down on the roadside. Kettering popped open the bonnet and managed to diagnose the problem, and thus began his fascination with the cars. He and a few colleagues gradually started meeting in a barn after work, where they would try to improve the cars of the age in different ways. This would later become a company that Kettering would name Delco.

It was to Delco that Henry Leland turned when he needed

help to improve – and above all to shrink – the electric starter that Cadillac had constructed.

It took Kettering three years to solve the problem. His innovation consisted of an electric engine that also functioned as a generator. It was a whole compact system that started the engine and then created its own electricity from the motion of the car. This in turn made the car's lights shine.

In 1912, Cadillac launched its Model Thirty, the first commercially produced car with an electric starter and electric lights. The company won the prestigious Dewar Trophy for its innovation. The new starter could be worked from a button on the dashboard or the floor, or with a pedal, all of which was obviously much easier than having to go out and crank. Cadillac immediately introduced the electric starter as standard in all of its car models, and many other companies soon followed suit. Some, however, hesitated, viewing Kettering's invention less as an improvement for everyone than a concession to women. While certainly elegant, the contraption was hardly necessary, they thought.

The *New York Times* described the innovation as 'a further item of ease and convenience for the lady'. The subtext being that it was women who couldn't crank, women who made all these demands that driving be easy, and women who had had to be accommodated with the electric starter. The electric starter only became standard in the Ford Model T in the 1920s. Until then, anyone who wanted to start their Ford without a crank had to buy an additional product.

'Women can drive Ford cars with perfect freedom and comfort if they will be sure to see that the car is equipped with a Splitdorf-Apelco electric starting and lighting system,' read one advertisement. 'Let *Her* drive your Ford,' read another.

But what Kettering had in fact done was take one of the

refinements of the electric car (the ability to start the engine from the driver's seat) and integrate it into the petrol car. Thus a product was born that had the benefits of the petrol car combined with the comfort of the electric. Is it really any wonder that this was the car that would come to take over the world?

Still, the question remains: why did the car industry for so long insist on there being two car markets – one for men, and one for women? The majority of families could only afford one car, after all. So why hadn't they previously attempted to create a car that appealed to men as well as women?

While the American electric-car industry was busy grumbling about its feminine connotations, Charles F Kettering had taken the 'feminine' notions of comfort and security and integrated them into the petrol car. This was the beginning of a long process by which many of the feminine 'frills' the car industry had initially sneered at eventually became the standard. As the years passed, the petrol car became increasingly electric. It was 'feminised'.

And it took the market by storm.

This transformed driving from an extravagant upper-class hobby to an activity for the population at large. So long as petrol cars needed cranking, they were of no use to anyone who needed to get to work on time, and thereby remained an object of leisure or sport. By integrating what had long been perceived as 'feminine' values into the petrol car, its manufacturers increased the size of their market and took the car from niche product to the object we now see on every drive.

'We must conclude that the feminine influence is quite largely responsible for the more obvious changes that have been made in gas car design from year to year,' *Electric Vehicles* reported. The magazine gave as examples of this influence softer and deeper upholstery, more beautiful lines, simpler controls and automatic ignition. All of this was described as 'evidence of concessions to the softer sex'.

Interestingly, the industry long continued to attribute this kind of demand for comfort to women alone. It was women who wanted comfort, not to mention safety, in their cars (apparently men were perfectly fine with dying). It was women who didn't want to get oil on their clothes, and women who wanted to be able to start the engine without breaking their jaw. This is, of course, bizarre. Why was comfort so long considered a feminine frill as opposed to a cutting-edge technological innovation? Why were convenience, effortlessness, beauty and security something that women alone could conceivably demand? Why was it so implausible that a male consumer might want a car that he could start without risking a gangrenous death? Why was it so long assumed that men wanted to get soaked to the skin when driving in the rain? And why was it taken for granted that they wanted a car that roared and stank by default?

As the historian of technology Gijs Mom sees it, it was the electric – not petrol – car that won out over the horse as a means of transport. The petrol car of the day was simply too technologically inferior. Once the horse had been defeated, however, the petrol car took over. Mom points out that this had nothing to do with petrol cars being cheaper to manufacture: they only became cheaper once they had more or less edged the electric car out of the market. In other words, the triumph of the petrol car was not one of price, but of other factors.

One important reason was of course the electric car's many

battery issues. Battery technology was still in its infancy, and the proponents of the electric car didn't succeed in building an infrastructure that could compensate for these problems – a network of battery exchange points, for example. But there was also a 'cultural' factor.

And this was almost exclusively to do with gender.

What electric- and petrol-car manufacturers had in common was a shared tendency to look down on things that they had been taught to view as 'feminine'. The electric-car industry built cars for women, but they failed to see that many of the 'feminine' qualities their cars possessed were in fact universal.

In the same way, many petrol-car manufacturers clung tooth and nail to the idea that a real man cranked his car. In doing so, both sides limited the size of their market. All to uphold an idea of masculinity that was essentially pointless.

For Henry Leland, it was only when his friend Byron Carter died of gangrene from a broken jaw that everything changed – according to the legend, at least. That was the tipping point that put him in touch with Charles F Kettering, prompting him to assimilate so-called 'female' and 'male' preferences and create a product for people. Which, as we know, is a big market.

Even today, more than a century later, historians and journalists often describe the electric starter as an innovation intended for women. Kettering is described as a hero because his electric starter (plus the artistry of male engineering) gallantly opened the door for women drivers.

When commissioning the electric starter for Cadillac, Henry Leland was probably thinking along similar lines. The manner in which he framed the story of Carter's death undeniably points that way, suggesting the electric starter was a necessary measure to prevent more men dying when helping hapless women with a crank.

But Kettering's innovation was actually something quite different. His invention redefined the boundary between men's and women's driving, thereby creating a new market for everyone.

This is why the electric starter was so groundbreaking – not because it allowed women to drive cars. They were already doing that pretty well.

Just ask Bertha Benz.

Which begs the question: might things have turned out differently had our view on gender been different? A hundred years ago, electric fire engines, taxis and buses roamed many of the world's major metropolises. Then they disappeared. Instead, petrol-powered technology became the dominant form of technology, bringing pollution, noise and odours with it. Had early twentieth-century society not looked down on the electric car as feminine, would history have followed a different track?

There's no denying that the electric-car infrastructure of 120 years ago contained elements that still feel strikingly modern today. For example, in the early 1900s you could hire electric cars, or pay per mile to drive them. Electric taxis milled around many cities, picking up passengers. What the customer wanted, as many electric-car entrepreneurs argued, was transport from point A to point B, not an expensive machine outside their homes. Rural aristocrats were overjoyed to be able to trust in a network of new electric cars, and not to have to take their horse and carriage into town.

In other words, our entire concept of transport could have developed more around ideas of car sharing and car pooling from the beginning, had the electric car won out. Or at least not disappeared. This world would have been no less technologically advanced than the world we ended up building. It would just have been different.

In the USA, way back in the 1800s, one such electric-car company constructed a central New York garage with a state-of-the-art, semi-automatic system that could swap car batteries in 75 seconds flat. Then – as now – the battery was the electric car's main issue. But, while electric batteries by their very nature took time to charge, it was at least theoretically possible to build a system to compensate for this. This was precisely what this company tried to do. Cars would drive in, have a freshly charged battery installed in a matter of minutes, and then zip out again. It was simply a different way of thinking. Had one of these business models succeeded, we might never have owned cars like we do today. It just wouldn't have been obvious in the same way that the good life necessarily involved every family having two almost identical cars at the ready on their front drive. Or that cities had to be car-dominated places where drivers would sit one by one waiting for traffic lights to turn green. Innovation lies not only in the machines we build, but in the logic born of those machines.

William C Whitney was an American investor who in 1899 raised $1 million to build a nationwide electric-car network in the USA. He had already played a role in electrifying New York's trolley network, which had been a big earner for him. Cars seemed like the natural next step.

Whitney's vision was an electric transport system that would link up the entire country. Electric trains would run from city to city, and within the cities electric trolleys and electric cars would take over. The idea was that city dwellers would never need to buy a car: they would be able to get wherever they wanted to go using the electric transport network. Horses and carriages would be replaced with quiet, clean, electric cars, he envisioned. Then the entire system would be exported abroad, to the likes of Mexico City and Paris. Whitney thought big. He was just one of those men: had he been alive today he would most certainly have given a bombastic TED Talk about it all.

But things didn't go so well for Whitney.

Just one year after the network's New York launch, the company had almost entirely lost its customers' trust. Operations were poorly managed, and the drivers didn't know what they were doing. Everything rested on their system of fast battery swaps working, but the expensive batteries weren't properly cared for, and many of them broke. By 1901 the company was forced to close. However, this is far from the first time in history that a grandiose idea has belly flopped due to a general lack of business acumen. Someone else could conceivably have taken the model further. Instead it died, along with the electric car.

So here we are, over a century later, trying to re-invent the wheel by starting over with electrics. Elon Musk, playing it safe, has designed his cars without a single in-built crystal vase, and today more men than women drive electrics. Meanwhile, young people are increasingly questioning the need to own a car at all. Still, everything from our modern idea of personal freedom to our community planning is deeply rooted in the logic of the petrol car. The same one that Bertha Benz drove to Pforzheim.

It was the petrol car's ability to drive off wherever you wanted that won out in the end. The electric car represented safety, silence and comfort. There is nothing essentially feminine in these values. They are, if anything, human values.

Unfortunately, that which we have chosen to call 'feminine' cannot be perceived as universally human. And if the electric car was 'feminine', then that meant it must also be 'inferior' – one of the notions that the early electric-car industry came up against. Had its technology not come to be viewed as feminine (and thereby of a lesser stature), would the electric car have made it? This is, of course, impossible to tell. Its battery problems were undeniable. Still, had society's infrastructure been built to accommodate these, it could have worked, at least in the big cities. But it wasn't to be.

What Charles F Kettering then managed to do with his electric starter was to turn the petrol car into a universal car. He refused to see the comfort of starting your car without risk of injury as a feature just 'for the ladies'. The electric-car industry didn't do anything similar to break out of its mould – if that were even possible, that is. Then petrol cars became cheaper and so did oil. Later attempts to revive the electric car were also met with powerful resistance from the oil industry.

In other words, we can't know if the electric car of the early twentieth century represented a world that could actually have existed. What we can say, however, is that few things shape our thinking as deeply as our ideas about gender. They influence which machines we choose to build.

And what future we are able to envision for ourselves.

TECHNOLOGY

3

In which bras and girdles take us to the moon

On the morning of Sunday 7 December 1941, Japanese planes attacked Pearl Harbor. Abram Spanel knew immediately that it would spell trouble for his business.

Spanel's company manufactured commercial latex products. His latest success had been the Living Girdle, a latex casing that sculpted American women's bodies into the hourglass figure dictated by the fashions of the day. The girdle held you in, compressed and made you slimmer, all without choking the oxygen supply to your brain.

Changing shape with the prevailing tastes had long been one of the female body's many duties. But the latex girdle was no whalebone corset: it was a revolutionary garment that not only slimmed a woman down, but also allowed her to bend over and tie her shoelaces. The innovative material gave her a new freedom of movement. She could even play tennis in the girdle, the adverts claimed. It was, admittedly, a sweaty affair, but even this aspect of rubber compaction was supposed to have its advantages: a woman who sweated was a woman who dropped the pounds, so went the logic. The latex girdle would massage away her rolls of fat, or at the very least coerce them back into their rightful place beneath her ribs.

Now, however, Japanese planes had bombed away any hope the USA had of staying out of the ongoing war. Dead bodies washed up along the Hawaiian coastline, and only one of the US Pacific Fleet's battleships managed to escape the Japanese attack somewhat unscathed. Spanel realised that for the foreseeable future rubber would be earmarked for truck tyres and military raincoats, not for ladies' waist-cinchers. What could he do?

He was no man to panic. Spanel had made millions in the vacuum-cleaner industry while still in his early twenties, and he was convinced that even after Pearl Harbor he would be able to find a way forward. But on 8 December 1941, Japanese troops attacked what was then British Malaya. Now Spanel really had a problem. You see, British Malaya was where the rubber trees grew. On Sunday Spanel had seen his home market decimated, and by Monday he had been cut off from his supply chain.

Business-wise, this turned out to be one of the best things that ever happened to him.

The rubber tree can grow to up to 40 metres in height. If you cut its bark with a knife, it will start to bleed latex into your hands. This liquid can then be coagulated and cast into anything from tyres to girdles to surgical gloves.

In the Amazon rainforest, nature had scattered these rubber trees over an area of millions of hectares. But in 1876, Englishman Henry Wickham managed to ship over 70,000 rubber-tree seeds to Britain, and in so doing profoundly shifted the balance of international trade.

Informed by his ideas on white superiority, Wickham

liked to pass this off as some intrepid, Victorian plant-smuggling adventure. The locals didn't even understand how valuable the trees were! Wasn't Wickham clever to trick them! But none of that was true.

In reality, Wickham had assistance from indigenous Amazonians in gathering botanical samples. Each seed was 2 cm long, so you couldn't exactly slip 70,000 of them into your pocket and do a runner. But why let the truth get in the way of a good story? In 1938 a German film depicted Wickham taking on an Amazonian anaconda in combat in the jungle. All of these stories obviously went down well back in England; they had the right racist overtones.

But their popularity made them no less fictitious.

Wickham was no swashbuckler; he was a pretty average British imperialist with a borderline knowledge of plants. Still, he did manage to reshape international trade . . . Eventually.

Trees, as we know, take some time to grow.

In these years, steelworks, railways and factories were all clamouring for rubber. Telegraph cables, irrigation hoses and – not least – tyres were made from the product. In light of such strong demand, the British shipped Wickham's seeds to their colonies in Asia, via the Royal Botanical Gardens at Kew in southwest London. In Malaysia they discovered that the latex could be harvested all year round, and that the local insects went easy on the new trees. The burgeoning rubber plantations proved capable of producing much more than the natural rainforests of South America.

It took a few decades – and a few financial rubber bubbles – for production to really pick up on the rubber plantations, but by the start of World War II some 90 per cent of the world's rubber came from British Malaya. Which was why

Abram Spanel found himself in such a tight spot after the Japanese attack on Pearl Harbor.

The USA started to quickly ramp up its production of synthetic rubber. Spanel, meanwhile, adjusted to the wartime economy. His company stopped producing rubber girdles, picnic blankets and latex nappies, and instead managed to stay afloat by manufacturing lifeboats for the US Marines and helmets for the US Air Force. When peace came, Spanel was ready for a new era of consumer products, as private consumption in North America picked up again.

Christian Dior dictated the postwar silhouette from a newly liberated Paris. Narrow waists and sashaying skirts were the order of the day, and Spanel's rubber once again enveloped the female body. The money came pouring in.

In 1947 his company, ILC, split into four divisions. The part that manufactured girdles changed its name to Playtex. Besides girdles, they also started producing bras, with great success. The name change was also accompanied by ambitious branding efforts aimed at the female consumer market. Playtex sponsored a homely afternoon TV show for housewives, and continued its aggressive advertising in the weekly magazines. The company quickly succeeded in making its name synonymous with female underwear, not unlike the way the Spanx brand is today associated with a certain type of body-shaping pants.

But after the war Spanel also retained the military division of his company. It had been doing well, after all, and there was no reason to shut it down. The armed forces were still buying enormous amounts of gear. So ILC invested into a research programme that would take this side of operations further. Soon it was developing helmets and attire for the air force and marines. Body-shaping ladies' undergarments and war munitions may seem like two very different things to house under one commercial roof, but flexibility was in the very nature of the product. The business model grew from the material, so to say.

And that was how it came to be that when Neil Armstrong descended the steps of the lunar module in July 1969, he did so in a space suit made by female seamstresses trained in the gruelling art of sewing ladies' undergarments.

In an absolute vacuum there is no temperature. Space, therefore, has no temperature. But there are, of course, individual particles in space that do. Heat is absorbed and emitted through radiation, and so the astronaut's temperature is dependent on the balance between the heat radiating out of her body and the radiant heat of distant stars.

Temperatures on the sunny side of the moon can reach 120 °C, while on the dark side they can drop to −170 °C. The universe's background temperature, meanwhile, is less than three degrees above absolute zero – the point at which nothing moves. In short, for a human to survive in space, she needs to be wearing clothes.

The only question is, what type?

It would be one thing to build a metal suit of armour, a hard construction in which the astronaut can urinate, defecate, breathe and survive. But an astronaut also needs to be able to move: to bend, twist, stretch and jump, to reach down to the lunar sands, take a fallen screw between her fingers and fix it back in place. All this, while at the same time being protected from micrometeorites that hurtle past at 36,000 kilometres per hour.

The USA decided to send a man to the moon in 1961. That it would be a man was decided the same year, with the ruling that only US fighter pilots could become astronauts. And as American women couldn't become fighter pilots, that left only the men. As early as 1963 the USSR sent a female cosmonaut, Valentina Tereshkova, into space. But – unlike virtually everything else the Soviet Union did when it came to space – this doesn't appear to have given the USA much pause for thought.

Nevertheless, an American man was to go to the moon, and he needed something to wear. So in 1962 NASA asked eight private companies to help them develop a space suit. One of these companies had zero experience with space, but a lot of experience in latex. We are, of course, talking about Abram Spanel's ILC, proud producer of hit female undergarments under the brand name of Playtex.

ILC presented a space suit that, unlike the other designs, was soft. This was the company's specialty, after all. The suit consisted of 21 layers of fabric and was to be sewn by hand. This soft space suit was the one that won out. NASA, however, was wary, and wasn't about to trust an underwear company with its space suits.

Their solution was to make ILC subcontractor to Hamilton Standard, a company that specialised in military technology. The idea was that the companies would simply work together to develop the new space suit. But the culture clash between the bra makers at ILC and the weapons makers at Hamilton proved monumental, and the space suits that came out of this enforced collaboration were unusable.

But Neil Armstrong still needed something to wear.

In 1965 NASA organised another competition. In Houston, three different suits from three different companies underwent 22 separate tests. The soft, hand-sewn suits from ILC once again won by a country mile. In the report submitted to the air-force general, it was noted that none of the other options were even comparable to ILC's suit. 'There is no second place,' the report stated. Presumably this was in reference to things like the helmet of one of the alternative suits flying off in one of the tests, or the shoulders of another being so wide that the astronaut couldn't get back through the hatch of the lunar module. Had that exercise been the real thing, the poor man would have been left stranded on the moon for ever . . . But thankfully he was just in Houston, Texas.

Whoever said that clothes didn't matter?

ILC were now victorious a second time round, but they still didn't dare believe that they would actually get to be involved in taking humanity to the moon, especially given how badly their forced collaboration with Hamilton Standard had gone. So they invested in even more research.

In 1968, ILC wanted to show NASA what they had managed to achieve. Instead of sending a report, they drove their new space suit out to a local high school's football pitch. One of ILC's technicians put on the suit, and they filmed him running, kicking a ball, throwing and passing. The man twirled around, stretched, and bent down and touched his toes. This was no whalebone corset.

This was how the Apollo space suits came to be soft, hand-sewn garments made by seamstresses specialising in women's underwear. And lucky they did: before Neil Armstrong and Buzz Aldrin stepped out onto the moon in July 1969, they had to change suits in the lunar module – a process that took three hours. In the end, one of them managed to turn in such a way that his oxygen tank snapped a circuit breaker. Unfortunately, as Aldrin dryly remarked, it was 'the one vital breaker needed to send electrical power to the ascent engine that would lift Neil and me off the moon'.

Whoops.

Back on the ground in Houston, technicians worked through the night trying to solve the problem. In the end, Aldrin fixed the issue by simply shoving a pen into the breaker. This allowed him and Armstrong to take off from the moon. Still, it's easy to imagine just how much damage the astronauts could have wreaked had they been winging around in hard metal armour for the entire voyage. But they weren't.

The soft space suits were sewn by women, as women made up most of the seamstress profession at the time. ILC transferred its best seamstresses from bra production and latex-nappy assembly to its space division. Naturally this required some adjustment – the seamstresses were given special sewing machines, for example, repurposed to sew just one stitch at a time. This was the only way to ensure perfectly straight seams. Ultimately, space suits have a quite different set of requirements than bras, even if both serve to mitigate the effects of gravity – or a lack thereof.

The seamstresses were also forbidden from using pins – despite each space suit comprising some 21 layers and 4,000 pieces of fabric. If you stick a pin in a space suit, it creates a hole. And however small that hole may be, it risks allowing the cold, deathly space to sneak inside and kill you. For this very reason, ILC installed an X-ray machine that scanned every layer of fabric for pins and holes.

Still, on the whole, the suits were not the problem. Nor the sewing; nor the machines. No, the main issue throughout the entire stressful production process was communication with the client.

So, NASA.

More specifically, NASA's engineers didn't know how to talk to ILC's seamstresses. And the seamstresses in turn didn't know how to talk to NASA's engineers. They talked past each other most of the time, often leading to grave misunderstandings. And it simply boiled down to the fact that they weren't speaking the same language.

NASA demanded technical drawings; the seamstresses used patterns. NASA required a detailed paper trail for every component used in the suit, including its origin (the done thing when building aircraft motors!). The seamstresses, respectfully, couldn't care less. They had 4,000 pieces of fabric to fit together, and a knowledge of how that fabric behaved that often couldn't be expressed in engineering terms. They had no use for technical drawings. Their knowledge came from another world, one of soft fabrics and sharp needles.

When ILC delivered its first moon suit in 1967, NASA initially refused to accept it. Not because of any technical flaws, but because the documentation requirements for the production process were 'not being met'.

After much ado, ILC eventually hired a separate group of trained engineers that it brought into the fold. Their job was to function as a buffer between NASA and the seamstresses. They were to translate the language of needles and thread into that of engineering, and in doing so keep NASA's bureaucrats happy.

To NASA's great delight, the newly appointed engineers produced huge reams of documents, which was just what NASA was after. One gigantic pile of paper for every one of the space suits, complete with masses of technical drawings.

But these technical drawings were not used by the seamstresses. As one of them put it: 'It might look all right on that piece of paper, but I'm not going to sew that piece of paper.'

Still, the piles of paper filled an important function: they reassured NASA. The technical drawings communicated the seamstresses' competence to the client in a language the client understood.

This proved crucial.

Today those white suits are what we tend to think of when someone mentions the 1969 moon landing: an image of soft fabric against the grey, crater-filled landscape of a foreign celestial body. The moon suits became the icons of that expedition, and they are what we have folded up and filed away in world history as the very embodiment of Apollo 11.

Had it not been for the 1,000-year-old technology of the needle and thread, we would never have reached the moon. This is a technology that tends to be associated more with women than with men. Historically, the task of making clothes for the family has fallen to the woman, and as a result, sewing is a technology that we don't tend to view as a technology per se. This, however, doesn't change the fact that spaceships still need wrapping up in precision-sewn sheets of soft, shimmering materials for thermal insulation in space.

NASA still uses and employs seamstresses to this day. If you want to take a digital camera into space, for example, you will first need to have a cover sewn for it, and the cover will need to be such that you can use the camera and change its battery without removing your gloves. Which makes that camera cover no easy thing to construct. Despite this, we often regard things that are soft as being in some way less technical.

An attitude that is largely to do with their associations with women.

Technology is that which men make from hard metals to kill big things, we are taught. It may not be expressed quite that explicitly, but this is nevertheless the narrative we are fed as children. Once upon a (prehistoric) time we all sat shivering in caves, until one of our forefathers thought to fix a pointy stone onto a stick and use it to kill a mammoth. And so began our long journey of technological advancement.

We thus imagine our desire to innovate as being inextricably linked with our desire to kill and subjugate the world around us. But is this narrative really true? And what are its economic consequences?

———————

Most of us will have heard the old adage that everything from mass-produced penicillin to Pilates reformers were first created for the military. The major powers' battle for dominion of the skies led to the development of aviation, and their race to the moon gave us rockets, satellites and Velcro. Without the atomic bomb we would have no nuclear energy; without the radar, no microwave ovens. Submarines, radios, semiconductors, even the internet – all were born, directly or indirectly, of the twentieth century's great wars.

In World War II, Winston Churchill personally devoted time to inventing a gigantic trench-digger originally known as 'White Rabbit Number Six'. It was no great success. Still, the fact that the British prime minister put his own time into overseeing the construction of a single machine in this way illustrates just how crucial innovations were considered to the war effort.

The one with the best gadgets would win.

The reality of the battlefield was considerably less high-tech. When Adolf Hitler invaded the Soviet Union in 1941, he did so with 3,250 big, strong German tanks, yes. But also with 600,000 horses. World War II wasn't nearly as mechanised as we are led to imagine. When visiting a war museum we see row upon row of shiny machines standing proudly on display, but the animals used to tow the artillery to the front don't feature to the same degree; these aren't zoos, after all. And so to some extent we are deceived.

Moreover, many of the inventions made to win the war didn't significantly contribute to this goal. The development of the atomic bomb cost $2 billion. With the same resources, the USA could have bought planes and bombs enough to inflict just as much death. If bombing Japan to the ground was the aim, that is.

Which leads us to the economic crux of it all: war by its very nature destroys far more economic value than it creates through innovation. Most economic historians are in agreement here. Truth be told, it's actually pretty obvious. So why do we think we need violence and death in order to create something new?

Sir Henry Tizard was chief scientific advisor to the UK's Air Ministry and Ministry of Aircraft Production in World War II. As such, he played an important role in the development of everything from radars to jet engines to nuclear power. Sir Tizard's conclusion, as given in a 1948 speech, was that, with the possible exception of a few specific branches, war didn't advance science in the slightest. On the whole, he felt that in wartime conditions 'the advance of knowledge is slowed'.

You blow the world into smithereens, but then succeed in mass-producing penicillin from the devastation. Of course the mass distribution of penicillin was a blessing, but there is no law of nature that states that good can only come of evil in this way. That you must kill 6 million people to get the internet – an immense human sacrifice to the gods of technology, who in return reward you with Velcro and radar.

Necessity is the mother of invention, the saying goes, but it also helps if she has money. War – or the threat thereof – tends to mobilise states to throw all they have at innovation. Where would we now be, had we invested as much into doing something about the climate emergency as we did into the Cold War? Presumably a bit further along the way to a solution. Yet somehow we are mired in this idea that human ingenuity requires some degree of blood and death to kick into action. This comes back to our gross misunderstanding of our own technological history.

One caused by our stubborn insistence on excluding women.

If that which women engage in cannot be deemed technology, while men are increasingly forced to specialise in war, then our understanding of the history of technology will place all too great a weight on violence and death.

Our ability to make and use tools dates back millions of years. Even our relatives the chimpanzees create tools. This has led scholars to believe that the first tools were probably not made of stone, but instead fashioned from branches, twigs and other highly perishable materials. 'Highly perishable' in this context means unlikely to survive more than say

350,000 years. That's the reason we don't know much about these tools – they are very much gone.

But it isn't by any means evident that the first tools we invented were for hunting and thus (probably) invented by men. Take the digging stick, for instance: wooden sticks that we sharpened and hardened with fire into stiff points. These sticks opened up a whole new world for humankind. With a digging stick in hand you could suddenly get underground, where there were delicious insects to sink your teeth into, not to mention yam roots: a type of sweet potato that could grow to be almost a metre long, making it almost impossible to unearth with bare hands.

We don't know what came first: the spear or the digging stick. What's interesting is the narrative: we assume that the spear must have come first. Human innovation must have begun with a weapon. The first inventor must have been a man. However, it's just as possible that sharpened sticks were originally invented by women to gather foods, and were only later adapted for hunting.

The reason we think women invented the digging stick is because of the division of labour in most hunter-gatherer societies. Men tended to hunt and women gather. This is different from the animal kingdom: just ask any lioness, tiger, leopard, wolf, bear, fox, weasel, porpoise or killer whale. There were female hunters among humans as well: the recent discovery of a 9,000-year-old skeleton of a woman with hunting gear has led to some rethinking of our assumptions about gender roles in ancient tribes.

We don't know how it happened, but among humans, the women at some point started spending most of their time raising young children and preparing food and household clothing. This is why, scholars believe, it was probably women who invented both the mortar and the quern-stone, and who figured out how to gather, transport and prepare foods.

Just as it was most likely women, given that this is what they specialised in economically, who discovered that you could smoke food, or preserve it in honey or salt. Cooking is a technology. It involves a great many physical and chemical inventions, and it also gave rise or contributed to other technologies like smelting, pottery and dyeing. Cooking involves techniques and processes that you don't just have to discover: you need to experiment to formulate them into effective, repeatable systems. The invention of cooking was much more than somebody accidentally kicking a pig into the fire and realising they liked the smell of crackling.

So why do we assume that clubs and spears were our first tools? It makes us buy into the notion that the driving force of human invention is somehow linked to a drive to dominate the world around us. When women are removed from the narrative, humankind becomes something else. And so we continue, in this way, to deceive ourselves about our very nature. One of the gravest consequences of the patriarchy is that it makes us forget who we really are.

If we instead took those aspects of the human experience that we have coded as female and recognised them as universal, we would change our entire definition of what it means to be human. The crux of the problem has always been that the human has been equated to the male. Woman is some sort of supplement, made, as we know, from a single rib.

We see this all the time in culture. In William Shakespeare's play, Hamlet, a white Danish prince, gets to speak for all humanity in his existential angst. Which to some extent he of course does. The problem is all the people who are not accorded the same right to be universal, and how this in turn limits our idea of what it means to be human.

Narratives about someone who gives birth, for example, are not seen as universal in the same way as narratives about men on the battlefield. Birth stories, apparently, can't tell us about human joy and pain, the violence of the body, or the things we do for those we love. Birth narratives are in modern culture invariably seen as 'feminine': they aren't expected to resonate with someone who isn't giving birth, hasn't given birth, or won't one day give birth. As if coming out of a vagina and meeting the light isn't literally the most universal experience there is.

We do precisely the same thing with the history of technology: man's tools are allowed to belong to '*his*tory', while woman's are passed over to 'women's history'.

The one small problem with this is that we thereby misinterpret everything.

Enlightenment philosopher Voltaire famously wrote: 'There have been very learned women as there have been women warriors, but there have never been women inventors.' This was of course entirely false: Voltaire even had a girlfriend who once invented a new financial product just to get him out of prison after he ran up some colossal gambling debts. But Voltaire wasn't thinking about this. By 'inventions' he probably meant 'big machines'.

Perhaps we shouldn't blame him. After all, in school we were taught that the Bronze Age was followed by the Iron Age, in precisely those terms: 'bronze' and 'iron'. But in all honesty we could just as easily have called them the 'Pottery Age', or the 'Flax Age'. That someone discovered that clay hardens in heat – and that she could therefore use it to store food and water – was a feat no less technological than those of bronze or iron.

Historian Kassia St Clair has discussed how textiles and pottery most likely played a more pivotal role in people's everyday lives than bronze and iron, yet aren't viewed as era-defining advancements in the same way. True, unlike their metal counterparts, the traces of this technology have long since perished underground. But it is also worth remembering that these objects predominantly belonged to the woman's world. And what belongs to the woman's world cannot, by definition, be technology. Over the course of history we have put a great deal of effort into keeping things this way.

For instance, when you go to see a midwife in many parts of Europe, she will place a wooden horn against your round belly. This helps her to hear the foetal heartbeat chugging away like a train inside. That this horn is made of wood and not metal has to do with wood being considered more appropriate for women. There is a difference between materials and *materials*, you see. Throughout history, certain materials have come to be regarded as feminine and others masculine. As a result, some of them have also come to be regarded as technological. And others less so.

When modern midwifery emerged in the nineteenth century, most midwives were women, while all doctors were men. It was deemed important that the midwife's work be distinguishable from that of a doctor, not least in economic terms. (How else would they justify doctors' high salaries?)

So in most European countries, midwives were banned from using metal instruments. Should a baby need to be delivered using forceps, this would be performed by a male midwife or a male doctor. Sweden was the exception: in 1829 Swedish midwives were granted the internationally unique right to use metal instruments – but only if no doctor was available. If a doctor was present, the midwife couldn't so much as take her own tools out of her bag.

This was stated very clearly in the official rulebook.

Despite this, in the 1920s and 1930s amazed delegations visiting Sweden from England and the USA reported on how differently things worked there. They arrived in the country to find a healthcare system that allowed female midwives to place metal forceps around babies' heads and pull. Shocking. But it also seemed to work: maternal and infant mortality rates were lower in Sweden than in both England and the USA at the time, despite the latter countries having both more doctors and higher standards of medicine.

Still, in most countries the aspects of midwifery that were seen as 'technical' were being handed over bit by bit to the doctors. Who was allowed to use which tools became key to the negotiation of status within the medical community. That the money then went to the one with the metal tools in his hand was simply an organic result of the 'natural' order of things – one carefully crafted through bans and regulations. In such a way, an economic logic was upheld that dictated male supremacy through the very definition of what was technology.

And what wasn't.

This is a logic that we have upheld.

Today's economists often explain away male–female salary discrepancies with the assertion that women 'choose low-paying sectors'. Women simply insist upon becoming nurses instead of consultants, midwives instead of pharmaceutical lobbyists. But our entire definition of the 'work' different professions involve is intimately linked to our views on gender.

The division of labour between doctor and midwife could

have been entirely different had we had a different perspective on gender. Perhaps then the midwife's role would have been the one to develop into the high-tech, well-paid medical specialty in the delivery room. The midwife might have done everything she does today, but she might also have been able to perform C-sections, say. This would have called for more training, and a much higher salary.

Had we not literally taken the metal instruments out of women's hands, it would have been much harder to take it as given that a midwife should earn less. Or that what the midwife does during a delivery is any less highly skilled.

Had we not had this need to designate one job as 'technical' and the other not, and differentiate between the two hierarchically, our entire healthcare system would have looked different.

Does it even follow that a job performed with tools, for example, should necessarily boast a higher wage or status on the job market? A task isn't by definition more demanding simply for requiring the use of tools. A midwife will reach up a birth canal and deliver a baby whose posterior shoulder is caught by pulling on its forearm, which is no piece of cake. It takes years of training. But one of our economic assumptions is that tasks performed with the hands as opposed to tools somehow require less expertise. The 'feminine' is equated to the low-paid as a direct result of our refusal to view what a woman does as technical.

Similarly, churning butter and skimming cream were jobs long performed by a predominantly female workforce. Women milked cows, made cheese, lugged troughs and hauled huge dairy bowls for straining. They kept accounts on butter production, lifted 50 litre pots of milk and turned enormous wet cheeses on high shelves.

Milk was something that could spurt from a woman's breast, after all, so it followed that curding, churning and pressing should also lie within her skill set. Had God not wanted woman to tend to cheese production, he shouldn't have furnished her with milk-spouting breasts!

Then industrialisation came to Europe, and in the nineteenth century the production of butter, cheese and cream moved off of the farms and into inner-city factories. The old order of things changed. Men started to take an interest in cheese.

One might have thought that women's dairy skills would have brought them some economic benefits. When the butter that they had been so dedicatedly churning started to increase in economic value, women should have stood to gain from it. But that wasn't how it went. When the machines arrived on the scene, the scene started to be taken over by men.

The narrative around milk changed. From cows' udders no longer flowed the feminine mystique in liquid form: milk was now seen as a chemical combination of water, fat, protein, lactose and salt. Which also turned milk into something men could break down and study at university.

In Sweden, two different dairy-related qualifications were introduced: one for men, and one for women. While the men got to learn about the technology, the women got to make cheese. Who came out better economically from this division isn't too hard to guess.

We see the same phenomenon in the art world.

When a man produces an abstract piece in oils on canvas, it is called Art. When a woman produces an identical piece in textiles it is called craftwork.

As a result, one is sold for $86 million at a New York auction house. The other is used as a tablecloth in a summer cottage.

Of course, our view on textiles hasn't always been so disparaging. In the Middle Ages, tapestries were status symbols that graced royal banqueting halls, and in Africa and South America textiles are still considered art in a way that they aren't in Europe. But the point remains that the economic consequences of what we choose to label as 'masculine' and 'feminine' can be enormous.

As a side note, the only reason that the female artist often worked with textiles was because, as a woman, she had been discouraged from studying painting. Because women have historically been excluded from many systems of education, they have been forced to rely more on so-called 'traditional knowledge'. This is still the case in many parts of the world. You learned to make cheese from your mother, not at university; you learned to weave from your aunt, not at art school.

It is this type of knowledge, the one passed from mother to daughter, that tends to be regarded as 'natural' as opposed to 'technical'. This, in turn, has a huge knock-on effect for women's economic opportunity. If a product or process is 'natural', if it has been gifted to you by your foremothers, then you can hardly patent it.

That's often the way with rules. They are built for men.

Decades after man landed on the moon, a myth spread that the reason we had Teflon pans in our kitchens was that NASA had used the material in its spaceships. In actual fact, we had Teflon frying pans in our kitchens years before NASA launched any rockets.

It was a Frenchwoman by the name of Colette Grégoire who in 1954 realised that the Teflon used to coat her husband's fishing gear could also be applied to her frying pans. Her husband became very rich on the idea. The company he founded, Tefal, exists to this day.

But it was easy for the world to swallow the myth that the Teflon frying pan was a by-product of the Cold War's space race. This once again comes down to what we have discussed in this chapter: our assumption that inventions first and foremost emerge from man's great triumphs. Eventually the odd crumb falls down to woman, who can gratefully fry her pancakes without them catching. The reality is, of course, much more complicated than that.

Which makes the possibilities much greater as well.

In the moon suit's final production phases, ILC's seamstresses worked on two specially souped-up Singer sewing machines. These were huge, bulky things: you can't exactly get a half-finished 21-layer moon suit under your average sewing machine foot, can you? The group's most skilled seamstresses spent many a long night with these Singers. By this point the time pressure from NASA was extreme: the rocket could hardly be delayed by Neil Armstrong's clothes.

Eleanor Foraker was one of these seamstresses. She had gone from latex nappies to space suits, and years later she described those long nights in the final stages of production. The thick, soft suits had to be manually lifted and turned to sit correctly under the foot of the machine, and the person who often stepped in to help on those long nights was Leonard Sheperd, head of ILC's entire moon division. In other words, the head honcho was the one to assist her at the machine. As he did, he would ask question after question.

This isn't so much a reflection of Sheperd's character as of the company culture. ILC was a company that expected its male engineers to take sewing lessons, often for weeks at a time. Seamstresses were taken seriously as the technical experts they were. They could almost always offer suggestions on how to improve the suits.

In other words, the garments that Neil Armstrong and Buzz Aldrin wore to the moon in 1969 were made by a company that had actually managed to break down many of the boundaries between what we perceive as 'male' and 'female' technologies.

ILC understood that the bra was a piece of engineering, just as they understood that their latex patent could allow astronauts to move on other celestial bodies – in addition to streamlining a woman's waist. They understood that sewing was a technology, and that soft things can perform hard functions.

Above all, they managed to build an organisation that reflected this.

That is why they could innovate. And that's what took us to the moon.

4

*In which we learn the difference between
horsepower and girl power*

In the summer of 1946, a now-legendary series of lectures was
held at the University of Pennsylvania. The course, which lasted
eight weeks, took place in an un-air-conditioned, red-brick
building at the university's school of electrical engineering. The
students had three hours of lectures in the morning, followed
by lunch, followed by informal seminars in the afternoon.

In the room sat 28 specially invited scientists, mathema-
ticians and engineers.

Those eight summer weeks in Pennsylvania would go
down in history as the Moore School Lectures. The lectures
were recorded on a stuttering tape recorder, and their tran-
scriptions would go on to be sold for exorbitant prices at
exclusive auction houses around the globe: this was the first
public course ever given on the computer.

It was here at the University of Pennsylvania that in World
War II engineers had developed the top-secret ENIAC
computer. Consisting of some 17,500 electron tubes and 5
million soldered joints, the computer was a sprawling, 30 tonne
machine that spread through the basement of the Moore
School of Electrical Engineering. When the news of this

mysterious machine went public after the war, an astonished American media wrote of a gigantic, electronic 'mathematical brain' that could calculate the trajectory of an airborne shell faster than the shell itself could fly.

Suddenly, delegation upon delegation wanted to visit the school in Philadelphia. While the university felt a responsibility to share its knowledge – peace had been made, after all – it didn't want to be left arranging continuous study visits, especially not during term time, when staff had their hands full with teaching. So it decided to hold a formal summer course instead. At 9 am on 8 July 1946, Dr George Stibitz stepped up to the lectern to open the historic course.

'Dr Curtiss has been called away rather suddenly and I have been asked to take his place,' he said.

Stibitz was not one of the school's professors. He had, however, spent World War II building both analogue and digital computers. How this came about is a long story, but by coincidence part of it involves him attending an experimental high school in Dayton, Ohio founded by Charles F Kettering – the same man who invented the electric starter that meant men no longer had to break their jaws when starting their cars.

At this experimental high school Stibitz had developed an interest in mathematics. This eventually led him to Bell Telephone Laboratories in New York, just as the telephone networks were beginning to be rolled out globally.

The more people who bought telephones and the more they used them, the more mathematical calculations were needed behind the scenes to make the network function. And the only tool the ever-sweatier staff had at hand to do these was the mechanical calculator.

People kept on calling, the networks kept on growing, and it became increasingly apparent that a new solution was needed. So Stibitz joined the scramble to build better calculators, the machines that would eventually come to be called 'computers'.

Now, in 1946, Stibitz stood at the lectern and looked out over the auditorium. After a brief historical overview, he soon arrived at the key question of his lecture.

'Is it worthwhile to develop and build more automatic computers, and if so, why?'

This was the question on the lips of everyone in the room that summer. The machine already existed: it was humming away in the basement. So the question was what use it would now have, especially seeing as the war was over. Calculating shell trajectories was no longer of the essence.

Building a computer was a substantial investment at the time. Was it really economically viable? Should we really continue to build these 'electronic brains'?

As Stibitz saw it, once upon a time humanity had started building computers for the simple fact that we found it amusing. Our early mechanical calculators were born of the same impulse that had led us to construct complex carillons of mechanised bells. In other words, the first computers were a type of spectacle. Nothing wrong with that, thought Stibitz. But it was 1946: time to grow up. Time to start seriously considering the economic aspects of it all.

'What is the value of a computing machine?' Stibitz asked. 'In other words, what is the value of the computation which it will do?' he continued.

The only way to answer this question was to consider how computers might be expected to save us money in the future, he noted. What we needed was an economic analysis. And so that's what Stibitz devoted his lecture to.

What were the findings of that first public economic

analysis of the computer and its value to society? Well, Stibitz started with a concrete example of a computer's capacity:

'The work done was the equivalent of four to ten girl-years,' he said.

Sorry?

Here a modern reader will stop short. What does Stibitz mean, exactly, by 'girl-years'? We are used to megabytes and gigabytes as measures of computer power. But 'girl-years'?

The audience at the lecture in 1946 didn't react at all. They went on listening as Stibitz noted that the computer in question had led to 'a saving of about four girl-years'. He then got down to the costs.

If amortised over three years, the machine would cost $4,000 per year. A 'girl', meanwhile, would cost $2,000, and you would need around three of them. Even taking into account the various rental costs for other supplementary machinery, the machine therefore represented a saving of 50 per cent. This was Stibitz's argument for why computers should be embraced by the world, and why, as it was initially suggested, they would 'eventually become a common feature of every large library'. So there we have it: the world's first public economic analysis of a computer, measured in something called 'girl-years'.

What the hell was he on about?

———————

When we invent a new technology, it is often the case that we don't know quite what we have invented. As we have seen, when Karl Benz's automobile first emerged from that barn in Mannheim, the inventor called it a 'horseless carriage'. We tend to make sense of the new through that which it is intended to replace. *Carriage minus horse equals car*, we reason, not quite realising that the automobile is something far greater than the subtraction of already-known variables.

Our contemporary talk of 'driverless cars' today is much the same. Who knows, perhaps our future selves will snigger just as much at that idea as we do now at Karl Benz's 'horseless carriage'? Then again, maybe not.

For in actual fact, we do still speak of 'horsepower'. It is the concept we use to describe the power of everything from our cars to our leaf blowers.

This is all thanks to a Scot called James Watt.

At the end of the eighteenth century, Watt came up with a new and improved version of the steam engine. As a businessman, he was obviously keen to sell his new product. But how would he describe its capacity to potential customers, when they had never even used a steam engine before? This was when Watt realised he should try to translate the advantages of the steam engine into a language that his customers better understood: horses. After all, these were what typically pulled the loads that Watt's steam engine was intended for. If Watt wanted an economic argument as to why potential customers should buy his steam engine, he could simply tell them how many horses it could replace.

So Watt came up with a fairly ballpark estimate of how much a horse could be expected to pull, and then figured out how many of these horses' work his steam engine could replace. The measure was instructive, if somewhat insulting to the horses: one horse does not in fact equal one horsepower. Arial, a famed Swedish stallion of the 1950s, could produce a whopping 12.6 horsepower, for example. Granted, Arial was a pretty extraordinary horse, but a more average creature might be able to manage 10.

That aside, Watt's concept was a measure of machine

power based on an estimate of the capacity of that which used to do the job – in this case the horses. This is exactly the same logic that George Stibitz employed when talking about his 'girl-years'.

You see, not so long ago, computers were in fact women. Literally. Before a computer was a machine, it was a job. You could get a job as a 'computer', and this would mean that you would sit in a room calculating equation after equation for someone else.

From the 1860s until some way into the 1900s, computing was one of a very small number of scientific careers deemed appropriate for women. As astronomer Leslie Comrie put it, the female computers were most useful 'in the years before they (or many of them) graduate to married life and become experts with the housekeeping accounts!'

The use of human computers originated in astronomy. Once humanity had discovered the laws of gravity, we could start calculating when a particular comet would cross the starry skies.

Although the astronomers knew *how* to do these calculations, actually doing them was another matter. That was when they realised they could break up the work into smaller tasks, and bring in dedicated staff to do it instead. All of a sudden they didn't need maths geniuses for the work, just anyone who could count and follow instructions.

A case in point: the French Revolution, among other things, led to a great drop in demand for wigs. Of course, aristocrats weren't the only people to prance around under great swells of false hair, but wigs bore an undeniable whiff of the upper class, whose bewigged heads had recently been rolling *en masse*. This had a knock-on effect for fashion as well as the economy. Many wigmakers lost their jobs, and a lot of them actually went on to become computers, trading in their false hair for trigonometric tables.

Computing work had a fairly low status from the start. It would often involve sitting for 8 to 10 hours doing the same calculation over and over again. By the turn of the nineteenth century, governments, universities and astronomical observatories had started to compile great swathes of data that needed processing and breaking down in order to be of use in, say, navigation at sea. Demand for human computers therefore increased.

So far, most of the computers had been young men. But by the end of the century employers had realised that if you hired women you could save some big money. And that was always an attractive prospect.

Women were paid less than men: you could pay a woman as much as half what you would a man and not hear any complaints. When the Harvard College Observatory started processing astronomical data from its telescope, it appointed a team of exclusively female computers. The director congratulated himself on his brilliant savings tactic. The computing sphere started to be filled not by the predecessors of today's hoodie-clad men (with sometimes questionable social skills), but by respectable ladies with corsets and dreams of science.

The computer's work was not seen to require any great intellect. Which was why it also came to be seen as a suitable job for women. In the USA, computing was also an important employer of African Americans, Jews and people with disabilities, precisely because it was low status. Groups that faced discrimination elsewhere could often get a job as computers, so long as they could count.

In short, these were the jobs that virtually no one else wanted. Of course, the work could be both laborious and dull.

Often you would simply follow instructions that someone else gave you, not unlike the way today's computers follow algorithms. 'Black plus black is black. Red plus red is red. Black plus red or red plus black – hand sheets to group two.'

You could sit doing this for 10 hours.

Even though many of the women now starting to enter the field had degrees in mathematics, and could execute complex calculations (to put it mildly), this brought with it no greater recognition – especially not if they happened to have the wrong colour skin. In the 1900s the industry only became more female-dominated, as increasing numbers of women started to apply for jobs outside of the home.

The University of Pennsylvania employed more than 200 women as computers alone. These were the 'girls' Stibitz mentioned in his lecture. They were there, flesh and blood, in the building. So of course his audience knew what he meant by the term 'girl-years'.

That wasn't the only such term used in those years: a 'kilogirl', for example, could be used to mean something requiring 1,000 hours of calculation work.

But the computers didn't simply replace the 'girls'. They came to be largely programmed by girls, too.

———————

Alan Turing suffered from acute hay fever. For this reason, the brilliant mathematician would often cycle the hills of Buckinghamshire wearing a gas mask. Even indoors, in a meeting, he might whip out the mask if he suspected pollen in the air. No explanation – on it would go, and he would carry on talking like nothing had happened.

The chain on Turing's bicycle had a habit of falling off,

but he refused to replace it. This meant he would often arrive at work with oil-blackened hands, which he would wash with a bottle of turpentine that he kept handy at his desk. He rarely locked his bicycle; his coffee cup, however, was almost always chained to a radiator, lest anyone should try to take it.

During World War II, Turing's mission was to try to crack the Enigma code. Nazi Germany encrypted much of its military radio traffic using a mysterious device known as the Enigma machine. Although the Allies successfully picked up the German radio signals, they couldn't make head nor tail of them. Doing so would mean being able to save their ships from German submarine torpedoes, but the radio traffic was essentially hogwash – all thanks to the Enigma machine and its 53 billion possible combinations.

The art of decoding enemy communications has a long-standing heritage in Britain. As far back as 1324, King Edward II of England gave the order that all international letters – be they incoming or outgoing – must first be collected and read in London. Unsurprising, then, that foreign diplomats at the English court started encoding what they wrote.

In response to this, Queen Elizabeth I later oversaw the establishment of an English secret service. Her personal astrologer was the one tasked with deciphering the letters that her spies managed to intercept. And so it has continued through the centuries. As the secrets grew in stature, so did the complexity of the code.

In 1938, British military intelligence service MI6 acquired Bletchley Park, a country estate in Buckinghamshire. It transferred its entire signals intelligence and cryptography division to this red-brick manor with its green copper dome. Code-breaking astrologers were no longer the order of the day, but men like Alan Turing: 'professorish' types, preferably geniuses.

And geniuses, as we all know, are entitled to their eccentricities, be that donning gas masks in meetings to some rather unconventional beliefs on other people's propensity for stealing their coffee cup.

It was this type of man who was now being tapped on the shoulder in the reading rooms of Oxford and Cambridge, and being asked to report to 'Station X', the military code name for Bletchley Park.

Before World War II, Polish mathematician Marian Rejewski had already succeeded in cracking the infamous German Enigma code. Polish engineers had constructed an analogue calculation machine that could decode the messages, but in 1938 the Germans rebuilt their machine.

The signals were once again indecipherable. In the summer of 1939, the Poles handed over Rejewski's work to the Brits (just prior to being invaded by both Nazi Germany and the Soviet Union). The machine the Poles had built eventually landed on Alan Turing's desk, and he was tasked with leading the work to build a new version. Over the coming years, this work would spawn over 200 top-secret machines that stood in different buildings dotted around Bletchley Park, endlessly cracking the Enigma code.

The men recruited to the code-breaking operation were, like Turing, mainly civilians. They were allowed to wear their own clothes and cycle to work (gas mask optional), and they could even take up their own research in their spare time, should they so choose. The unwritten rule was that these brilliant men from posh universities were excused from the more physically gruelling aspects of military life. This is an idea with some precedence.

In 1798, for example, Napoleon Bonaparte dragged more than 150 French scholars all the way to the pyramids in

Egypt during his military campaign. Everyone from astronomers to botanists were brought along for the ride, and the ordinary soldiers, bitter about the special treatment that the scholars' great intellect was seen to entitle them to, sourly took to calling them 'the donkeys'. Indeed, in battle Napoleon is said to have given the order: 'Donkeys and scholars in the middle!', which of course meant that they would be protected.

Following the same logic, the commanders at Bletchley Park hardly even tried to get men like Turing to march in step. The code-breakers were there to perform vital intellectual work: they couldn't be expected to do morning exercise drills on the front gravel.

But those who were expected to do such morning drills were the women. Women made up 75 per cent of the staff at Bletchley Park in the war years, and it was largely they who operated the huge code-breaking machines.

The engineers at Bletchley Park would eventually come to build the world's first electronic, programmable computer. It was programmed using levers and buttons, and operated by female volunteers from the Women's Royal Naval Service.

Which makes these women the world's first programmers.

The women would work in three shifts, seven days a week: 8 am to 4 pm; 4 pm to midnight; and midnight to 8 am. Even after a whole night working the machines, for much of the war the women would be forced to do the morning drills, as well as march in line to church on bitterly cold Sundays.

For a long time, programming was seen to merely require an ability to follow instructions. Women were good at that, society thought. Women were compliant, and they could perform tasks methodically in a set order. It was in their nature: they conscientiously knitted and sewed from patterns, and cooked from recipes. Plus they were good at explaining things to children.

In 1973 Ida Rhodes, one of the USA's great computing pioneers, compared her ability to program with her ability to teach. 'I had already had the great training of teaching how to do very complicated mathematics to people who knew no mathematics at all. So the machine was really nothing but the same sort of pupil.'

In the 1950s, IBM in the UK measured assembly costs for its computers in what it called 'girl hours'. Historian Mar Hicks has noted how the workforce building these machines was so female-dominated that the company could just as well calculate its entire staffing costs in the woman's lower hourly rate. Which it did.

Come the 1960s, the British civil service was forced to follow new government regulations on equal pay for equal work. This caused problems in public-sector computing, namely because there were so few men.

The Treasury therefore argued that the principle of equal pay for equal work should not be applicable to this particular field. There was, they declared, no 'men's pay scale' in computing that the women's pay levels could be raised to meet. And so the women's lower wage became the standard. Did women flock to programming because it was low-paid, or was it low-paid because so many women applied for these jobs?

It's hard to say.

Programming was a profession that hadn't existed before World War II. So it hadn't acquired any specifically masculine associations, either. No one had managed to come up with a reason why women were unsuitable or unqualified for these jobs: perhaps the men were too busy being blown apart on the battlefield for six years. The patriarchy took its eyes off the ball, so to speak. In addition, computer programming didn't seem to appeal to men as a career. It was considered boring, a job that was easy to combine with morning drills on the gravel during the war and housekeeping and childcare after.

In many ways, the whole business of tending to computers could actually be seen as an extension of woman's nature, it was thought. This is always a handy trope to crack out when justifying why a job should be low-paid. If the faculties required for the job could be defined as inherent to woman's biology, then she couldn't reasonably demand an especially high wage for it, could she?

The nineteenth-century hosiery industry, for example, employed both female and male workers. The women, however, would be put to work sewing up the toes of the stockings, which was the technically more complex task. They also turned out to be rather good at it, and because they turned out to be rather good at it, their employer started to view the ability to sew up a toe as a 'naturally feminine attribute'. And if something was a 'naturally feminine attribute' then it needn't be valued economically as a formal 'skill'.

Which meant the women could be paid less. This was all very practical. For the factory owners, at least.

This way of reasoning put women in an impossible position. If an individual female worker was bad at something, it was proof that womankind as a whole should be paid less. Just look – these womenfolk can't do the job like a man!

But now, simultaneously, the exact opposite was being argued: if a female worker was good at something, it was proof that women should be paid less. Whatever her aptitude for the task, it was taken as proof of why she should earn less money. The trick was always to define anything a woman excelled at as a 'naturally feminine attribute'. She simply couldn't help but have a biological knack for closing the toes of silk stockings, programming computers or looking after the elderly.

This mode of thinking persists to this day.

It isn't uncommon for society to fall back on this reasoning when it comes to careers in elderly care and childcare. We see women come into these jobs and do them well without a great deal of formal training. So we take that as proof that the jobs are 'low skilled' and therefore shouldn't be well remunerated.

If, on the other hand, a man is 'naturally good at something', it often becomes an argument for the exact opposite: for why he should be paid well.

In those nineteenth-century hosiery factories, much was said about the male workers' 'skills'. The female workers, meanwhile, were described in terms of 'speed' and 'accuracy', and the tasks they excelled at were presented as an extension of their nature. They remained passive objects that merely happened to have quick or accurate fingers. Bodies that all but worked by themselves.

The man, meanwhile, was an active participant in his work in a quite different way. He learned things and became 'skilled'. So it comes as no surprise that economic logic promptly demanded that he also be better paid.

At some point in the mid-1960s, computing's image started to change. Programming still broadly speaking involved the same work, but the industry had become more important to society.

Suddenly everything from state VAT-payment systems to cruise-missile programs were being processed through the new computers. It started to dawn on many male managers that these apparatuses were probably pretty key. Could they really be left in the hands of low-paid, chain-smoking girls in miniskirts?

Something had to be done.

A public scheme was launched to encourage men to take an interest in computers. Boys needed to learn to code. A little bit, at least.

The idea was that if they could just get enough promising young men from the right social class to learn the basics of programming, these men could go on to fill the public sector's management roles in the field.

The women who already knew how to program were now tasked with training up the young men to effectively become their own bosses. Management, it was thought, would come easy to the men – by virtue of their social class as well as their sex.

It was no big deal if they knew nothing about computers.

Perhaps it isn't so strange that women then started to leave the industry in droves. They had no real chances for promotion.

This sudden female exodus from computing was such a tangible phenomenon that young British entrepreneur Stephanie Shirley seized on it as a business opportunity. In 1964 she founded a company whose entire concept was to offer female programmers the opportunity to work from home. Her idea was to harness the wasted talent that had left the industry.

Her company, Freelance Programmers, was soon building software for public- and private-sector clients alike. All of their programmers worked from home – long before the days of email and Zoom. But it worked. The company recommended that its programmers play a recording of typewriter sounds in the background whenever customers called. This would give the impression that the work was being done at a 'real' office, while also masking the sounds of any crying children.

When the company went public in the 1990s, it was valued at £2.3 billion.

But what happened to those promising young men, the ones tipped to manage the computerisation of the civil service? Nothing much. As it happens, many of them weren't too fussed about working with computers. Most of them left the managerial positions they had been specially trained for as soon as they were offered other jobs.

In other words, the money the British state invested into training them could just as well have been poured down the drain, according to historian Mar Hicks. In many ways that would have been the smarter decision, economically.

By investing in young men while scaring off its women, Britain managed the spectacular feat of creating its own shortfall in the computing labour market, at the precise moment when the industry was truly becoming important to the economy.

People were terrified by the prospect of technological development leading to such unthinkable things as women getting managerial roles at the Bank of England. So terrified, in fact, that they were more or less prepared to jeopardise the technological jump-start Britain had gained from building the world's first programmable computer at Bletchley Park.

And we of course all know what happened to Alan Turing, that brilliant, pollen-fearing mathematician who was so key to the development of the modern computer. He was convicted of 'gross indecency' (i.e. homosexuality) and chemically castrated. On 8 June 1954 he was found dead in his bed, a half-eaten apple beside him. He is thought to have poisoned himself with cyanide.

Today Silicon Valley is not in Buckinghamshire.

For many reasons.

Throughout the world, the number of women in computing started to drop steadily from the middle of the 1980s, even as percentages of women in other technological and scientific fields grew. Programming went from being female-dominated to male-dominated at the very same time that it went from low status to high status, low paid to high paid.

Of course, this is not the first time in history that a profession has changed gender. From antiquity until the end of the nineteenth century, the position of secretary was a high-status role for men. Grand portraits of secretaries to kings can be found in most of Europe's national galleries, complete with long quills, and muscular calves bulging from their breeches. But at some point in the 1920s the profession became something for women. They sat in long rows, typed away furiously, and were poorly paid for it.

For centuries we allocated jobs by gender based on the physical strength required to perform them. The idea was that somewhere there was a physical order that also dictated the economic order of things. Women were often paid less because they could lift less – and therefore produce less.

But why do we take it for granted that economic value lies in physical strength, specifically? After all, strength isn't the only physical attribute that can bring economic value.

Having small fingers, for example, could be at least as valuable on many factory floors. It was simply a question of what was bring produced. But no one argued that women should be paid more for the slightness of their hands. No, it's the physical attributes typically possessed by men that we have learned to value economically.

Nor is it the case that all men are physically stronger than all women. Or that all the jobs we view as masculine require more strength than those we view as feminine. Women who care for the elderly are expected to lift patients who have fallen over or need turning in bed, and this has not led to any increase in salary or status for them.

Similarly, women were expected to be able to carry 50 litre cans of milk, but not 50 kilo sacks of cement. And just because milk has long been associated with femininity doesn't mean that 50 litres of milk magically stops weighing just as much as 50 kilos of cement.

Over time, we realised that lifting 50 kilo sacks of cement wasn't so good for male backs, either. So we started selling cement in 25 kilo sacks.

So there's that option, too.

The idea of physical strength as a guiding principle for determining female- and male-coded professions has now disappeared across much of the labour market, but it has been replaced with assumptions about 'technical competence' that we allow to dictate how well paid a job should be. Men are more technical than women, we think. If girls are to learn to code, they need encouragement from an early age, while for boys it comes naturally.

In 2017, engineer James Damore got fired from Google after writing a memo that implied that women simply weren't cut out for IT. It was all down to their biological make-up, he declared. Women typically prefer jobs that are social or artistic, and are more interested in people than things, he wrote. But they are also more neurotic, which is another reason why they should maybe stay away from computers. Or at the very least not be encouraged, against their female nature, to take a high-paying role at Google.

Damore's memo caused widespread outrage. But on some level many thought he was right. He took the fall for a very widespread attitude in the Western world that sees women and computers as somehow diametrically opposed.

Economists' standard explanation as to why women earn less than men tends to be that women choose less-well-paying industries. Sadly, girls just don't like computers. Some, like Damore, believe that this has something to do with how their brains are wired. Women simply don't have what it takes to think the way a programmer needs to. At least not a well-paid one.

When programming was low-paid, women unquestionably had what it took.

Others think that it's down to society not encouraging girls into these roles enough. Girls don't play enough video games: they should spend less time with cuddly toys, and more time massacring each other with digital weapons instead. Then they would suddenly get all the well-paid jobs while also 'softening' the hard tech industry by virtue of their femininity. This is something akin to sitting the gifted schoolgirl among the most unruly boys in class in the hope that she'll get them to calm down: the woman's task is to temper the man, not to be anything in herself. The thing is, those who think women aren't biologically wired to like computers and those who think women have been socialised into this dislike both confirm the same misconception: that technology and womanhood are somehow opposed.

That her sex is something a girl must overcome in order to take her place at the computer.

But barely 75 years ago the computer was a girl.

Literally.

FEMININITY

5

*In which a great invention is made in Västerås,
and we go on a whale hunt*

Aina Wifalk got sick in the autumn. Which was often the way with this particular virus. It was why parents told their children not to mess around in the autumn leaves, and not to eat any of the fruit that had fallen from the trees. They thought that polio was somehow seasonal. In Sweden the illness became known as 'the ghost of autumn'.

The disease would often start with a fever and a strange feeling at the nape of your neck. If you were unlucky it would get into your bloodstream. This would take three or four days, and that was when you might suddenly stand up, not knowing that the steps you were taking would be your last.

You fell to the floor, paralysed.

The polio virus was old: historians believe it had once even struck down an Egyptian pharaoh. But the first time the disease reached aggressive, epidemic proportions was in Sweden in the late nineteenth century. It was all rather strange: people had just stopped dying in droves from smallpox, dysentery and scarlet fever. They had learned to wash their hands with the new mass-produced soaps, and to dress in cheap cotton clothes that were much easier to keep clean. Then polio came along, and Scandinavia quickly got a bad name as a hazardous breeding ground for epidemics.

Aina Wifalk was 21 years old when she fell ill. She had just started studying in Lund, a university town not far from where her parents had rented some farmland when she was little. The year was now 1949. World War II was over, and Sweden had just stopped its rationing of soap and detergent. Swedish manufacturing was booming: unlike in the rest of Europe, the factories hadn't been bombed to the ground in the war, as Sweden had managed to stay out of the fighting. The Swedes now ate meat soup with dumplings and watched their economy grow, while the government started investing in a new and extensive welfare state.

Growing up, the young Wifalk didn't have any grandiose dreams. She didn't have time for such things. She had been far too busy working to put some money aside for her studies. Education, as she saw it, was the key to a better life.

She had just started at nursing school in Lund when, on 4 September, she came down with what she thought was a cold. She had a stiff neck and felt very tired. It was only a few days later that the pain started in her lower back, a radiating, cramp-like twinge that then moved down towards her feet with alarming determination. One week later she was in the hospital, unable to raise her right leg.

The paralysis attacked her body, affecting her right arm, abdomen and both legs. The pain was unbearable, especially at night and especially in the hips. Wifalk looked down at her legs. She knew that they were there, but she could no longer feel them.

By October Wifalk could neither walk nor stand. The doctors first put her in a fabric corset with leather panelling, and then one of plaster. She couldn't lift either leg with her knees straight, and could only sit up when using her arms to support herself. Four months later she started to walk again, with two walking frames that she shuffled in front of her. Every step was a struggle, every metre a victory. Few have given as much thought to what it takes for the human body to move through this world as those who have been sick in this way. By the end of February, Wifalk had swapped her walkers for two crutches. One under each armpit.

And that was how she would get around for the next 15 years.

Wifalk never did become a nurse. Instead she got a job as a hospital counsellor in the orthopaedic clinic of Västerås Central Hospital, and there, in that little town on the shores of Lake Mälaren, she started a new life. She moved into an apartment on the ninth floor, went for drives around the great lake, and walked the city streets on her crutches. By day Wifalk worked hard for her patients, and in the evenings she devoted her time to founding disability organisations. At times the hospital just didn't understand the reality of her situation, and when that happened she made sure they knew it: that ramps, for example, might be a good idea if they wanted people with mobility issues to be able to enter the building.

Every Sunday morning Wifalk went swimming. On those occasions the Red Cross would send volunteers to the local swimming pool to help her to get changed: getting in and out of her swimsuit was, in all honesty, more strenuous than the exercise itself.

As the years passed, Wifalk got an accessible ground-floor apartment, and a new job in social-services administration. She also wanted a dog, but knew that would never happen. In the

1960s she developed something of an obsession for improving the world around her, in matters both big and small. She fixed a cowbell to her patio door, for instance, so she would be able to hear any possible intruders. Although quite what she would have done if anyone did try to break in remains unclear. Similarly, she installed a roller blind under her sink, because she hated seeing the rubbish bags out in the open.

She didn't sleep particularly well: the nights were when the pain came. It moved through her body in waves that she would follow through the night, sleeping for around 90 minutes at a time, at most. She refused to take painkillers for fear of the side effects, and besides, she liked the company of her own thoughts. She knew that the crutches had worn out her shoulders, and that was why she was in so much pain. A body like hers was not meant to move freely in the world; it was supposed to be hidden away. That was what society had decided.

Wifalk, however, had other plans.

At the end of the 1960s, the now-41-year-old Wifalk got in touch with Gunnar Ekman, a designer at the county council's workshops. She asked him to build her a wheeled walker. It was to have four wheels, a handle, brakes, and a board to sit on. And it should be foldable: she wanted to be able to pop it in her car and take it with her wherever she went. Ekman designed and constructed the walker following Wifalk's instructions. And with this the modern rollator was born.

The lame cast aside their crutches and started to walk.

Or Aina Wifalk did, at the very least.

Whether the rollator born that day in Västerås was *actually* the world's first is difficult to say. As with many inventions throughout history, the answer is hard to unpick.

There were earlier patents for similar walking aids that Wifalk was unaware of, but none of these caught on in the same way. Having the idea to put wheels on a walker is one thing, but what Aina Wifalk had was a vision of a different kind of life for her and those like her.

Wifalk's rollator wasn't something that would stand gathering dust in a hospital corridor, a gadget that might occasionally help a weak-boned senior to walk the few metres from bed to bathroom in a dreary old age that was basically a waiting room for death. No, in Wifalk's eyes the rollator was a 'sidekick', a machine to *live* with. It would be at your side when you mangled your laundry, watered your plants or went for a coffee. The modern rollator was created in response to the limitations of Aina Wifalk's body, along with her desire for freedom. Had she belonged to a different social class, body or sex, people would have undoubtedly called her 'entrepreneurial'. But they didn't.

Instead she was forced, unwillingly, into early retirement.

───────────

It is often said that the Swedish summer is the best day of the whole year. Like most of Västerås's population, Aina Wifalk would gaze out over Lake Mälaren through the winter months, waiting for that cracking sound that announced the breaking of the ice. Six months of darkness make people thirst for sun.

Swedes had enjoyed three weeks of statutory annual leave since 1938. After the war it occurred to one eager businessman to make use of the many planes that had been grounded by the peace. He turned them into charter planes, and soon wide-eyed Swedes were able to go on group holidays to the sun of southern Europe. Hotels in Mallorca started serving Swedish coffee, Greek tavernas organised Swedish folk dancing, and ABBA did their very first gig for free, in exchange for a discount on a package holiday to Cyprus.

Wifalk, too, had dreams of Spain. But she had a problem: her rollator had nowhere for her to put a suitcase. And how else would she get there? She needed a walking aid with some sort of shelf on which to place her bag.

One day she noticed a book trolley at a local library in Västerås, which was used by staff to wheel the books around to the different sections. Wifalk mail-ordered the very same trolley frame and had someone help her screw wheelchair wheels onto it. A new rollator was born. Perhaps this would be the one to take her to Spain? She tested it excitedly, but no: when she put her suitcase on the new construction, its wheels stopped spinning. The weight of the suitcase was too great for the repurposed library cart.

But that was when Aina Wifalk opened her fridge. As it happened, on top of that day's other projects, Wifalk had also been defrosting her freezer. Now she took out one of the fridges rack's and attached it to her rollator. She put her suitcase on the rack and, lo and behold, the wheels started spinning.

She travelled to Spain triumphantly.

With time, Aina Wifalk's invention would help many of the world's elderly to realise a whole new freedom. With the rollator, anyone who suffered from osteoporosis, arthritis or dizziness could regain almost full freedom of movement within their homes. Suddenly they even dared to pop out to the shops for milk; if they couldn't make it the whole way, they could simply take a seat on the rollator and have a little rest. It was no coincidence that this invention was made by a woman who had struggled her way about town with a crutch in each armpit for 15 years. When you live in a world that isn't built for you, it's probably easier to envisage how it can be improved. Not just for yourself, but for everyone.

Today we type on keyboards partly thanks to Italian inventor Pellegrino Turri, who wanted a way of communicating with his blind friend Carolina Fantoni da Fivizzano. He built one of the world's first mechanical typewriters, which allowed the pair to write letters to one another without her having to dictate her words to a servant first.

Similarly, the world's first email protocol was written by the American Vint Cerf. He was hard of hearing, and could easily see the potential of email, since it would help him to keep in touch with his family while at work – without them having to scream into a receiver at full volume.

That you control your mobile phone with the swipe of a finger is down to a different American: Wayne Westerman. Nerve damage to Westerman's right hand prevented him from using a mouse, so he developed a technology that meant he could control his computer through the touch of a pad. In 2005 Westerman sold the technology to Apple.

Two years later, Steve Jobs could launch the world's first iPhone.

The global walking-aids market has been valued at $2.2 billion. This figure is expected to grow rapidly over the coming decades, as the world's population gets older and our perceptions of old age change.

In other words, Aina Wifalk's invention had a big impact on the world. But the same can't be said of its impact on her bank balance. Today there is no foundation in Wifalk's name that gives out grants to entrepreneurs with disabilities or finances research into accessible design. What little money Aina Wifalk earned from her rollator she bequeathed to the Swedish Church on the Costa del Sol.

She really did love those package holidays.

Aina Wifalk's problem was that she didn't have any money, which meant that she couldn't make any real money from her idea, either. Yes, she could produce one or two rollators for herself, enhance the design with some DIY fridge racks, and wheel them up and down the high street in Västerås as she went about her daily life. But to turn this into an export product that could be rolled out across the globe would require quite different sums of money. Which she didn't have. Nor was it particularly likely that anyone would want to invest in her. Of this she was well aware: 'Who would listen to me, a handicapped lady among all the lads?'

Aina Wifalk never patented her rollator. Instead she sold the idea for what would be around £750 in today's money, and a royalty of 2 per cent on that particular manufacturer's sales.

'I was almost a little too nice,' she would later recount.

Yes, Aina. That's one way of putting it.

Today there are probably those who would have recommended Wifalk a course on female entrepreneurship, who would tell her to 'lean in', 'make her voice heard' and 'believe in herself'. Who would hand her a book on negotiation techniques, and another on putting together a winning pitch deck. But that isn't what this is about. This is about our whole financial system.

And how it systematically excludes women's ideas.

Many small companies never make use of any form of credit. Let's say you sell apple juice. You put the money from each sale away in the cash register with a ding, and when your supplier comes by in the afternoon you take the cash out of the register and use it to pay her.

It is perfectly possible to run a company in this way, but it makes it pretty hard to grow: if you want to open another juice factory you may need a bank loan, and even if you have no plans of expanding, you never know what the future might bring.

Your supplier might get hit by a swarm of Asian hornets, and while they ruthlessly decimate the entire local honey-bee population, you are forced to buy expensive apples from far away. That's when you need a bank that will let you go into your overdraft for 90 days.

Your juicer might break, in which case you will need a new one if you are to prevent production from grinding to a halt. And if you don't have an arrangement that allows you to pay within 30 days, things could get pretty tight.

In other words, credit is a way of managing risk in the economy. At its best, it's a case of a stronger player (such as a bank) going in and helping out a temporarily weaker player (the apple-juice producer). But when the system breaks down – which it tends to do quite often – we get what is commonly known as a credit crunch.

The global financial crisis of 2008 is a classic example. It was brought on by the collapse of some fairly insane credit gimmicks on the American housing market. This meant that one day, banks were suddenly unwilling to lend money to other banks. The credit markets across much of the globe froze over, and companies that had previously been able to rely on access to credit could no longer do so.

Businesses couldn't expand, and many were forced to let go of staff. The people who lost their jobs no longer had salaries with which to buy products and services, which in turn forced the companies that had previously sold to them to let people go. Unemployment grew, which meant the state collected less money in tax, while also having to pay out more in unemployment benefits. The deficit soared. Credit crunches have a nasty habit of turning into vicious circles. Without intervention, entire economies can be held back for years.

The problem is that the women of the world live in a permanent female credit crunch. It is currently estimated that some 80 per cent of all female-owned businesses have an unmet need for credit. This is because our current financial system was never built for women.

A female farmer in Côte d'Ivoire can't get a bank loan because she rents, rather than owns, the land she cultivates. The bank says she has no 'security' with which to guarantee the loan. As women are much less likely to own things like land or property, they are also much less likely to be approved for credit.

Throughout the world, women are deemed a greater financial risk than men. They have less money, own fewer assets and, on top of that, their bodies often do things like carry and give birth to children, which come with their own economic risks.

In addition, many women start up beauty salons, cafés and day nurseries, types of companies that are considered less 'serious'. And if women aren't starting companies in these 'frivolous' industries, they will often establish boring, steady businesses like doctor's surgeries or accounting firms. These businesses lack the prestige of a tech start-up and are not thought to have growth potential that investors look for. As a consequence, they tend not to be prioritised in the same way, especially when it comes to the really big cheques.

For someone to give you money, you must first and foremost be seen to be economically competent. When we think of such a person, we think of a man. The person we choose to invest in or back with credit is the person we choose to believe in. And that person typically isn't a woman – if she is, she tends to be white.

There isn't a single country on the planet in which women collectively don't have less money and less economic opportunity than men. The fact that men have money and women don't is one of the factors that fundamentally shapes our world. Naturally, it also plays a huge part in determining which innovations become a reality and which ones don't.

There are, obviously, many perfectly rational reasons why female entrepreneurs may not get loans, credit or investments. But even when adjusting for these sorts of factors, the fact remains that women are women and are therefore treated differently. If you are a person of colour or have a disability then things get even harder. Much harder. All of this, despite the fact that businesses started by women generally turn a profit faster than those started by men.

The credit crunch of 2008 held the world economy back for 10 years. Meanwhile, the ongoing female credit crunch has been holding the world economy back since . . . well, for ever. Of course, sometimes having to build a company from scratch, without any external loans or investments to speak of, can be a good thing. But in many industries that just doesn't work: the risks are simply too great. Consequently, many women give up. And yet we aren't calling world leaders to sit, po-faced, before seas of microphones at emergency summits to discuss the female credit crunch. No central-bank governors stand ready to inject trillions to unblock the credit system for women. In a permanent female credit crunch, women do as Aina Wifalk did: sell their innovations cheaply, or let them die.

This has huge ramifications. But to understand just how vast these are, we must set out for the polar circle's coldest waters.

We're going on a whale hunt.

———————————

In the 1800s, whaling was one of the grubbiest, riskiest and most violent undertakings that anyone could engage in. It was also one of the most lucrative.

The American whaling ships would set out for the far north around Alaska or into the remote Pacific. When the crew caught sight of one of the magnificent creatures, they would hop into smaller whaleboats that would be lowered from the mother ship and row in reckless pursuit of the mammal through the waves and past the icebergs.

The aim was to get close enough to the whale to harpoon it: in order to do this, you would have to get the point of your spear to pierce the blubber while you also kept hold of the other end of the rope. Obviously it would be impossible to haul in a 45,000 kilo whale on a single line from a rowing boat. Instead, once the barb had caught, the crew simply had to hang on. The wounded whale would then try to thrash itself free. By all means, this was an intense experience, but the sailors in that little boat would just have to ride it out. The whale would drag them helplessly over the waves for two to three hours, and only once the creature had given up its dance of death could the crew – had they survived – hoist it up onto the mother ship.

The whale was killed because of its blubber, an important part of the economy of the day. The whalers rendered it into oil in gigantic vats on deck, and this oil was used to illuminate much of the world at the time.

You see, whale oil can burn with the most unfailingly white light. The lighthouses that guided the great ships to shore blazed with boiled blubber, as did the street lights in New York City and the lamps that miners carried as they crawled through tunnels to hack the coal out of the earth's underbelly. The cogwheels of the Industrial Revolution were (literally) hot stuff, and when production ramped up, so did the temperatures in the machines. These wheels needed to be kept well oiled, and whale oil turned out to cope very well with this kind of heat.

This was why the whale had to die.

Since the products that came out of whaling were so important to society, whaling became an industry with extremely high profit margins. In the mid-nineteenth century, an investment in an American whaling expedition could offer three times the return that the same investment in agriculture would give. But this was a game that you needed big money to play.

To send a whaling ship to Alaska required an initial investment of $30,000 – almost 10 times what it would cost to open an average-sized factory. Yes, there were rich families in the USA and yes, they were interested in whaling, but they didn't have limitless wealth.

It was also a very risky type of investment. It isn't hard to see that a lot can go wrong when you're being churned around for hours in a rowing boat in the Arctic Ocean by a whale in its death throes. One in three whaling expeditions ran at a loss. And it was from this combination of potentially enormous profit and enormous risk that a new industry was born: venture capital.

A new group of investors came up with the idea to go to several rich families and ask them to cough up smaller pots of money. In his authoritative book on American venture capital, Professor Tom Nicholas recounts how these early 'venture capitalists' would pool this money into a fund, which they would use to buy a ship and recruit a captain. The captain would be responsible for taking the ship out to the whales and then home again. If the captain succeeded, the venture capitalists would split the carry between their investors. 'Carry' is the term used in venture capital to this day.

This new system made it possible for the rich to spread their investments across several different whaling expeditions. If two ships went under but a third came back to harbour, the profit made from the third ship would often more than compensate for the money lost on the first two. Thanks to the venture capitalists, more and more whaling ships could now be financed.

And in the end they practically cleared the seas.

Eventually we stopped illuminating our cities with boiled blubber. Women did away with their whalebone crinolines, factories started using other lubricants for their machinery, and the venture-capitalist model only really resurfaced a century later.

But it did so with a vengeance.

It was when personal computers were developed in the decades following World War II that the venture capitalists, those old whalers of yore, set sail for California.

The place where they came ashore would come to be known as Silicon Valley.

Nowadays many young people want to become entrepreneurs, but in the USA of the 1950s this kind of career choice was seen as rather nutty. Why 'work for yourself' when there were millions of well-paid jobs in big, stable companies that would look after you for the rest of your life and give you a gold watch on retirement? Entrepreneurship was something for eccentric hippies who built computers in their garages. Still, an economy needs people who are willing to throw money at such oddities.

The economy needs people who might contemplate investing in previously untried people, technologies and products. That was how the American tech scene came to be the new whaling: an industry that demanded great investment at great risk, but which also offered the potential for enormous profit to those who bet on the right venture.

The venture capitalists came up with the money, and helped new companies in Silicon Valley with contacts and business plans. An alliance was formed between tech entrepreneurs and venture capitalists that would change the world, becoming fundamental to the digital economy we live in today.

When the whaling ships returned to shore in the 1800s, the crew would usually take 20 per cent of the carry to the investors' 80 per cent. The ship's captain, however, would get 2 per cent of the entire investment in advance, the idea being that this would compensate him for having to stock the ship with food and other supplies for the long journey. In other words, the captain would take his 2 per cent regardless of whether the expedition was successful. In many ways this is still how venture capital works today.

Around 2 per cent of the money that venture capitalists take from their funds and invest into a company tends to go into their own pockets, regardless of how that venture goes. This 2 per cent is the fees for their services. While these services can often play an important role in a company's success, what sort of incentive does this actually create?

The answer, of course, is that venture capitalists want to make their investments as big as possible. If they put £10 million into a company, then every year they will make their 2 per cent on that £10 million, whether or not the company ever turns a profit.

If, on the other hand, they were to invest £500,000 into a much smaller company, their guaranteed annual income would only be £10,000. As such, it makes more sense for them to make 10 gargantuan investments than 100 smaller ones. Even if only one of these 10 gargantuan investments makes it safely back to shore, so to speak, the venture capitalists will get 20 per cent of the carry, which will probably more than make up for none of the other companies ever turning a profit.

All of this means that smaller investments into companies that don't have their sights set on world domination become rather unappealing. The investors want the potential for extreme growth: they want to find the next Facebook, spear the 40,000 kilo whale, and take home the whole damn jackpot. The venture capitalists are very comfortable playing this risky game, especially since – unlike the captains of the old whaling ships – they aren't risking their own skins.

Or even their own wallets.

But what does all of this have to do with Aina Wifalk and her rollator? It's not as though there was a great deal of venture capital floating around central Sweden in the 1970s. The funding Wifalk applied for was an entirely different kettle of fish. But Wifalk herself noticed that no one wanted to invest in a 'handicapped lady among all the lads'. And this economic fact – that only ideas from a very small subset of the population stand a chance when it comes to investment – has been scaled up to bewildering levels thanks to venture capital. On top of a system that already put woman at a disadvantage, venture capital and its whaling logic has created something quite extreme.

Less than 1 per cent of venture-capital funds in the United Kingdom go to start-ups founded entirely by women. Eighty-three per cent of deals made by British venture capitalists had no women at all on their founding teams, according to a 2019 report commissioned by the Treasury.

For every pound of venture-capital investment in the United Kingdom, all-female founder teams get less than 1 pence, while all-male founder teams get 89 pence, and mixed-gender teams 10 pence.

'The distribution of Swedish venture capital remains skewed between the sexes,' wrote financial newspaper *Dagens Industri* in 2020. In 2019, just over 1 per cent of Swedish venture capital was invested into companies founded by women. The choice of the word 'skewed' here is in itself interesting: we're talking about money in over 98 per cent of cases going to men. But fine, let's call it 'skewed'.

In the rest of the European Union a very similar 'skew' emerges: venture-capital-backed tech companies with all-male founder teams get 93 per cent of the capital, for example. In the USA, less than 3 per cent of venture funding goes to businesses with all-female founders, which is quite shocking, considering that nearly 40 per cent of all businesses in the USA are owned by women. Things are changing, but very slowly: at the current rate it will take 25 years for women even to get their hands on 10 per cent of the money.

But does this really matter? At the end of the day, companies financed by venture capital are a very small fraction of all companies.

It matters because we have given these companies power to set the rules of the game for the rest of the economy. The tech revolution of the past few decades has seen industries that used to be part of the physical economy become part of a new digital economy, one that exists solely on the devices in our pockets.

For the first time in history, a company can actually *create* markets with billions of customers. Nowadays it's possible to found a social network with 800 million users, a dating site that operates in 190 countries, or a video platform for almost the entire world. These are the types of colossal beasts that venture capitalists are hoping to catch.

It's all in the whaling logic.

Today's entrepreneurs are more dependent on venture capital than ever before. The matter of who gets this capital is what determines what cars we will get to drive, what groundbreaking medical treatments we will receive, and what logic will guide the robots to whom we are yielding increasing power. This is why it is such a problem that women have hardly even a foot on this playing field.

Around the turn of the millennium, it used to take about three years for a tech company to return to shore (i.e. go public). Now it takes almost a decade. Google received less venture capital on its entire voyage to the stock exchange than what Swedish electric-scooter company Voi received in 2019 alone. How can other entrepreneurs compete with a bunch of guys who suddenly have $85 million with which to shower Stockholm's streets in electric scooters?

They can't.

The one with the cheque for $85 million is unbeatable. He is the one who gets the chance to rewrite the rules for everything: from Stockholm's pavement traffic to how we buy books, run election campaigns or finance our media.

Or consider WeWork, the now-infamous start-up that failed spectacularly with its IPO – initial public offering – in 2019. This disaster made its investor SoftBank pour at least $5 billion into the imploding company – about $1.5 million more than was invested in all-female-founded companies by venture capital in the USA during the same period.

Since over 97 per cent of all venture capital goes to men, it follows that our software, apps, social media, artificial intelligence and hardware are now being created, financed and developed by men. There's nothing wrong with men. But there is something wrong with a system that shuts women out.

The alliance between venture capital and Silicon Valley has meant that the rules for an entire industry can now be decided by a single company's business plan. And when this venture capital is almost exclusively going to men, we face a problem that is infinitely bigger than a young woman not getting financial backing for her new app, Aina Wifalk never getting rich from her rollator or women not getting loans to expand even profitable nail salons.

When ideas and inventions are created by such a small, homogenous group, it's unsurprising that our world is suddenly filled with services and companies built to cater for a certain urban white middle class. The founders of these companies are praised as great entrepreneurs, but can we genuinely not do better?

In the past few years we have started to equate innovation with things like 'Uber for catsitters', 'Tinder for farmers' and 'Netflix for historical documentaries', a fourth and even better camera on our iPhones and a type of economy that has made a handful of men richer than anyone on earth has ever been before. These men have then been able to fundamentally change the rules of the game for the labour market, democracy and media. Was it worth it? And could we do things differently?

It can escape no one who hears Aina Wifalk's story that the rollator was possible precisely because of who she was. Her experience of illness and disability is what made her think the way she did. Diversity is absolutely crucial to the best ideas coming through. This is not the case today, and it's far from just a question of discrimination: it lies within the backbone of our very financial system.

The companies that struggle to find backing are the more modest projects: practical innovations that it is quite easy to see turning a profit. To a large extent these are the types of companies that women establish, and they don't fit within the whaling logic.

That women are shut out economically is a waste that we can ill afford, especially since we are now facing perhaps the greatest collective innovation problem in history. Since the 1860s we have emitted over 500 billion tonnes of greenhouse gases into our atmosphere, while simultaneously clearing the forests and exploiting land in unprecedented ways. This makes it increasingly difficult for our planet to absorb carbon dioxide, and the consequences are threatening to render earth uninhabitable for humans. Innovation and new technology are a key part of the solution to the climate emergency. We need all the good ideas we can get.

But instead of changing the financial system, we are trying to teach women to take more risks. To stand before male investors and present ideas with the potential to 'crush!', 'disrupt!', 'dominate!' and 'own it!'. That's how they speak, ergo how you must speak if you want backing. Facebook's motto was 'move fast and break things': if you grow big enough and fast enough, the profits will eventually follow. Don't get caught up in the consequences, just pursue a monopoly and crush everything in your way. The entrepreneur is portrayed as a superhero who, in the name of innovation, has the right – nay, the duty – to disregard the rules that apply to everyone else. This is the ideal that has led us to where we are now. But it didn't have to be this way.

The tragedy of the patriarchy is that we have taken the human experience and split it in two. We have said that certain aspects of what it means to be human are female and others male, and that the male must supersede the female. This not only takes shape in men being given precedence over women in society, it also finds expression in values that we call 'female' being pushed aside in the economy.

The way we traditionally raise boys has, more than anything else, been about telling them to shut down, deny and repress everything that can be seen as 'feminine' within themselves. Don't cry, don't be so sensitive, don't stand there admiring the flowers. But all of these are, of course, also facets of being human.

Ones that we are denying men.

In economics we do the same: female-coded values such as feelings, dependence, connectedness and anything considered to be 'soft' are not regarded as things that create economic value – or even have the right to exist in the hard world of economics. If they do, they must certainly be secondary. Corporate social responsibility, environmental considerations and social justice are all well and good, but they are small fry compared to things like market dominance and winner-takes-all competition to the bitter end. In our attempts to uphold this economic logic at all costs – a logic in which the male supersedes the female – we lose so very much.

Including ourselves.

Couldn't innovation just as well 'repair' as 'crush'? Or new inventions just as well 'help' as 'disrupt'? Couldn't they 'contribute' to the market ecosystem instead of 'dominating' it?

What we choose to invest in as a society says a lot about what we value – and what we don't. What problems are we currently throwing millions at in our attempts to solve? Or, rather: whose? And whose problems are we *not* seeing?

The whaling logic is masculine. Not because it is biologically inherent to the male, but because it embodies a number of values that we have learned to code as such and, therefore, also accord more value than those we code as female. As a result, companies that try to operate outside of this logic don't enjoy the same opportunities. In fact, we have as good as excluded the values that we describe as 'feminine' from economics. We have dismissed them to the private sphere – a place where it is acceptable to 'care' and 'repair', 'help' and 'conserve'. Required, even – at least if you are a woman. The market, meanwhile, is a place for 'crushing', 'disrupting' and 'dominating'. As we have seen, this definition of what innovation 'is' excludes many female entrepreneurs. But that isn't even the worst of it.

The worst of it is the wealth of innovation that remains untapped.

In 1998, 88-year-old Queen Ingrid of Denmark arrived at a lavish wedding ceremony at the Danish royal family's summer residence. She was wearing a turquoise lace gown, which she accessorised with a matching mint-green rollator.

This was a big moment for older women's mobility in this part of the world. For women across large swathes of northern Europe, the images of Queen Ingrid unapologetically wheeling her rollator to the big palace party normalised it as a walking aid.

Just because you are afraid of stumbling doesn't mean you have to miss the ball. Just because you don't walk like everyone else doesn't mean you have to hide away at home, or give that lacy turquoise gown a miss for anything in the world.

On that day, when her invention really broke through into the mainstream, Aina Wifalk had been dead for over 15 years. Yes, her rollator rolled out into the world. But how many ideas from others who – for whatever reason – didn't 'fit in' never saw the light of day?

Aina Wifalk's story can at least be written. What cannot, however, are the stories of all of the solutions that never were. Who gets to play a part in inventing our world? And who doesn't?

And what is the cost to us all?

6

In which influencers get richer than hackers

The first three lipstick shades cost $29 each and sold out in 30 seconds. The next day you could find them on eBay at almost 10 times the price. The market was crying out for these kits containing a lipstick and matching liner. The idea was that you would apply the pencil just outside the natural lip line and then fill it in with the lipstick, thus making your lips look fuller than they were. The technique was nothing new, nor were the colours, but the enormous demand sent prices soaring on every buying and selling site on the internet.

When Kylie Jenner launched another three lipstick shades four months later, they were gone in 10 minutes. Then just 20 years old, within a few years she would go on to sell half her company for $600 million. It didn't matter that people whispered about her business largely being built on exaggerated figures and the odd lie. The money she had made from it was still just as real.

Kylie Jenner first appeared on TV at the tender age of 10. She made her debut playing the role of herself in a reality-TV show about the family she happened to be born into. At the time, the show was broadcast in 160 of the world's 190-odd countries. Every week the world could tune in and follow Kim, Kourtney, Khloé, Kendall, Kylie and their mother Kris Jenner as they went about their daily lives. The men of the family essentially served as props in the series – the show was all about the women: Kim and Kourtney working out at their home gyms while sipping on frappés and scrolling through Instagram, Khloé picking her way through a huge bowl of takeaway salad on the sofa, Kendall zipping off on a private jet in tracksuit bottoms and super-long eyelashes made of glued-on mink hairs.

These North American sisters came to define the Western world's feminine ideal in the 2010s, not unlike how British model Twiggy had defined it in the 1960s. Back then it had been a thin silhouette and doe eyes against a backdrop of a swinging London. Now it was flawless skin, cat eyes, high cheekbones, tiny waists and big lips. Not to mention the booty. Musicians sang song after song in praise of the female posterior. Not since baroque painter Peter Paul Rubens laid down his brushes in the 1600s had the derrière occupied such a central place in mainstream culture. Kim, Kourtney, Khloé, Kendall and Kylie were heralded as symbols of this new ideal.

The sisters helped millions of women to discover their own eyebrows and start diligently grooming them with special brushes. They normalised Botox by broadcasting injections of the poison into their faces, and they made it acceptable to spend 90 minutes in front of the mirror applying different shades of blush to their cheekbones. They also became incredibly rich.

Above all Kylie. The youngest of them all.

In the 2010s, it was fairly easy to start a successful company if you, like Jenner, had more followers on Instagram than Germany had residents. If that was the case, then you already possessed the object of the fiercest competition – attention.

Kylie Jenner captured the imagination of young women at a time when they were becoming increasingly difficult to reach. They had retreated into their own digital worlds, beyond the grasp of traditional advertising strategies. That Jenner could still speak to young women gave her economic power – a power that surely surprised even her.

In February 2018, Jenner wrote on Twitter: 'Sooo does anyone else not open Snapchat anymore? Or is it just me . . . ugh this is so sad.' This was immediately taken to mean that Jenner no longer liked the social platform Snapchat, which triggered a whole chain reaction of 'SELL SELL SELL!' on the market. Before the day's end, Snapchat's share value had caved by 6 per cent, $1.3 billion wiped from its market value.

When Jenner started selling lipstick in 2015, people on the internet had already been discussing her lips for two years. Had she, or had she not, had filler injections? People put their lips inside glasses and sucked until their lips looked just as inflated as hers. This happened just as the make-up industry was going through big structural change. Young women were abandoning their mothers' L'Oréals and Maybellines in favour of new products from new brands, things that they had heard about on social media or in make-up tutorials on YouTube, where women of their own age contoured their eye creases and shaped their eyebrows in front of smartphone cameras. It was this move away from the old and out into the digital that Jenner managed to tap.

The attention surrounding her person – the same attention that would drive Snapchat's shares into the ground – she now harnessed for the sale of her own products, which also happened to be linked to the body part she was most known for: her lips.

And the money came rolling in.

In 2018, American magazine *Forbes* named Kylie Jenner the world's youngest self-made billionaire, a title that had previously belonged to Facebook founder Mark Zuckerberg. The path to the greatest possible riches at the youngest possible age appeared to have changed, from building websites in student dorms at Harvard à la Zuckerberg, to selling lipstick à la Jenner from her mother's much-filmed kitchen table in Los Angeles. The influencer appeared to have beaten the hacker at capitalism, and who could have imagined that this was where the digital revolution would lead us next?

In 2010, renowned American investor Peter Thiel muttered in disappointment: 'We wanted flying cars, instead we got 140 characters.' He was of course taking a dig at the social platform Twitter, which had found success by letting users express themselves in 140 characters. Was this really the apex of innovation? Today Thiel could just as well have remarked: 'We wanted flying cars, instead we got Kylie Jenner behind five different glittery Instagram filters.'

The 2010s were when the internet showed it could do something new: combine television's ability to reach people with the intimacy of your average phone call. This was social media. And it gave birth to an economy largely dominated by women.

The decade saw blogpreneurs, mumpreneurs, influencers and Instagrammers come to represent female business success, all while the numbers of women at major tech companies like Apple, Google, Facebook and Microsoft remained shockingly low.

Social media also brought about a sea change in activities that had previously belonged to the private sphere. All of a sudden, making food, planning family holidays, setting the table, arranging flowers or picking out clothes for the kids could be something you could build a business around. Social-media platforms made it possible for relatively normal women to earn money from their marriage, their children and their consumer choices in a completely new way.

What was interesting was that this was happening in a society that generally didn't value women's traditional labour all that much. Things like making food, planning family holidays, setting the table, arranging flowers or picking out clothes for the kids aren't counted as 'economic activities' in standard economic theory. They are invisible and assumed to lack 'economic relevance'. But now, suddenly, entire businesses could be built around them.

Without even being a man. In the past, it was often only when men stepped into traditionally female-dominated fields – from dairymaking to food preparation – that the money started to come. Not this time round. These new business models started cropping up, from Nyköping to Nairobi and from Århus to Moscow.

For someone who wasn't Kylie Jenner, things might go something like this: a young Chinese woman comes to Italy to study biochemistry. A fan of shopping, she soon discovers how much cheaper it is to buy European designer goods in Europe than in China. She also knows how much demand for luxury products among the Chinese middle class is growing. So why not buy Armani skirts and Chanel shoes in Milan and start selling them to Chinese consumers?

The 2010s saw the widespread emergence of this sort of professional buyer of Western luxury products, who sold to the Chinese market with the help of social media. They took a skill that they had developed in style and fashion, and offered it as a service that others could buy, using their own lives as shop windows.

They photographed themselves in fitting rooms and filmed themselves strutting down cobbled streets. They staged a life to match the products they were selling, becoming living mannequins in their own digital boutiques.

What had started as a private interest in fashion could suddenly become five different buyers across Europe and a dedicated customer service line in China.

'Glamour labour' is a term for the type of labour pioneered by female influencers in the 2010s, and it is now a prerequisite in an increasing number of industries. Glamour labour is the curation of your body and self to appeal to followers in the version of your life that you present on social platforms. This includes all the effort that goes into your make-up, styling, workouts, eyebrow tattooing and anything else that makes your physical self match your virtual self. But it is also all of the strategies in your head: the thought that goes into making your life appear a certain way on the screens in other people's hands.

Glamour labour is what Kim, Kendall, Kylie, Kourtney and Khloé have demonstrated such outstanding stamina in. Their strategy has been to build a personal brand, spread it across different platforms, and then sell products through the sheer force of the attention they have managed to generate around themselves.

It is often said that the Kardashians are famous for being famous. But that isn't true. Kim, Khloé, Kylie, Kourtney and Kendall are famous for what they consume. They are a form of idols of consumption. And it's no coincidence that the business model they played a huge role in creating was born in a matriarchy – a strictly controlled organisation with the mother, Kris Jenner, at its head.

———————

'The proper study of mankind is man . . . but the proper study of market is women,' wrote *Printers Ink*, the first trade magazine in the world dedicated to the burgeoning advertising industry, in 1929. The message couldn't have been clearer: the consumer is a woman, even if mankind is, of course, always a man.

In many countries men now spend more money on clothes than women. Women, however, tend to spend more time shopping. And it is women who control the lion's share of all consumption in the world. It is the woman who buys the food, clothes, nappies, coffee tables, detergent and contact-lens fluid. Not because she has the most money, but because the economic task of procuring goods for the household has fallen to her. This points to the fact that consumption is to some degree a job.

Shopping is one of the many things that has to happen for a household to work. Someone must notice that the eggs are out, the fish tank needs a new algae magnet, or that if there were some sort of mat beneath them, the kids might get less bruised from falling off the kitchen chairs.

Today women are expected to think of these things more than men: it's part of the mental and emotional labour of being a woman. More often than not, it is the woman who makes sure the toilet paper doesn't run out, which, as we know, no one misses until it actually runs out. But the role the woman performs as society's consumer-in-chief isn't something she gets any special medal for. Quite the opposite: private consumption is often framed as something dirty or frivolous.

It was the man who went to work, the man who built, banked, constructed and invented, or so the traditional narrative goes. Then the woman spent his money and that kept the economy afloat. The political left and right were long in agreement on the key points of this story. Conservative thinkers saw the man as representing the high and the intellectual, while the woman represented the base and the material. Socialists, on the other hand, often thought of production as something collective, male, creative and useful, while consumption was female, individualistic and in many ways meaningless.

Even today many men instinctively distance themselves from the concept of shopping. When a man spends £100 each month on vinyl, it isn't called 'shopping', but 'an interest in music'. If he spends hours looking for the right accessories for his motorcycle, he has 'a passion for speed' not 'a passion for shopping'. A female head of state with a handbag that cost £5,000 will be dragged in the media as a shopaholic, but no one will bat an eyelid at a male politician owning 12 suits at £1,000 or more apiece.

The very image of the shopaholic woman with a wardrobe full of designer handbags has become a shorthand for economic irresponsibility. Yet the second-hand value of a luxury handbag is often greater than its purchase price. Compare that with your shiny new Volvo, which starts to depreciate in value at an alarming rate the second you leave the dealership.

Consumer power was one of the earliest forms of economic power that women actually possessed. At the start of the twentieth century Swedish women didn't have the right to vote, but they did get to establish consumer associations. If the milk was full of liquid manure, say, or a merchant had sold them sausages filled with waste, it was in their roles as consumers that they could try to affect change.

Similarly, back in the 1700s a popular form of protest emerged in England whereby women would buy brooches, snuffboxes, fireguards and cushions with anti-slavery slogans embroidered onto them. Obviously this type of activism was often dismissed as the gushy passing fad of a 'virtue-signalling' cultural elite. After all, these women were the very people who had likely benefitted from the economic system of slavery. An embroidered cushion wasn't going to change this.

Nevertheless, some British women went on to boycott sugar, the raw material harvested by slaves in horrific conditions. Similar forms of consumer protest took place in other parts of the world. The African-American journalist Francis Harper would write: 'Oh, could slavery exist long if it did not sit on a commercial throne?' How much of a difference such movements made is debatable, but these examples suggest that some women had started to recognise and wield their consumer influence.

Similarly, women have historically taken more of an interest in price development than wage development in the economy. The cost of goods has simply had a greater impact on their everyday lives. Notably, it was often when the price of bread went up that women took to the streets. This was seen during the French Revolution of 1789 and in Russia's February Revolution of 1917. In other words, female consumer power has long been a force to reckon with. In spite of this, female consumption has often been used to characterise a moral decline in society, as opposed to, say, a progressive development.

When the modern department store was created in Paris in 1852, the talking heads of the day declared that French women would never be able to cope. The allure of the shop windows was almost sexual for the ladies, they suggested. Woman by her very nature was vain and impulsive. Drawn to beauty, sensuality and convenience, she was generally not to be trusted when it came to temptation.

We all remember who made Adam take that bite of the apple, don't we?

When the department stores first opened their doors, they housed several important innovations that were deemed particularly dangerous, at least for those who were weak of mind (i.e. female). One key feature of the department-store concept was that you could enter without having to buy anything.

The department stores were built as spectacles in and of themselves, entertaining worlds designed to keep the customer within their four walls for as long as possible. There were fancy staircases, glittering mirrors and enticements from every corner of the world. And, crucially, it was perfectly fine to simply come in and gawp. With this, shopping became a pastime. Many wondered where this shocking development might lead.

The other important innovation that came to be associated with the new department stores was fixed prices. At the department store you didn't have to haggle or negotiate to get the hat you wanted, no: you could see what it would cost straight away. This increased the pace of trade.

The department store's entire concept was also its size:

you were forced to make your way through floor after floor to find what you needed. It was almost as though they wanted women to get lost.

Émile Zola wrote his classic novel *The Ladies' Delight* on Paris's burgeoning department-store scene. The eminent French writer spent weeks doing research at Le Bon Marché, an illustrious department store in the capital's Rive Gauche. As Zola saw it, the department store arrived just as the Frenchwoman started to abandon the Church. In his eyes this was no coincidence: shopping had to some degree become woman's new religion, he wrote.

Woman had stopped perfecting her soul and was instead encouraged to perfect her body. A new worship of fashion, the body and beauty emerged, with the department store its temple.

But what Zola failed to explore in any depth was the fact that there was something very concrete that churches and department stores had in common, something that went some way to explaining why women were drawn to both places. Namely, these were public spaces that the female body could navigate in relative safety. The new department store gave the more affluent Frenchwoman a right that she hadn't previously enjoyed: the right to *flâner*. Suddenly woman could wander aimlessly in a public space without having to weigh up the risk of sexual assault or harassment. She could stroll around as though she were on the street, while enjoying far more protection. The department store was, quite simply, a public space that woman could frequent without a man and without fear.

Working-class women, however, continued to get pawed at behind the counters as usual. The department store by no means represented freedom for everyone – far from it – but when the state wouldn't create a public space that was safe for women, the private sector tried.

And it was paid handsomely for it.

When American Harry Gordon Selfridge founded his vast department store Selfridges in London in 1906, he saw it as something of a feminist act. At Selfridges, the department store that still crowns the west end of Oxford Street, the woman's duty to shop would become something to enjoy. The American entrepreneur filled Selfridges with elegant but affordable restaurants in which the female consumer could eat both alone and undisturbed, something that was genuinely not possible in most other London establishments. Selfridge had a library installed from which she could borrow books, and created a reading area and a first-aid facility. In the middle of the building there was also a quiet, gently lit space where, he imagined, a woman could sit back in the warm embrace of a soft chair and close her eyes.

Before going back to the day's shopping.

There was obviously a commercial logic behind all of this. Businessman that he was, Selfridge naturally wanted to keep consumers inside the store for as long as possible. Even so, the fact remains that he created a city space in which at least some women could move with much more freedom than before. In other words, the idea of shopping as part of the path to female liberation, at least for white, affluent women, is nothing new.

Consumption is something shameful that can corrupt an entire society, Émile Zola warned, while others, like Harry Gordon Selfridge, imagined it as a possible avenue to women's liberation. On many fronts this debate is still raging, only it sounds more like this: is Kylie Jenner a role model or a worrying case in point? Is it 'inspiring' that she flies around in a pink private jet that cost $50 million – or simply another symptom of late capitalism? We can't decide. Neither then, nor now. But the question may be even more important today, for this is no longer a question of a well-delineated department store on one of Paris's avenues. New technology has seen the consumer logic spread through our lives in entirely new ways.

In the nineteenth-century department store, fixed prices were the big story. But these days you can read a magazine article online, click on the image and immediately end up on a sponsored link that takes you to a page where you can buy what you have just seen. This is generally how the social platforms on which we are spending increasing amounts of time make money. And this integration of commerce with the technology we carry around in our pockets has become a central part of how we experience the world in the early twenty-first century.

If the consumer is a woman, and more and more of our world is consumable, does this give her more power, or does it come at her expense? This question is important.

An influencer gets paid to live a life whose components are up for sale. Your followers are keen to hear what you have to say about your panic disorder or your new cat, but they also want to be able to buy the sofa you're sitting on when you talk about it in those posts.

The development of social platforms is such that it is no longer a matter of simply showing different consumer choices – 'Look at this blouse I bought!' Rather, it's about people getting the chance to see your consumer choices and imme-diately buy themselves a 'part' of what you represent to them. This is actually something of a commercial revolution.

There are now smartphone apps capable of 'scanning' the

world around you. The idea is that you will be able to see where you can buy the carafe you are admiring by taking a photo and then running the image through the app. As such, the retail industry now has dreams of transforming our entire world into a single clickable shop window. If you see someone in town wearing a jacket you like, you will be able to take a picture of them and immediately get a link to where you can buy it, thus making the real world shoppable in the same way as the digital. Everything will be like Harry Gordon Selfridge's department store – all subordinate to a single commercial logic.

The 2010s blurred the borders between consumption and production, and we increasingly started talking about a new category of 'prosumers'. These were people who were neither consumers nor producers, but a combination of the two. It was in these borderlands that many women built their companies.

An influencer is a prosumer. She consumes vitamins while producing ads for the same pills by photographing herself as she takes them. Her primary job is to convince her followers that she would take the vitamins anyway, whether she was getting paid to or not. The trick is to persuade your audience that you are a normal consumer just like them. Which you are. And also are not.

Indeed, every Instagram user is to some extent a prosumer. We use the platform, while also creating the platform through our content. The question is of course if this is really anything new: many innovations of the past century have been about pushing the boundary between consumption and production in various ways. Take the fast-food restaurant, for example: here the consumer becomes co-producer in their own meal-time. Customers must carry their food to their table and clear up after themselves, which allows the restaurant to offer lower prices.

Or Ikea, where the consumer also becomes furniture-maker when attempting to screw together her set of shelves as best she can in her living room.

Although we often think of consumption and production as two separate entities, they rarely are. But in the 2010s this line undeniably blurred even further, and this created many opportunities for women.

After all, the fundamental narrative of a woman in the economy has been that she belongs to the private sphere – that the man goes out and does paid work, while the woman stays home. Even though this hasn't been the case for any extended period of history – woman has almost always worked in the formal economy, too – this is undeniably our perception of how things stand. The man is out there in the public sphere, while the woman is assumed to belong to the private.

But what happened in the 2010s was that new technology made large parts of our private sphere public. You could snap a picture of your breakfast and post it online for all to see, and some people discovered that they could even earn a pretty penny from posting such photos. If they had a flair for chopping elaborate strawberry shapes and arranging them atop soggy chia seeds, at least.

Similarly, your marriage and children could become a full-time career, if you were good enough at creating ongoing lifestyle reportage about them online. What was distinct about this new economy was the way in which it was based almost entirely on an ability to build an emotional bond with your audience. 'Being personal' in these years took on a whole new commercial meaning.

Take motherhood. The 2010s was a decade in which the Western world was obsessed with motherhood. Which female celebrities were pregnant, fertile or infertile, or how they chose to raise their children or not – were all huge talking points. People updated their profile pictures on social media with ultrasounds of the child they were carrying in their wombs. When motherhood as a concept, idea, challenge and problem was played out in the public eye in this whole new way, it often saw the digital and the intimate merge.

For female celebrities, this type of digital motherhood was often a way of transforming themselves from unattainable dream woman to someone a consumer could relate to. Motherhood was a way of combining the glamour of celebrity with the internet's demand for intimacy. Kim, Kylie, Khloé, Kendall and Kris together have a total of 12 children. Motherhood is central to their brand on almost every level. They represent a type of glamorous, entrepreneurial motherhood in which you name your latest product after your daughter and then pose with her online while the orders come rolling in.

Young women bought lipstick from Kylie Jenner because they saw her as authentic. She was real to them in a way that L'Oréal's latest billboard model was not. Even if that model looked exactly like Kylie Jenner, the young women wouldn't have heard her talk about her relationships in the same way, or seen her pregnant belly smeared in blue gel at an ultrasound appointment. Jenner became relatable because she shared things, and her motherhood was a big part of that.

This is ironic in many ways. Motherhood, so long perceived as the opposite of everything the hard market stands for, now suddenly had a not-insignificant commercial weight.

Historically, woman's identities as parent and professional have been seen as intrinsically opposed, in a way that could not be said of man. Having a job and providing for the family is part and parcel of what it means to be a good father, we believe. The same does not apply for woman, and for many women in the 2010s, starting a company around one's identity as mother became a way to bridge this gap.

Kylie Jenner's company was started at a kitchen table – but it was a kitchen table that was constantly being filmed and photographed. The private sphere was still the woman's workplace, but technology had suddenly brought it into the public realm. In some way this was the entire revolution: more women could create themselves an alternative to a labour market that was never built for them.

To some extent, entrepreneurship has been one such 'way out' for women. In Africa, the continent with the highest percentage of female entrepreneurs, entrepreneurship is often a response to discrimination. Women have more difficulty finding jobs and more often lack the sorts of formal skills that many employers require. Women also take primary responsibility for the home and children, which means they need jobs with a flexibility that doesn't exist. So they create them for themselves.

Similarly, in Europe, women often decide they want to work differently: a female lawyer may be tired of being paid less than her male colleagues, or simply not see the point of a company culture that requires employees to be in the office 12 hours a day.

Tech developments gave us more female entrepreneurs because it made it easier for them to both start companies and run them from the home. Indeed, in the 2010s entrepreneurship was often hailed as the new feminism. Of this new breed of female entrepreneur, the most talked-about was, unsurprisingly, the woman who worked from home, and who made her living showing off what she consumed while sharing snippets from her family's everyday lives. Of course this also happened to be the type of entrepreneurship most easily combined with the female gender role, if not simply presented as an extension thereof. But there was a price to pay. Your intimate life became public, and the details that you shared online then belonged to the big tech companies. Kylie Jenner – a woman – might have been the biggest earner on Instagram.

But Mark Zuckerberg owned it.

In these years, sharing very personal moments became a business strategy. The trick was to combine a flawless exterior with a vulnerable inner world that revealed the flawless exterior as something that was *external* – and could therefore be achieved by buying the products being promoted. This type of intimacy can work as a business strategy, but it can also push you into giving up more and more of yourself. The intimacy that your followers feel they share with you can even lead them to feel a certain sense of ownership.

But perhaps we're getting ahead of ourselves. After all, intimacy as a sales strategy is nothing new. Men use it, too. Building emotional relationships with clients is far from something that women have discovered or by any means hold a monopoly on. In the same way that a woman might use social platforms to build relationships that can turn into sales, a man might also try to create intimacy through varying means in his business.

Going out and getting spectacularly drunk at a business dinner is one example of a strategy for building intimacy in potential business relationships, one as classic as it is perceived as traditionally male. You get smashed and therefore develop a bond. The strip club – arguably the most clichéd place for men to do business – is another.

For what is it that might compel someone to take a client out to a heterosexual tit show? The answer is intimacy. Not with the women on stage, of course: they're there for looking at. No, a strip-club expedition is about building intimacy with other men. You share an experience that exposes you, and that intimacy can provide the foundation for a future business relationship.

That there are some major pitfalls here is easy to see.

Studies show that teenage girls' self-esteem decreases the more time they spend on social platforms. At the same time, the development of such platforms can also be seen as a way for women to earn money from traditionally female skills. And what is wrong with building a company around beauty, your house, child-rearing, baking, or wanting to be at home when the kids get back from school? We tend not to judge male celebrities like George Clooney for making half a billion dollars from commercialising his hobby (tequila!). But there is, of course, a difference.

From childhood, women have been encouraged to always think about how they come across to others. Historically, attractiveness has been an economic necessity for women in a way that it hasn't for men. Since women haven't had the same economic opportunity for independence as men, they have had to rely more on the goodwill of others.

To this day, in many parts of the world the unpopular widow is often driven from her community if there aren't laws or institutions in place to ensure her right to inheritance. Similarly, Jane Austen's books describe the direct relationship between being popular at the ball and being able to provide for yourself in the autumn of life. It all comes down to pleasing man – or, failing that, at least not alienating those in your community. Is it so strange that women then obsess over what others think of them? For centuries being liked has determined women's chances for economic survival.

It's unsurprising, then, that many women developed a sixth sense for how they were perceived. Then it turned out that this was something you could put to good use in the digital economy. With social media, a woman's ability to make herself likeable and build emotional bonds could suddenly be monetised. Had Kylie Jenner been born two decades earlier, she would probably have become rich anyway. But not as rich. Female supermodels and TV stars could become millionaires back then, but almost never billionaires.

The influencers who made the most money in the 2010s were those who, like Jenner, assumed the role of an idol of consumption. That people lost in product jungles might turn to someone they trust to recommend a pushchair isn't strange. So why shouldn't a blogger mum get paid to advertise products? Weekly magazines owned by men have been doing the same for decades. Why shouldn't a film star be able to take the interest in her person and use it to sell her own line of trainers? Why should it be primarily the male-owned Hollywood studios that get to make money from the public not being able to take its eyes off her?

Consumption is something we have coded as female. But we can hardly say that this consumer logic is one that we reject or ignore, like we do with most other things associated with women. Quite the opposite: the consumer is one of very few female-coded identities that is actually starting to become universal. And with it, private consumption has come to play an increasingly decisive role in our economy.

On 10 May 1940, Winston Churchill became prime minister of the UK. War was raging in Europe, and in a parliamentary speech the new premier uttered the famous words: 'I have nothing to offer but blood, toil, tears and sweat.' Sixty years later, US president George W Bush gave a speech in a different crisis situation, following the terror attacks of 11 September 2001. Here, Bush called on the American people to do something quite different: he told them to 'go shopping'. Churchill appealed to his people's work ethic, while Bush spoke to them as consumers. And in many ways that made sense.

The economy of the UK of the 1940s was fuelled by precisely the type of self-sacrificing work ethic that Churchill was trying to speak to. In the United States of 2001, however, much production had been shifted to workers on the other side of the world. Which isn't to say that many Americans didn't work incredibly hard in these years. But that work was often done in low-paid jobs in the service sector, meaning consumption was what drove growth, fuelled by credit and low interest rates – everything that would eventually lead to the financial crisis of 2008.

In recent decades, a number of economists have talked about the 'feminisation' of the labour market. By this they mean that there are more women in paid work, but also that the entire labour market has become more 'feminine'. This doesn't mean that the labour market is getting pinker and cuddlier or hysterical once a month.

It means that it has become less secure.

The jobs that we have are increasingly flexible, low paid and home-based. What was traditionally meant by a 'job' – going to a factory for eight hours a day and then being able to provide for your family on your wage – has become increasingly difficult in many economies. Instead, low-paid, part-time work is becoming more widespread – the sort of work that was previously considered suitable for women. Women, after all, didn't 'need' to earn as much as men, it was thought.

Similarly, many economies have been 'feminised' by becoming increasingly consumption-driven. Men and women alike have been encouraged to see their economic identity as consumers, above all else. This was what made it so natural for George W Bush to usher Americans into this very role in 2001.

In his book *Art & Energy*, Barry Lord discusses this shift, which he believes started in the 1970s. Our identity as consumers became increasingly important culturally at around the same moment that our societies started being powered by oil.

Oil facilitated a full-on explosion of cheap consumer products, the buying and selling of which became an increasingly significant part of our economy. This seeped into our cultural identity, too: we stopped seeing ourselves primarily through our relationship to production and instead as consumers. That was your primary role in the economy, and so in a time of crisis the contribution you could make as a citizen was to shop. Therein lay your power, and in that sense, we have all to some degree become 'women'.

The department store consumed us, as it were.

Lord's point is that our identity is enmeshed with our consumption of energy. Today's extremely strong consumer identity sprang from our fossil-fuel society. We won't be able to extricate ourselves from fossil fuels without also finding ourselves a new economic identity.

If we continue to view ourselves first and foremost as

consumers, we will never be able to see the solutions to the climate emergency. We must go from consuming the world to protecting it. And Kylie Jenner probably isn't going to help us here.

This book has so far argued that many of the things that we have learned to code as female are due an upgrade in our estimation. That looking down on everything from bags with wheels to women in electric cars has not only been unhelpful but has actually held us back. As has our stubborn insistence that only hard things like metal can be technology, or that the spear must have come before the digging stick.

Meanwhile, the logic by which innovation must 'dominate', 'crush' and 'disrupt' has created an economy that is in many ways inhumane. Finding an alternative will require us to think differently about gender, because our ideas on gender dictate to such a great extent what we value and what we don't. In our personal lives, and in the economy as a whole.

But earning $600 million from selling lipsticks doesn't automatically spell liberation just because a woman is the one doing it. Kylie Jenner's private jet produces no less emissions simply because its upholstery is pink. In other words, this isn't a matter of painting the same world pink and calling it progress.

Kylie Jenner represents an extreme version of the consumer role that woman has been allocated in our economy, combined with very traditionally male symbols of material success such as private jets – albeit in a different colour. In itself this is perhaps nothing to get outraged at. We've probably devoted quite enough time to outrage at female consumption as it is. But we shouldn't confuse it with liberation, either.

Liberation for the woman is not expanding the department store's consumer logic to encompass the entire world. It is giving women access to the rest of the economy on the same terms as men.

And that is a much bigger project. One that will change almost everything.

BODY

In which the black swan turns out to have a body

In the beginning there were only two things in the cosmos: ice and fire. There was the blazing realm Muspelheim to the south, and the frozen realm Niflheim to the north, and from fire to ice stretched Ginnungagap, the gaping void in which wisdom resided. It was from these three sources – ice, fire, and nothingness – that the Vikings believed that the world came to be.

One day, sparks from Muspelheim's fires met the ice of Niflheim. Presumably this would be only a matter of time, even if *time* as we now know it didn't yet exist. Where the ice and fire had mixed there formed a body of water, and from that water now emerged two creatures: a cow and a giant. The giant's name was Ymir. He drank from the cow's udder and then fell asleep. From the sweat of his armpits sprang the frost giants, and together his feet begat a terrible being with six heads.

Such was the chaos of the meeting of ice and fire, which set in motion the creation of the world.

The giant Ymir drank of the cow's milk, and the cow, in turn, licked salt stones for nourishment. One day her big wet tongue managed to lick the god Buri from the stone.

Buri went on to have three grandsons: Odin, Vili and Vé. These were the first gods, and they grew up in the void of the Ginnungagap with the frost giants as cousins. It was Odin, Vili and Vé who would later decide that Ymir had to die, and with swords that they themselves had forged they slayed their progenitor. From the carotid artery that they cleft in two gushed a cold blue blood that drowned the other giants.

Now they took Ymir's body and from it they created the world: Ymir's flesh became the earth, his bones the mountains, his blood the seas and lakes. They lifted the crown of his head towards Ginnungagap's peak and with it they formed the skies, adorned with sparks from Muspelheim's fires as stars. They took four of the maggots that were feasting on Ymir's corpse and placed them at the very edges of the sky. These became the four compass points: east, west, north and south.

From the rich soil now grew the tree of life, the immense ash tree Yggdrasil. Yggdrasil's branches stretched across the skies, embracing both the fires of Muspelheim and the ice of Niflheim. This was when Odin took two pieces of wood and with his axe whittled forth the first people: the man, Ask, and the woman, Embla.

As you may have noticed by now, the Vikings certainly weren't lacking in imagination. Which is why it's especially interesting that their idea of how humanity came into being is so unimaginative. Odin didn't sweat or lick us into existence, no: he whittled us with an axe; humans were a product of technology rather than mystery. The world may have sprung from salt-licking cows and stomping frost giants, but the gods created humanity in roughly the same way that the Vikings themselves created their boats and their houses.

George Zarkadakis, an expert on artificial intelligence, has pointed out that our ideas of where we come from often tend to be suspiciously similar to the dominant technology in our societies. In the Bible we are told that God 'formed man of the dust of the ground'. Similarly, the early Greeks thought that Prometheus moulded us from water and earth. In Egyptian mythology the gods sculpted children out of clay before slipping them into women's wombs, and in Sudan it was said that God used clay of different colours, which explains why humans had different-coloured skin. Zarkadakis writes that this sort of clay metaphor was especially common in agrarian societies where survival was dependent on the crops, and where pots made of clay were high-tech wonders.

Then our metaphors changed.

In ancient Greece, engineers developed complex canal networks, aqueducts and irrigation systems. Ctesibius of Alexandria created a water clock with a moving indicator, and a water organ that could play music using the water's weight. The first steam engine was invented in Egypt, and in Upper Mesopotamia Ismail al-Jazari constructed a boat with four automatic musicians that floated on a lake, playing mechanical ditties for the king.

If water, steam and some skilled engineering could make things move, was it not then logical that humans worked the same way? We started to see ourselves more and more as constructions powered by liquid or steam.

Hippocrates advanced medical science, and came to see the body as essentially controlled by four different liquids: blood, yellow bile, black bile and phlegm. Indeed, hydraulic metaphors are still used to this day, especially when it comes to describing our emotions. We might feel 'pumped' for something, say, or that 'the pressure was too much', or simply voice the need for an emotional 'outlet'. To some extent we still think that emotions build up inside us like steam in an engine.

In the seventeenth century, French philosopher René Descartes promenaded through the royal gardens of Saint-Germain-en-Laye, which were built by the famous Francini brothers from Florence. These Italian brothers specialised in fountains, but when I say fountains I don't mean a stone frog idly spitting out small jets of water, or a limply bubbling pond that serves as a toilet for the local birds. I mean hydraulic statues: water-driven automata that could move, play music and dance. The gardens in Saint-Germain-en-Laye were veritable labyrinths of mysterious passages and grottos where you could come face to face with mechanical animals or hear the tinkle of water organs. These were some of the age's most spectacular technological feats, and they were built across much of Europe, at the behest of princes and popes.

Descartes would eventually come to formulate the very influential idea of the body as no more than 'a statue or a machine'. Look at these hydraulic statues, he wrote, see how they move and play! See how they appear to come to life! If humanity could build this type of machine, then surely it was only logical that God could build even more complex things? And is that not what humanity in its essence is – a complex machine?

In the Middle Ages and the Renaissance, mechanical figures danced on clocks and organs all across Europe. The machinery was often sponsored by the Catholic Church, which invested heavily in the development of this technology, funding new editions and translations of antique manuals on its construction. There was even a crucifix on which poor

Jesus writhed and grimaced while dangling in mechanical suffering for all our sins.

In the large cathedrals, the clock wouldn't just strike twelve with an abrupt ding-dong, but with an all-out mechanical spectacle. Angels would open doors for Holy Virgins made of wood, then bow their heads and raise their trumpets. A cogwheel-powered Holy Spirit would come flying past, while an automaton Gabriel would spring out as horrifying beasts rolled their eyes and stuck out their tongues. Finally, Saint Peter would march out with the other apostles, and with twelve hammers they would strike the hour. Naturally, these technological spectacles made a huge impression on the people of the day. Just as the Vikings once believed that the gods had whittled us with axes, people now started to imagine God piecing us together with a big mechanical toolkit. For why couldn't our muscles, bones and organs be theoretically interchangeable with cogwheels and camshafts?

Walking in those gardens, Descartes noticed the same source of water could make different statues do completely different things. One single force powered both the lyre-strumming Apollo and the flapping birds in the next grotto, a single stream of liquid that appeared to bring an entire world to life. Descartes started to picture the human body working in the same way. Our nerves ran through our body like pipes, he reasoned, and through them flowed something that powered the entire system. The only question was what. Meanwhile, our muscles and tendons were like 'engines and springs', while within our chests our hearts ticked away like clockwork.

Nerves were laid from our brains out to our bodies, just like the water pipes in the hydraulic statues, he thought. If something touched us, it would set off a reaction back up through the nerves and to our head. Later he would come to believe that our feelings probably worked in the same way, too: everything from our fear and vanity, our grief and love had to be some form of mechanical reaction. From our tears to our guts, everything could be understood and explained in the same way that a clockmaker could understand and explain their clock.

It may be easy to snigger at Descartes' ideas today: clearly he was perhaps a little too taken by his hydraulic statues. But to him it all seemed perfectly logical, for he saw himself in the machines: something we humans have continued to do.

For example, in the early 1900s it was common to speak of the brain as some sort of telephone exchange – a phenomenon that stemmed from the increasing importance of telecommunication. Our nerves were no longer pipes through which liquid flowed, we thought, but something that sent signals to the biological exchange we carried in our heads. If you touched a hot stove, say, a signal of 'ow ow ow' would be sent to the brain, which would in turn send a lightning-fast order to the hand to move. With time, of course, we realised that the whole process was considerably more complex. We were neither hydraulic statues nor telephone exchanges. Yet still we continued, time and again, to picture ourselves precisely as a more complex version of the most complex machine we were then capable of building.

And why did we do that? Metaphors are one thing – they can often be handy – but why do we choose the metaphors we choose? Why have we been so very eager to see ourselves as products of technology in our creation myths? Why not, for example, imagine something along the lines of the gods bringing humans into this world in the same way that we humans bring children into this world? It's at least as logical as all of the scenarios of gods whittling, moulding, building or drilling us. Of course, such a metaphor would place the power of creation in the female womb instead of in the hands of man.

And wouldn't that be scary.

―――――――――

L Ron Hubbard founded Scientology in 1954. The controversial movement grew from a self-help book that the successful science-fiction writer had published four years earlier. The book was called *Dianetics: The Modern Science of Mental Health*, and it is of interest to us here because of the metaphor that Hubbard uses: the human brain, he declares, works like 'a computer'.

Hubbard goes on to consistently describe human thought in terms of 'processes', 'circuits' and 'memory banks', all of which are lifted straight from the world of computers. A person could 'fix' her mind in the same way she could fix a computer, Hubbard suggested. You see, when performing optimally, our brains can bring up all the relevant data and solve every imaginable problem for us. Unfortunately our systems are full of bugs that we have picked up over the years, but these can be cleared. You can 'de-bug' yourself, so to say, and thus perform better.

'As a Scientologist, I have the technology to handle life's problems,' film star John Travolta declares on the movement's website. Indeed, to this day Scientologists often describe their secretive methods as 'the tech'. Humans are computers with the power to reprogram themselves. Scientology may be an extremely modern form of religion, but in this respect it harks right back to the Viking god Odin and his axe: we see ourselves in the dominant technology of the day.

Nowadays everyone is a bit of a Scientologist, in the sense that we tend to talk about our brains as 'biological computers'. We imagine that we 'process information' or 'reboot' just like computers do, co-opting terms like 'hardware' and 'software' and applying them to ourselves. In computing physical components like the computer processor, screen, graphics card and motherboard are usually called the 'hardware', while the instructions that you then code the machine to follow are the 'software'. Similarly, in recent decades we have been encouraged to think of our bodies as a form of hardware and our thoughts as a form of software. Obviously our brains need a body, we think, but only in the same way that a computer program needs a machine, or a parasite needs a tree. This has in part led us to now think of intelligence – or humanity, for that matter – as something independent of the body. The body becomes something of a robot that carries our 'self' around, a concept we have extrapolated from wildly. Some of the great thinkers of our time, like the physicist Stephen Hawking or cosmologist Max Tegmark, have predicted that in future we will even be able to 'upload' our consciousness to something other than the human body.

This conclusion is drawn from the idea that humans function like computers. If our intelligence and personality are a form of software, it follows that it should be possible to 'run' these on a machine other than the body. Humanity's essence is simply some sort of advanced software trapped in a biological prison. But thanks to technology, in the future it will be possible to swap out the body for something better. Kind of like transferring the content from your old computer onto a new and better model. In doing so, we will be able to escape our bodies and everything they entail by way of frailty, sickness and, finally, death. Which brings us undeniably back into religious territory. This is a wondrous story of how humanity will eventually achieve eternal life on earth, only this one tends to be told in the language of science.

The question is whether posterity will find these ideas just as bizarre as we now find René Descartes' ideas of humans as a form of hydraulic statue, or if we see them as a step towards a better understanding of our brains and of ourselves.

That computers were called 'electronic brains' when they first arrived on the scene does indeed make a lot of sense. They effected logical processes, took in raw data and produced new knowledge, seeming, quite simply, to 'think'. As early as 1958, mathematician and computer pioneer John von Neumann wrote the book *The Computer and the Brain*, which drew parallel after parallel between the computers of the day and the human brain. And while this new language paved the way for several scientific breakthroughs, that a metaphor proves useful doesn't also make it true.

The brain is no digital gadget; its cells are not binary objects that can be turned off and on. There are countless differences between our brains and our computers, the main one being that the brain has a body. It is, in fact, a body – a body that exists in a context, at that. Our brains are interacting with the rest of our body and with our surroundings from the very moment they start to develop inside the womb.

That fact can't just be abstracted away.

Once upon a time, we stopped thinking of ourselves as dust and water power. And, just as we gave up on the idea that we were telegraphs, telephone networks or electrical gadgets, one day we will probably stop seeing ourselves as computers, too. A new metaphor will have taken its place, one that will most likely reflect our future technology in the same way that the idea of humankind as a computer reflects today's.

But the idea that the human is 'like a computer' has already had consequences. The notion of us being akin to program-mable flesh-robots has had a huge impact on how we organise our economy. To see these consequences, we need only take ourselves back to early spring 2020, and the moment when the great pandemic struck the world.

On 11 February, the number of confirmed Covid-19 cases outside China was 400. Five weeks later it was 90,000. On 22 January, the UK raised its risk assessment from 'very low' to 'low'. Thirteen weeks later, 41,000 Brits had died. In other words, everything was under control until it suddenly wasn't. The virus seemed to come from nowhere. Which obviously wasn't the case.

When teachers explain this type of growth, they often describe the water lily. Picture a lake with a single water lily in bloom on a mild summer's eve. Now imagine that today is 1 June, and that every day the number of water lilies in the lake will double. By the time your diary says 30 June, the water in front of you will be entirely covered in water lilies. So when was the surface of the water only 50 per cent covered? The answer is 29 June.

For most people this isn't hard to get their heads around: it's only logical that if the number of water lilies is doubling every day, then between 29 and 30 June they will go from covering 50 per cent of the lake to 100 per cent. No one on the shore would be able to help but notice this type of drastic change, but in actual fact the water lilies have 'only' doubled in number, just as they did between 1 and 2 June.

To the next question, then: if the surface of the lake was completely covered in water lilies on 30 June and 50 per cent covered on 29 June, on which day was only 1 per cent of it covered? The answer here is 24 June. Now, unlike the previous answer, to most people this will seem instinctively wrong. How can the coverage go from 1 per cent to 100 per cent in only six days? This, however, is precisely how exponential growth works.

On 24 June, when 99 per cent of the lake was water-lily-free, you would never in your wildest dreams have imagined that just six days later it would be entirely covered by flowers. This was exactly where many of us found ourselves in February 2020 with the pandemic: we gazed out and saw a few water lilies, but couldn't conceive that in just a few weeks they would be everywhere – that we would be encouraged to shelter in our homes, while people were fighting for their lives in intensive-care units across the world.

This was when economists and financial analysts started to shout about 'black swans', their go-to expression for anything they haven't managed to predict.

What is a 'black swan'? Yes, it's another metaphor, one popularised and redefined by Nassim Taleb in 2007. In the opening chapter of his book *The Black Swan*, Taleb tells the story of how Europeans were long convinced that all swans were white. Until they came to Australia, that is, where they suddenly found that swans could also be black. In one fell swoop, the sighting of a single black bird rendered all of the Europeans' former conclusions utterly invalid. Yes, their old belief that all swans are white was based on millions of observations over the centuries, but all it took to disprove that conclusion was a single black swan. It changed everything.

Taleb uses the term 'black swan' to describe the things we cannot predict. The things that lie beyond our notions of what 'could happen', but which, when they do, are the ones that impact us the most.

A black swan is, firstly, something you cannot imagine. Secondly, it is something with enormous consequences that change the world as we know it – like two planes flying into the World Trade Center, for example, or a world war breaking out after the assassination of an Austrian Archduke called Franz Ferdinand at a crossing in Sarajevo.

Thirdly, black swans are something we try to explain retrospectively. We should definitely have seen that Osama Bin Laden was a threat, we think, or that it was a Bad Idea for Franz Ferdinand to travel to Bosnia. Taleb suggests that this is simply human nature: once the inconceivable has happened, we are desperate to be able to explain it, even when we can't.

In short, black swans are something quite different from the water lilies on the lake. That the water lilies will cover the entire surface of the lake on 30 June is entirely predictable, so long as we know that they double in number every night. A black swan, on the other hand, cannot be predicted. Which is why it is less a question of being able to spot specific black swans before they land, and more a question of organising our societies and lives so as to withstand unpredictable events.

This is Taleb's main point.

Was the pandemic of 2020 a black swan? No, it wasn't. A black swan must be impossible to predict, and the possibility of a global pandemic of this nature had been discussed for years. Many had predicted this particular swan. Taleb himself wrote of the risk of a future global pandemic as far back as 2007. In our globalised world, the question was never *if* we would experience a major pandemic of this scope, but *when*. In short, the 2020 pandemic was your average white swan.

But we still ended up where we did.

Leading hospitals found themselves without established methods to treat the new virus, nurses in New York wrapped themselves up in bin bags for want of PPE, people sewed masks in improvised home factories, and in Western economies, where it had seemed possible to order anything you might want with just a couple of clicks on your phone, flour vanished from the supermarket shelves. For the first time since measurements began, growth fell throughout the world, in countries rich as well as poor, as the service sector, the modern economy's biggest employer, was forced to shut down from Malmköping to Mumbai.

In purely economic terms, this was a crisis like no other. Economic crises usually tend to go from the abstract to the concrete. The global financial crisis of 2008, for example, started with financial products so complex that not even the financiers who sold them understood what they consisted of. When the market eventually realised that the gold was in fact repackaged mortgages from people who would never be able to repay them, investors panicked. The commotion toppled a few American banks in quick succession, and the crisis then rippled through the economy, where it had devastating consequences for very real people, who lost jobs, savings, houses and, in some cases, even lives. This is how we have come to think of economic crises – with human bodies coming last in our order of priorities.

But the 2020 crisis was the exact reverse. This was a global financial crisis that originated in the human body. Some of the most vulnerable humans in society started dying in their droves from a new virus, so we decided to close down large parts of the formal economy, voluntarily slamming the brakes on this economic juggernaut that had been built for one thing and one thing alone: growth.

And with a giant screech it all came to a halt.

This served as a huge reminder of one very basic fact: the economy is based on the human body. This may seem obvious now, but just think back to March 2020, when the market crashed 1,500 points in shock at this insight. Back when economist after economist suddenly started calling the fact that a virus could infect people, spread and prevent them from working a 'black swan'. In other words, they saw it as a high-profile, hard-to-predict and rare event. But that bodies can infect other bodies with a virus – that humans are in such a way both vulnerable and bound to each other – is no black swan. These are the very conditions of all human life.

How the hell could we have forgotten that?

———————

The digital revolution of the 2010s seemed to transform our smartphones into a kind of remote control. With one in your hand, you could book anything from a cleaner to a driver in just a few taps. Or why not someone to pick up your dry cleaning, or do your make-up? All you needed was the right app and – of course – the means to pay. We called all of these new app-based services 'innovations', and a number of them were certainly ingenious. The only problem was that we tended to forget that there were people on the other end of them.

Even if you summoned your cleaner with the tap of a

button, and even if she was a different person from the one who came last week, she was still a person. But the workers in this type of gig economy are treated like an extension of the technology that summoned them. They weren't even called workers, just people who fulfilled different 'tasks'.

The companies they worked for could exist by virtue of five other innovations. One: the smartphone, which made it possible for customers to tap a screen and order whatever it was they wanted to their home. Two: digital map technology that could tell the one-off gardener where to go. Three: algorithms that could manage the work and match the right person to the right customer. Four: huge piles of venture capital that the founders of the company could burn through until they had hopefully achieved something of a monopoly in their sector, as per the whaling logic. And finally: enough people prepared to take on insecure and low-paid work.

Ride-sharing app Uber, for example, organised the work of its 3 million drivers through an app that – completely digitally – instructed them which passengers to collect and which route to take. This meant that if you worked for Uber, you could decide when you wanted to work, how much you wanted to work and who you wanted in your car. Many of the drivers liked these aspects of the job. On the other hand, it also put them under constant surveillance. The app would know where they were, how fast they were driving and which customers they were choosing. If they didn't follow its instructions, they could be penalised or even blocked from the platform.

In the same way, workers picking goods at Amazon's huge warehouses walked routes plotted almost entirely by algorithms. The small, handheld machine that you used to scan goods was, in essence, your boss. It kept an eye on whether you were picking your 400 items per hour and that it took you seven seconds to take each item off the shelf. It registered when you went to the toilet, and whether you were walking fast enough on your routes.

Carers in the home-care service of the famously well-funded Swedish welfare state worked under similar conditions. They often received their day's schedule by phone just five minutes before their shift. From this digital system you would receive the schedule that would then direct your movements for the entire day. Your work was sliced up into different tasks, with the smartphone in your hand telling you exactly how long each should take.

The system told you that Mrs Almqvist on the third floor needed help showering once a week. This should take 0.45 hours. She should then have three meals a day, which should take 0.15 hours per meal. Then there were the toilet trips, for which the app instructed you to help her five times per day. The entire schedule was a way of describing the work down to the smallest possible component, almost as if someone had tried to write it all in code. Not that a robot could currently perform this type of work (we'll discuss this more in the next chapter). But anyway.

In the UK, home carers are often paid only for the exact number of minutes the app allocates them for each client. The journey time between clients is then calculated using GPS, a calculation often made without any real consideration for traffic or the time it takes to put on your coat and hop on your bike. Similarly, the computerised schedule leaves no leeway for the unforeseeable – bedding that may need changing or coffee that may get spilled – let alone card games or small talk about puppies and geranium cuttings. And so the job you are doing changes, becoming less about care and more a set of individual tasks that the technology guides you through. It perhaps isn't strange that this would wear you down: after all, you are no algorithm-driven robot. But that's how the system sees you.

This way of organising work is intended to make staff interchangeable. It shouldn't matter who knocks on Mrs Almqvist's door that Thursday morning, since that person is only there to assist her with a 0.45 hour shower and a 0.15 hour toilet trip. This was what the 2020 pandemic brought to a head.

In Sweden, for example, it emerged that elderly people who received care at home – i.e. some of those who needed protecting the most from the virus – were on average coming into contact with over 16 different people in any two-week period. In other words, it made no difference that they were shielding: the virus came into their homes as stranger after stranger turned up to help them with a 0.15 hour toilet trip, as instructed by an app.

In the middle of a global pandemic, you cannot pretend your staff are robots. Even if the person delivering a package or cleaning your home came at the tap of a screen, like a mere extension of that digital service, she wasn't. She still had a human body. This was why, in the face of this new virus, all of the problems of the gig economy were suddenly laid bare. People being able to stay at home if they were sick was now of the utmost national importance, but the gig economy's workers couldn't do that in the same way. They had no entitlement to sick pay, and often they didn't even have a human manager who was accountable or could at least make sure they had hand sanitiser and face masks to hand.

In Italian and French cities where everything else had locked down, these gig workers still fulfilled their deliveries.

Many felt that they had no choice: staying at home and taking responsibility for their own and others' health would mean losing their entire income.

In Sweden, carers in the home-care service spoke of feeling like potential angels of death whenever their digital schedules instructed them to enter yet another vulnerable elderly person's home without protective clothing. They were not machines, even if their work was organised as though they lacked human bodies.

Home-care services that had formerly regarded their staff as interchangeable performers of specific work tasks could no longer do so – not if they wanted to protect their elderly from death. Taxi apps that had for years been putting up legal fights to shirk any and all employer accountability were forced to change their ways, albeit temporarily. At least if they didn't want to spread the virus further. The economic crisis that followed was no 'black swan', either. It was a knock-on effect of our economy's fundamental dependency on the human body.

And of our attempts to forget that.

In the 2010s we thought we were creating robots that were like humans. We believed that soon all of society would be automated, and that machines would soon be better than us at everything, thanks to the number of transistors we could stuff into the microchips in their electronic brains. But it turned out it wasn't that easy. We still haven't created machines that are like people. Instead we have organised humans like machines.

And called it innovation.

———

We thought that the way we organised workers in these years was a result of the new technology, whether it was applied to the Swedish home-care service or a business model in the Dutch hairstyling industry. But it wasn't.

Just because digital technology exists that enables delivery people to be more autonomous, doesn't mean they should also be made responsible for finding a substitute for themselves if they get sick. One doesn't follow from the other. Today many workers in the gig economy are forced to pay fines to the company they work for if they don't find a substitute for themselves. What this inevitably leads to is people being forced to work when they are sick. Similar systems are found in everything from start-ups to established companies owned by the French government. The logic is the same.

And that's precisely the problem.

One of the many risks is that this holds back true innovation. There is no incentive for these companies to really think out of the box; we have made it all too easy for them to fiddle their employees' basic employment conditions and make money on that instead. The companies get almost all the benefits of robot staff without having to either invent such robots or pay for their use. Instead they just pay a human minimum wage, or less, to act like a robot.

But the fact that you pretend someone is a robot does not make them one. Nor does building an app give you the right to treat the women who work in elderly care like robots. One does not follow from the other. Exploitation is not the same as innovation. Nor is human exploitation anything particularly new.

It's basically the oldest business model in the world.

At the same time, there are of course lessons to be learned

from the gig economy. A number of studies have indicated that people who work for these companies can feel a greater sense of satisfaction, despite also having more anxiety about their finances. Many people clearly value the flexibility that these jobs can offer, and that is worth taking seriously when reflecting upon the future of the labour market.

These studies, however, tend to focus on human workers driving taxis or delivering packages. We know far less about the opinions of women who work in a care system that is increasingly in thrall to this way of thinking. Yet in international debate, much is said about the opportunities that the gig economy offers – to women in particular. Since women typically bear the primary responsibility for the home and childcare, it is hard for them to have careers in the same way as men. This is where the gig economy can supposedly come in and save the day.

A woman who formerly worked full time as a cleaner can now find opportunities to earn money here and there, making it much easier for her to combine work with motherhood. And to some extent this is true: the gig economy has helped many women earn money that they would otherwise not have had.

Women ask for flexibility, and the new technology can provide this without them having to start a company themselves. The only problem is that they still have to deal with extremely inflexible things like food prices and rent every month. So long as so many of these women live on the margins, no app in the world will be able to offer them true flexibility. They will simply take every gig they can get. Whether or not they are sick. Whether or not their children are sick. Whether or not they feel physically safe working for that client.

We are racking our brains trying to come up with complex technological solution after complex technological solution to help women, when the good old invention of cold, hard cash could actually go quite a long way. Why not start by paying women a decent wage for the jobs that play such a key role in keeping the world going?

This isn't to say that we need to go back to a world of lifetime employment and nine-to-fives. That was a model built on another society. The point is simply that, when trying to create something new, we have to work from reality.

And our reality is the human body. Our economy is the human body. Bodies that work, bodies that need care, bodies that create other bodies. Bodies that are born, age and die. Bodies that need help throughout many stages of life, and a society that can organise this. The thing is, the body is radical. Admitting the existence of the body has a major impact on our economy. A society organised around the needs that human bodies have in common would be fundamentally different from the society we see today and consider to be the only one possible.

To take the body seriously is to create an economy that puts human needs front and centre. Physical things like hunger, cold and sickness, or a lack of healthcare or childcare, suddenly become central economic problems.

To be reminded of the body is to be reminded that helplessness and complete dependence are also part and parcel of the human experience. To be reminded that the body is born of another body, and that when it comes out of the womb and into the light it is at the complete mercy of its surroundings. Illness can make it dependent once again, just as age almost always does. And there is nothing wrong with any of this.

It's part of being human.

The body reminds us of all those things we find uncomfortable: our vulnerability and our reliance on others. The very things that we have been taught to see as 'female'. After all, this is what the patriarchy has always been about – taking the parts of the human experience that scare us, labelling them as female and marginalising them. And, as we have seen, this means we lose sight of ourselves, but it also means that we build an economy that doesn't accommodate that one minor detail: the existence of our bodies. The pandemic of 2020 showed that this situation is not sustainable with all the clarity we could ever wish for.

The hierarchy we have created between what we consider feminine and masculine is once again rearing its ugly head. It makes us run from everything we call 'feminine' in ourselves, which leads us to see the brain as a computer and humanity as some kind of algorithm-controlled robot, hydraulic statue, telephone exchange or whatever it might be that bears no relation to the bodies that actually bring us into this world. Everything seems easier than actually looking down at our own bodies and accepting what their existence means. Whatever your gender.

Not just for ourselves, but for society as a whole.

It isn't a matter of there being some 'truth' in the womb that we have misplaced, or need to retrieve through some energetic goddess dance in the light of the full moon. It's that we let the female body represent the bodily essence of humanity. And then go on denying our bodily reality precisely because of these female associations.

The consequences are enormous. Not least economically.

Much of what unites us begins in the human body. Our health is not our own. This was the inconvenient truth of the pandemic. Our health is linked to the health of others, to the health of the planet and of the earth, to the health of our ancestors and of our future children. Not to mention the health of the economy. We are, quite simply, part of a greater whole.

René Descartes pointed at the hydraulic statues in Saint-Germain-en-Laye and said that humanity was a variant of these. What is the difference between him and the futurists of our day, who point at algorithms and computers and claim that we are just like them? This is a sincere question. And a call for humility. We know, in fact, quite little about how we work. So why deny the obvious: that we have a body, and that this makes us both vulnerable and reliant on each other?

The Viking gods didn't whittle you with an axe. You are no hydraulic statue, telephone exchange or computer. You came, kicking and screaming, out of a pulsating, blood-red womb.

Deal with it.

And create an economy based on something we actually know to be true.

In which Serena Williams beats Garry Kasparov

A nine-year-old Serena Williams is throwing an American football across a tennis court in Compton, south of Los Angeles. It is around this time that her father declares to the world that one day Venus will hold the top spot in women's tennis, and that his youngest daughter Serena will probably be even better. It is only some seven years later, when Venus comes from nowhere to reach the US Open final, that anyone really starts to believe him.

Serena and Venus throw the American football back and forth to each other. Having started about one metre apart on either side of the net, the sisters move back slowly, throw by throw, until they find themselves at opposite baselines, the ball spinning through the air between them.

Their father, who is coaching them, had only taken up tennis in middle age, using videotapes borrowed from the local library. It was on one such tape that he saw the drill involving the American football. As it turns out, getting an American football to rotate in a tight spiral across a tennis court requires almost exactly the same hand motion as landing an overhand serve.

What makes the tennis serve such a difficult shot to master

is that it involves not just hitting the ball over the net at high speed, but also landing it in the service box on the other side. This should be practically impossible: you have to whack the hell out of the ball to get it over the net, which can in turn make it sail across the court at such speed that it doesn't drop into the box in time.

Of course, if you're tall enough it's much easier to land the serve with some force: you simply hammer it down from your full reach. Serena Williams, however, will only come to be five feet nine inches tall. Which is where the American football comes in.

You see, it's all a question of spin.

When serving in tennis, the trick is not to hit the ball flat. Instead, you have to extend, jump and all but fling your racket at the ball. This throwing motion is what makes the ball spin, which in turn makes the air around it do the same. A pocket of lower air pressure forms beneath the ball, and as the air is pulled upwards the ball is pulled down, causing it to almost stop and drop in the right place.

Sir Isaac Newton, the father of modern physics, observed this phenomenon back in the seventeenth century from his window at Trinity College, Cambridge, which just so happened to look out over a garden where tennis was played. Serena Williams' father understood the same thing from the videotapes he borrowed from the library in Compton. Anyone who can learn to spiral an American football across a tennis court will be able to incorporate that same hand motion into their serve. The key is repetition: doing the same thing again and again until it imprints itself in the body.

Many of our human faculties build on this form of body intelligence or muscle memory. Indeed, every day we rely on this knowledge to get us through life. Yet the human body is a detail that often gets ignored when trying to invent machines that resemble ourselves. This has created technical problems in everything from AI and robots to driverless cars, which is what this chapter is all about. Many of these problems can be traced back to our ideas of gender, since they relate to the distinction we make between mind and body, which often posits the mind as male and the body as female. From here on out, the ideas we will be discussing might prove a little trickier to take in. For it is one thing to look at the electric cars at the dawn of the twentieth century, to chuckle at people's notions of the female and the male, and see how the ideas of the day – that cars had to be loud and dangerous to be *real* cars – tied in with the prevailing ideals of manhood. It's much more difficult, however, to recognise how we make similar mistakes today.

But that doesn't mean we don't make them.

So let's get back to Serena Williams on that Compton tennis court.

In those days, the Williams family had a yellow Volkswagen van and would use it to ferry their youngest daughters to and from tennis practice. One of the van's seats had been removed to make space for an old shopping trolley full of tennis balls that Serena and Venus would use to practise serve after serve and shot after shot, day after day and year after year.

After passing the American football back and forth, the two sisters stand side by side and serve tennis ball after tennis ball over the net. Now, this type of serve practice may sound like a monotonous way to while away the hours, but that's because we don't know what's going on in Serena Williams' head. Every shot Serena hits is packed with information that she is constantly responding to through small adjustments. She listens to each stroke, feels it. She knows exactly where her racket is at all times and never takes her eyes off the ball. She repeats each stroke time and again so that this knowledge becomes second nature. Which it isn't – not by any stretch.

At least, not if you think about it theoretically.

To win at tennis, the very instant the shot leaves your opponent's racket you have to figure out roughly where it's heading, an equation that requires you to gauge the ball's initial speed and rate of deceleration, factor in any wind or spin, and weigh up the possible trajectories of the ball, all while taking into account the surface you are playing on, from Wimbledon's lawns to Melbourne's acrylics. Then, finally, you have a millisecond or so in which to manifest the result of all these calculations with your racket.

But the only number crunching you'll find Serena Williams doing on a tennis court is counting: one, two, three, four, five. The greatest tennis player of all time always bounces the ball five times before her first serve, twice before her second. It turns out that forcing the mind to focus on a simple, repetitive task is one of the easiest ways to silence it.

When out on court, Serena Williams isn't thinking in equations. Her serve consists of a series of movements that, repetition by repetition, drill by drill and year by year, have gradually become one with her body. Even if Serena Williams were to sit down with you and explain everything she does on a tennis court – even if it were somehow possible for her to communicate everything she knows about the sport – that doesn't mean you would be able to use a racket the way she does.

'We can know more than we can tell,' wrote Hungarian

philosopher and economist Michael Polanyi. This is what we tend to call 'Polanyi's paradox'. Just because you know everything there is to know about driving a car – you've read all the books and manuals and can draw the inside of a spark plug blindfolded – doesn't mean you can *actually* drive one. Most of us who can drive do it without necessarily being able to express everything we do behind the wheel. What exactly are you looking for when you glance in the rear-view mirror? What sounds are you subconsciously listening out for? Why did your hand just move to the gear stick?

Every day, we humans do things we can't describe, whether that's beating Maria Sharapova in straight sets or catching the crystal bowl that has just toppled off the kitchen shelf. You wouldn't have been able to calculate the trajectory of the falling bowl, but you still managed to catch it, right? This is Polanyi's paradox. It simply means that you can do more than you can explain. Now, this may seem like an obvious enough statement, but when it comes to the work that can or cannot be performed by machines, the consequences are huge.

You may perhaps remember American computer pioneer Ida Rhodes from the chapter on girl power and computer power. She likened her ability to program computers to her ability to teach mathematics, and they essentially come down to the same thing: the ability to explain how to do something in a way that the other party can grasp.

To get a machine to do something, you must first explain what you want it to do. This involves breaking the task down into smaller steps, and then writing a program that requires the machine to complete them one by one. So for a long time, if we couldn't explain something to a machine in this way, it wasn't able to do it.

This is a consequence of Polanyi's paradox.

If you can't explain what you do in order to *see* that chair in the corner, it's hard to get a computer to do the same. How can you tell it's a chair, as opposed to a turtle? It's hard to say. Which is precisely why it has been very tricky to get machines to do something like *seeing*.

On the other hand, some things have been reasonably easy. For one, it's pretty easy to explain how to calculate that 450 divided by 5 is 90. As a consequence, we have long had machines that can help us with this type of problem. The fact that it is easier to get machines to do some things and much harder to make them do others has fundamentally shaped technological development. Polanyi's paradox means that a robot will find it hard to compete with Serena Williams and replicate what she is good at. Serena Williams sees, feels, weighs up, adjusts and acts instinctively on the information coming from her senses, but she can't explain what she does because it's 'second nature'. However, there are other sports that machines are better at.

Take chess.

The year is 1985 and Garry Kasparov is 22 years old. The young Soviet has been invited to Hamburg, in what is still West Germany. Later the same year, Kasparov will become the world's youngest ever World Chess Champion.

Kasparov is standing in the middle of a carpeted room, dressed casually in a striped shirt and green summer jacket. A set of tables have been arranged around him, holding 32 chessboards in all. Kasparov is here to take on 32 computers at chess, and he will win every match. Even if the world's press is more interested in what Kasparov has to say about the political situation in the USSR to *Der Spiegel* (a surprising amount) than his showdown with the computers, the chess match is what makes this visit historic.

In the early 1980s, the best chess-playing machines available to the public at large were produced by five companies. These companies sent all of their best computer models to Hamburg. It took Kasparov five hours to beat them all, and no one was surprised. At no point could Kasparov have imagined that just 12 years later he would lose to a single computer.

But that was precisely how quickly the tables would turn.

In 1997, then 34 years old, Kasparov would lose his infamous match against IBM's supercomputer Deep Blue in New York. This time the match made front pages across the world, with the newspapers reporting the result as the final nail in the coffin for human ascendancy on earth. If a computer could outplay a brain like Kasparov's, then the rest of us might as well just give up, it seemed.

It was the machines' time now.

Deep Blue cost $10 million in 1997. But today you can download an app onto your phone that would be capable of beating Kasparov. In fact today, a single computer could quite easily accomplish what Kasparov achieved in 1985, but in reverse: it could take on 32 human grandmasters at chess, and win every match. So much has the balance of power between human and machine shifted.

Or has it?

For if we give this a little more thought, it's clear that no computer could actually do what Kasparov did in Hamburg in 1985. Picture him standing there, 22 years old, surrounded by tables in that carpeted room. He isn't just playing against

32 computers: he is also walking from board to board, picking up the pieces with his very own hands. And this, as Kasparov himself has noted, is where today's machines would struggle. The physical process of picking up a chess piece and placing it on the board without toppling it may be something a child could do, but for a machine it poses problems. Precisely because it is a physical process.

This is a widely known phenomenon in robotics. It is fairly easy to teach machines advanced mathematics and chess; it's far less easy, however, to teach them motor skills. Kai-Fu Lee, one of China's foremost investors in AI, recently stated: 'AI is great at thinking, but robots are bad at moving their fingers.' So what does this mean for us economically?

Let's take cleaning as an example. We imagine cleaning to be easy, or in any case that's how it's valued economically in today's world. The people whose job it is to clean homes and offices are predominantly women, for one. They also tend to be among the worst paid on the whole labour market, and often have a skin colour that others discriminate against. The economic logic behind the low status of cleaning is that we think it's a job that 'anyone could do'.

If a deadly virus shuts down the entire British economy, then yes, Professor Needhorne in Warwick would be able to clean his own house. It might not be as spotless as when his cleaner does it, but he would manage.

Cleaning doesn't require any specialist training, we think. But that's because we are humans and not machines. We take our own inbuilt bodily genius for granted. But think of it from the poor robots' perspective: Polanyi's paradox makes it much easier for a computer to learn everything Professor Needhorne knows about the fossils of this world than how to clean his house. Much, much easier. In the same way that you wouldn't be able to play tennis like Serena Williams just because she tells you what she thinks on court, the robot won't be able to clean Professor Needhorne's house just from us explaining how it's done.

Cleaning is actually a pretty complex thing.

One evening, Professor Needhorne is reading in bed upstairs. Overcome with excitement at something in his book, he accidentally knocks over the teacup he has beside him. The hot tea spills over the bedside table and down onto his blanket and rug. Now, if for some reason his mother were to enter the room at that moment, she would start three different parallel processes without giving it a second thought.

First, she would get a cloth to wipe the tea off the bedside table, then a sponge to soak up the tea that had dripped down onto the rug, and then she would start stripping the bed.

While scrubbing the rug, she would instinctively feel how much pressure she should apply to get it clean. And if at any moment she should start to suspect that her scrubbing might negatively affect its dyes, she would immediately apply less pressure – almost without thinking. In fact, she would do everything almost without thinking, including giving Professor Needhorne a piece of her mind. To a robot this is more or less miraculous.

Like beating Maria Sharapova in straight sets.

In short, there's a reason why the robot maids we used to see in comics are still just a pipe dream. The main issue the machines face here is the unpredictability of our homes. Cleaning a house involves a wide range of different situations. You can't simply tell a robot to 'do the laundry': if you do, it has to first know how to move and where to point its various cameras and sensors. It needs to understand the difference between socks and pants, red napkins and white sheets, wool and cotton.

We humans find it very easy to navigate unpredictable environments. Which isn't surprising, considering we're a product of 200,000-odd years of life in this unpredictable environment called earth.

The machines don't have the same advantage. It would probably be easier to construct a self-cleaning house than a robot capable of cleaning our current houses in any satisfactory way. If you were to build a self-cleaning house from the ground up, you would be able to adapt the environment to the machine, instead of vice versa. You would be able to put different sensors in the floors, and get the furniture to send updates on their dust levels to a central hub. Or something along those lines.

This has traditionally been our approach to remedying the difficulties machines experience in coping with the unpredictability of our world. We tend to simply put them in their own 'universe', an environment more tailored to their needs. Otherwise known as a 'factory'. Here robots can excel undisturbed by the complexity of the world outside. So it isn't particularly surprising that the jobs in our economy that have been automated the fastest are those in factories.

These are the jobs that have been the easiest for the robots to take from humans. Later on in this book we will explore this in more detail, in particular the economic studies that show that robots are more likely to take jobs from men than women. But this does also link back to Polanyi's paradox: if the machines can do what a human does in a factory, but not what she does when cleaning a home, then in the future cleaning jobs may be more secure than many factory jobs.

And if the men work in the factory and the women in the home, then you can see how things might go.

But more on that later.

Let's stick with the body for now. For if AI is great at thinking but bad at moving its fingers, then why didn't we prioritise physical concerns as much as, say, chess when trying to develop this technology? Instead we thought that if machines could simply learn to succeed in the 'difficult' things (like beating Garry Kasparov at chess) then they would almost automatically be able to take on the 'easy' things like sorting laundry.

That wasn't the case.

Despite the great advances we have made in developing machines that can make complex medical diagnoses, a robot would still struggle to do the work of the waiter at your local restaurant.

In fact, the robot would rather calculate a comet's precise trajectory across the skies than have to predict how a restaurant's interiors will be affected by a couple of three-year-olds on the loose. These are the unpredictable things that we humans manage instinctively.

Roboticist Hans Moravec famously wrote that the explanation to this phenomenon lies in evolution itself. The skills a waiter uses may seem simple at first glance, but they are of course the product of billions of years of development, through which the human race has drilled and refined the art of survival on earth. We know how to move through spaces or lift glasses of different weights from a table, and we understand that water on the floor equals a risk of slipping. The complexity of seeing, or climbing, or instinctively understanding that the ball flying towards you is heading straight for your head may be something that we take for granted, but that doesn't mean it isn't there. It just makes it invisible. Chess and mathematics are something else.

We haven't been doing either very long, Moravec notes.

And because we haven't been doing them for billions of years, we have learned the laws of mathematics and the black-and-white logic of chess through more conscious processes. We have all plodded through our times tables, and had the rules of chess explained to us. Which means that we can also explain these things to a computer. And so the machines got good at algebra and chess, which is amazing, of course. But it didn't automatically lead to them being able to do everything in the economy. And why did we think it would?

The match that Garry Kasparov played and eventually lost against Deep Blue lasted only an hour, but in the media it was presented as some sort of existential struggle between human creativity and the computer's cold and calculating way of moving through the world. If the computer won, then an army of faceless machines would soon take over. Humanity would simply have to come to terms with our new lower status in this world. Our lone hope against the machines taking over was a knight in shining armour from the recently collapsed Soviet Union: Garry Kasparov. Such was the existential drama that we projected onto this match. What would win out? Humanity's ability to solve problems with feeling and instinct? Or the brute force of millions of equations per second?

As we know, it was Kasparov who lost. And with that, some part of the world thought that the rest was a foregone conclusion. If a computer could beat Garry Kasparov at chess, it was probably only a matter of time before machines could do everything else.

'Excelling at chess has long been considered a symbol of more general intelligence. That is an incorrect assumption in my view,' wrote Kasparov in 2018. We made a big deal of his matches against Deep Blue because we thought our humanity lay in our intelligence. And that intelligence equalled an ability to win at chess.

But there are a plethora of other things that machines do better than us that haven't led to such dramatic conclusions. The first time we built a forklift that could transport more than a human could, we didn't witter on about the end of our dominance on earth. Bats see better in the dark – does that mean in 50 years they will be our overlords? Why did we think that a machine that could beat us at chess would develop an ability to do everything else, too?

This is where gender comes into it.

Roboticist Rodney Brooks has written that AI researchers long regarded intelligence as the ability to tackle 'the things that highly educated male scientists found challenging'. This was why computers were tasked with playing chess, proving mathematical theorems and dabbling in complex algebra. In the world of the male scientist, these tasks were deemed high status.

But that world turned out to be pretty small.

We wanted to build 'human machines', but our definition of 'human' was based on a certain type of rational, academic masculinity. Computers were reserved for the problems that we deemed 'challenging', and in our minds these were interchangeable with the activities that we had learned to view as 'male'. Then we drew the conclusion that if the machines could negotiate these 'male' problems, then they would obviously be able to dominate the rest of the world, too.

But they couldn't. And we got stuck on this hurdle for a long time.

Of course, the question is if having more women in AI would have made a difference. Had the early AI pioneers not been a narrow group of white male professors, would research have started to see cleaning as an equally legitimate problem as chess? And would we have come further in our technological development?

Possibly.

We now have ways of getting around Polanyi's paradox, but they come with their own limitations. Certain machines can teach themselves to do things by simply practising them. This is called 'machine learning', but for it to work you need such vast quantities of data that this in turn can prove problematic. Data in our world also tends to be based on men, not women.

But above all, this is a process that you are almost constantly having to redo. If you have trained your robot to teach itself to pick up a bottle from the ground, for example, then in principle you need to start from scratch if you want it to pick up a coffee cup instead. As we all know, that isn't how humans work: we can apply a general ability to pick things up to other things in a fairly natural way.

Just watch a one-year-old toddle around with her toys, drop them and pick them up again. She may well take a tumble, or fumble the rattle as it falls to the floor, but she has no difficulty applying what she learned from picking up the spade to the problem of picking up the ball. A robot who saw her would think she was an absolute genius of bodily intelligence.

Now imagine you have a self-driving car. This car needs to teach itself to read road signs. But for the machine to be able to follow the command: 'If you see a stop sign, stop,' it first needs to know what a stop sign looks like.

You, a human, simply see a red sign. But your self-driving car is controlled by an algorithm, and the algorithm instead 'sees' different clusters of lines. This is how we have taught it to break down images into mathematics in order to gradually understand them.

Now imagine that you are driving your new self-driving car down a country road. You activate the autopilot and sit back and relax while the car drives and the sun shines. Suddenly two road signs on either side of the road inform you that the speed limit is about to go from 50 kilometres per hour to 30 kilometres per hour. But something has happened to one of the signs. Someone has stuck some tape across it, probably because it's damaged in some way: perhaps it was butted by an elk, or vandalised by a local teen. Now, a human can instinctively see that something in this vein has happened, and we hardly give it any notice. Our brains automatically read the sign as '30 km/h' without a second thought. But not your self-driving car – for it doesn't think, it calculates. Which means that piece of tape causes real issues for the system. The algorithm suddenly interprets the sign as '80 km/h' instead of '30 km/h', just because there's a bit of tape on it. Your car accelerates merrily away and crash, bang, wallop, you fly straight off the side of the road on the tight bend.

'Polanyi's paradox!' you might have exclaimed, were you still conscious.

In short, reality isn't as black and white as a chessboard. And this constantly creates problems for our machines because they calculate their way through existence, while in many respects humans *feel* their way with their bodies. This is why machines like it best in factories.

Now, we could obviously do the same for self-driving cars that we have done for other machines. We could build them a dedicated 'universe' of special roads that only they can use, thus sidestepping the real-world problems they currently experience with everything from snow-flecked signs to unpredictable pedestrians. The roads would be made so that these algorithm-driven vehicles could travel in peace, away from all the complexity of human-driven traffic. But if we were to do that, what would be the difference between a self-driving car and, say, a train? Couldn't another name for this sort of road be, well, tracks? Yes, we might be able to travel in individual vehicles in a way we don't currently do on our train lines, but that isn't how the idea of self-driving cars has been sold to us. Tech entrepreneurs have promised us self-driving cars that can get around in normal traffic just like our cars do today, without any changes to society, but with the added bonus of being able to play video games in the back seat. These cars don't exist, and many doubt they ever will.

'Elephants don't play chess,' says Rodney Brooks. And elephants are pretty damn smart anyway. They are in many ways smarter than our fastest computers, though in other ways much less so. In a nutshell: it's complicated. Dogs seem to be able to understand when their owners are sad, but computers find that challenging. Which one is smarter, really? Just because a machine can beat Garry Kasparov at chess, that doesn't mean it can beat Serena Williams at tennis. What she expresses is a different form of intelligence. A corporeal intelligence. And in that also lies a great deal of what makes us human.

But somehow we have trouble admitting that.

Chess is a game of war, the squares on the board a battlefield. When chess was invented in India in the sixth century CE, all of the pieces were men. It was only when the game reached Europe 400 years later that one of the pieces started to be called a queen. In those days she was the weakest piece on the board.

The only woman in the game had the least mobility of them all. She could only move one square at a time, and only diagonally. But then in the fifteenth century something changed. The queen's power grew on the chessboard, just as it did in reality.

Europe's elites were suddenly dominated by figures like Catherine the Great of Russia and Isabella I of Castile. As a result, the chess queen also started to take up more space on the board. Suddenly she was the only piece that could move in whatever direction she wanted, and as far as she pleased. Today the king in chess is just a glorified pawn, in spite of his title. Still, those who play chess remain primarily men, and the type of intelligence required in chess is something we associate with the male.

In other words, when it came to creating a thinking machine, we turned it into a man. Or what we implicitly considered one to be. And in doing so we overlooked so many of the faculties that actually allow us humans to function in the world. All because we had coded them as 'female', and therefore something that it was fine to take for granted.

In the economy, as well as in our machines.

Serena Williams on a tennis court is one of the purer expressions of the type of human intelligence that machines have the most difficulty replicating. Yes, a machine can hit a ball harder. And yes, robots may one day be able to play brilliant tennis: a tennis court is, after all, a rather predictable environment compared to the rest of the world. But that isn't the point.

The point is that we saw the world as a chessboard, and incorrectly assumed that what kept it turning was rational thought alone. The fact that we anchored ourselves to this kind of fallacy is bound up with our views on gender.

———————

David Foster Wallace once wrote a celebrated essay on male tennis star Roger Federer. In it, Foster Wallace states that at Roger Federer's elite level, sport is nothing but an expression of human beauty. For yes, men happen to have bodies, too, though we may view Roger Federer as 'less body' than Serena Williams: he is a white man, after all, and she a black woman. In 2018, the *Herald Sun* published a cartoon of Serena Williams which the US based National Association of Black Journalists described as a 'racist, sexist caricature' that was 'unnecessarily sambo-like'. Black women are frequently reduced to this idea of pure and threatening physicality, which is somehow deemed more primitive.

In his essay, Foster Wallace discusses Federer's beauty in particular – a beauty that has nothing to do with sex or cultural norms. When playing at his best, what Federer expresses with his tennis is, according to Foster Wallace, a beauty that is universal.

Sport can, in its greatest moments, become a means of reconciling the spectator with the fact that he has a body. Great players like Federer can catalyse our awareness of how wonderful it is to stretch, feel, see and move in this world – to simply interact physically with matter. Think of the moment when a baby realises that she can raise her hands to her face. *That* feeling. As adults we need Roger Federer for that.

Obviously Serena Williams and Roger Federer can do things with their bodies that the rest of us can only dream of. But these dreams are important, says Foster Wallace. Why? Because they put us in contact with our own humanity by putting us in contact with our bodies.

But he also notes that for many men this can be very uncomfortable. The body reminds man of his weakness. As we all know, it is the body that will one day die. But not only that: it is the body that may one day make man dependent on others and his surroundings, through illness and age. He doesn't want to be reminded of this. Dependence doesn't fit within his gender role.

And that is why, as we have seen, the body has been coded as female for millennia. Woman has been perceived as more bound to the reality of her body through birth, leaking breasts and the blood that can flow from her womb. Woman had to be body, so that man could be something else. We still teach men that overcoming the body is synonymous to becoming a man. But a pair of testicles is in no way less corporeal than a pair of ovaries. Still, we largely regard maleness as some form of rational intellect at the controls of the machine that is his body. The woman, conversely, is entirely reducible to her physical self.

And now we find ourselves back at the fundamental tragedy of the patriarchy: that when genders are defined by their oppositions, no one gains access to the full spectrum of what it means to be human.

David Foster Wallace writes that, while many men may long to see Roger Federer on Centre Court, they can't accept the sporting experience of beauty for what it is. And so they have to project sport as some sort of war. This is a distancing technique.

Men often talk about their 'love' of sport. But this is a love that must be expressed through the syntax of war to be acceptable to other men. The man conceals the experience of physical beauty his soul is searching for in sport by the way he talks about it, discussing it in terms of hierarchies, technical analyses, or a nationalistic or tribal sense of us against them. But the compulsive reeling off of sporting statistics, the chest-pumping, the face-painting and the bellowing of fight songs from the stands are all things man resorts to in order to make the sporting experience that puts him in contact with his own body compatible with his own idea of masculinity.

It was this male ideal – which is terrified of admitting the importance of the body – that tried to build technology in its own image.

And so we got machines that could defeat Garry Kasparov. But not Serena Williams.

FUTURE

9

In which we forget to ask after Mary

The year was 1842 and Friedrich Engels was 22 years old. It was, as his father saw it, high time for his son to get over his youthful radicalism. So he packed him off from the family home in what is now western Germany to spend two years in Manchester in the north of England. Here in the English textile city, young Engels was to work at the offices of a mill that produced sewing thread. Having enjoyed the benefits of middle-management life, he would return to Germany reined in, industrious and conservative. At least, that was his father's plan. This proved to be something of a miscalculation: the trip to Manchester would instead lead to Engels founding modern-day communism with his friend Karl Marx.

Engels the younger was in many ways the first real champagne socialist, a man who enjoyed fox hunting and lobster salad throughout his life. But when he arrived in Manchester it was to a city swept up in the Industrial Revolution – often known as 'the first machine age'. What Engels saw in Manchester would make him choke on his lobster salad.

The new machines had well and truly reached that northern city, and industrialisation was going at full tilt. There were steam locomotives, factories, and gigantic chimneystacks that blurted smoke up into the sky. People were leaving their small country cottages and home-produced goods for an entirely new life in the city. The technology appeared to be trailing all of society in its wake, on a wild and bumpy ride towards – well, no one quite knew what.

Economists like technological development: innovation is what can bring about higher living standards for everyone, they tend to think. And they are probably right about this. As the economist Joseph Schumpeter put it, capitalism isn't about producing 'more silk stockings for queens but [about] bringing them within the reach of factory girls'. And if factory girls in silk stockings is your goal, then you will definitely be in need of some technological development.

For it is innovation that increases productivity in the economy, which means the girls' wages can go up: suddenly they can produce 20 silk stockings in the time that it once took to produce five.

And if the machines can take on the factory's most arduous, dangerous jobs, then half of the girls can go on to do something else, too. When society gets richer, it can invest in their education, for example. Before you know it, half of the girls will be textile engineers and editors of fashion magazines instead. This, in any case, is how it is supposed to work.

We invent new machines, and they in turn free us from the jobs we would rather not do. And since these machines also make us richer, this new wealth creates demand for new things, too – like grooming salons for dogs, imported ceramic vases and chocolate-chip cookies. Which creates new jobs blow-drying dogs, serving cakes and selling ceramics, jobs that are more enriching and better paid than the ones that came before. Meanwhile the price of silk stockings will drop

– we can make them much faster, after all – and so factory girls will be able to wear silk on their legs, a luxury that just a generation before was reserved for but a handful of queens. This is the rough idea of how it should go. Of course, a lot can go wrong along the way, as Engels was made acutely aware in Manchester.

The future communist worked in Salford, just west of the city. At the time he was a confused radical who had met Karl Marx just the once. But on the factory floor in Salford he fell in love with a young, politically active Irish woman, who would take him by the hand and show him the first machine age.

Or perhaps, above all, its shocking cost.

Engels would come to see Irish migrants dwelling in ramshackle houses with broken windows, families in dark, damp cellars, living in stench and squalor. Factory floors where the air was so dusty that workers were coughing up blood, or where the machines were so tightly packed that the bodies of workers would sometimes get caught in them. Around town, he noticed how common it was to see human bodies that had been completely deformed – knees that bent backwards, ankles with thick swellings, spinal columns bent in unnatural angles. He met children who were forced to work 12 hours a day and were whipped if they couldn't keep up. He walked down to the river and took in the dreadful stench of waste and its blackish-green slime, and saw how the chimneystacks hid the summer sun behind black clouds of smoke.

Engels became like a nineteenth-century Dante, stepping down through circle after circle of a hell of inhumane conditions. Then he wrote it all down. His book, *The Condition of the Working Class in England*, was a furious journalistic indictment penned by a now 24-year-old expat German middle manager who dealt in sewing threads. Karl Marx, who had been suffering from writer's block in London, was so enraged by Engels' depiction of the terrible conditions in Manchester that he took to the page once again to finish his great work, *Das Kapital*.

With time, millions would be murdered in Marx's and Engels' names, under some of the world's most brutal dictatorships. But that doesn't mean that the young Engels didn't see the awful things he saw in 1840s Manchester. The suffering that trailed in the wake of the first machine age was horrifying.

Worst of all, things could have been different. The machines needn't have destroyed people's lives. We could have banned child labour, dumping waste in rivers and 12 hour working days. We could have built decent housing and legislated for health insurance, job security and fire escapes. Then we would have not only saved millions of lives but perhaps even succeeded where Engels' father failed: at preventing his boy from becoming a revolutionary.

In such a way, the story of the twentieth century could have been very different. The great lesson from all this is that there is always an alternative. It isn't technology that decides how we organise the economy. It's humans.

———————

Many experts say that we are now living in a 'second machine age', an age at least as dramatic as the one that Engels bore witness to. The robots are coming, so they say, and soon it will be possible to automate most tasks. Today we have technologies that can understand what we say, react to it and report back to us, algorithms that can sift through millions of legal documents to find precisely what we are looking for, 3D printers that can print out spare parts for jet engines, and surgeons that can operate remotely using robot arms fitted with knives.

And just wait till that new technology really ripples through the economy, they say, then *everything* will change. The second machine age won't just lead to truckers and fast-food cashiers losing their jobs: it also spells the end for patent lawyers, management consultants and human-resources specialists. This time the robots are out for the middle-class jobs too.

You may have a hard time really taking this in. For yes, your mobile phone is more advanced today than it was yesterday, and yes, you have noticed that many new cars can parallel park by themselves, and yes, it does seem like we're constantly being shaken by political crisis after political crisis. But an industrial revolution? The end of our old ways? Surely this doesn't match up with the radical nature of what Engels observed in the 1840s?

But this may depend on where you are.

Industrial revolutions tend to strike very regionally at first. Economist Carl Benedikt Frey has described how the rural English high society of Jane Austen's novels sat in their southern counties proposing to each other over their floral teacups, pretty much oblivious that the entire textile industry in Northamptonshire – just 100 miles away – was on the brink of collapse. Similarly, great swathes of the world woke up in shock in November 2016 to the news that Donald Trump had become president of the USA. What exactly were the societal tensions that we had missed?

The robots were definitely one of them. Economists were

quick to point out that the American states that voted for Donald Trump in 2016 were also the states in which the most jobs had been replaced by machines. In recent years we have seen a gradual concentration of the highest-paying jobs and the greater part of all capital into the big cities, while other regions have been left to their fates. We have subsequently seen many of these very regions take revenge by voting for various populist parties. And if this really is the start of a second machine age, then our economies and our lives will be changed for ever.

The only question is how.

One of the more influential analyses posits that the economy will split into three. First we have the elite: the already super-rich will, unsurprisingly, continue to get even richer on the back of technological improvements. This will lead to them pulling away from the rest of society, not only economically and socially, but even biologically, a number of futurists say. They will even be able to apply the new technology to themselves, in so doing becoming some sort of super-humans who can bio-hack their bodies into everything from eternal life to the ability to see through walls. The effect will be the rich literally breaking away from the rest of mankind and irreversibly rewriting humanity's biological fate.

At least for themselves.

In group two, just beneath the elite, we have another class of people who will also have it pretty good, or so the futurists think. This class will consist of all the people who will manage to make a living by selling various personal services to the elite. Think Pilates instructors, couples' therapists, private-school teachers, stylists and life coaches. The people who will perform these jobs for the elite will form the new middle class in society, and the elite will undoubtedly have plenty of money to spend on them.

Then we have the third group. And this is where things start to get problematic. This group consists of all the people who the robots have put out of jobs along the way – the people who used to drive taxis, work in newsagents, write legal contracts and pick goods in warehouses. Billions of people who will no longer be needed in the economy, for the simple fact that we will have machines that can do everything they once did on the labour market, only much better, and much cheaper.

In such a way, billions of people will become permanently unemployed. They will simply no longer be needed, and no growth in the world will be able to get them a job. Futurist Yuval Noah Harari calls this group 'the useless class'. So what are we going to do with all these people we no longer need? In recent years this has become one of the major issues discussed at tech conferences on the future, tickets for which will set you back a neat $10,000. And it has got the billion-aires in the audience thinking.

What will all the people the economy no longer needs actually do with their days? Can we really trust them to sit nicely in their homes and play their computer games? Or will they – shock horror – revolt? March on Silicon Valley, pitchforks in hand? Vote in political leaders who are bad for business, or who think tech companies should pay taxes like everyone else? Will this 'useless class' riot in the streets and smash up our flying cars? And will this force the elite to move out to self-sufficient, environmen-tally friendly bunkers with solar-cell-lined roofs and armed robot guards at the door? A bunker can be bought, of course. But it's no fun sitting down there long term: the palace is never safe when the cottage is not happy, and all that.

Which is why a large number of well-known tech billionaires have recently started to embrace the idea of a universal basic income (UBI). This would mean that everyone, whether they have a job or not, would be guaranteed a certain income from the state every month. The idea is that if millions of people become 'superfluous' to the economy then it's probably best to pay them so at least they won't starve. Hopefully that will also mean they don't start a revolution. In other words, the elite are stumping up in order to be left alone: take your universal basic income and leave us in peace with our bio-hacked bodies and army of robot servants. If you please.

Different variants of this story – that the second machine age will split society into three groups – have been raised time and again in recent years. People may disagree on what action to take, but the narrative itself is often the same: the second machine age will lead to permanent mass unemployment on a scale never seen before. But is it really true that such a huge group of people will actually become 'superfluous' to the economy? In order to consider this question, we must look at a perspective often missing in the debate on the second machine age: that of women.

So let us return to Friedrich Engels' book on his experiences in 1840s Manchester and turn to page 154. Here young Engels tells a story that was previously recounted to him in a letter. It goes something like this.

Once upon a time there was a man called Joe. He was travelling through Lancashire, and on the outskirts of

Manchester he decided to seek out an old acquaintance by the name of Jack. After a bit of asking around, he was eventually given his old pal's address. But something was wrong. Jack appeared to live in a damp cellar consisting of a single, scantly furnished room. When Joe stepped inside he saw his friend sitting by the fireplace. But what on earth was he doing?

Jack was sitting on a footstool, mending his wife's stockings! Joe almost fell flat in shock. Jack, mortified, immediately tried to hide the stockings behind his back. But of course, it was too late.

'Jack, what the devil art thou doing? Where is the missus?' Joe asked. 'Why, is that thy work?'

Jack was then forced to confess his shame. Sniffling, he explained to Joe that of course he knew mending stockings shouldn't be his job, it was just that his poor wife Mary worked in the factory all day. She left home at 5.30 am and didn't get back until 8 pm, and by then she was so exhausted that she had no energy for anything else. So Jack had to look after the home as well as Mary, seeing as he had been unemployed for over three years. Since the machines had come to Lancashire the only jobs to be found were for women and children, he moaned.

'Thou mayest sooner find a hundred pound on the road than work for men,' he said.

Then he burst into bitter tears.

'I should never have believed that either thou or anyone else would have seen me mending my wife's stockings, for it is bad work. But she can hardly stand on her feet; I am afraid she will be laid up, and then I don't know what is to become of us.'

Jack then mournfully described what family life had been

like before the machines had come to town. He and Mary had had a little cottage, and furniture, too. Back then it was he, the man, who went to work and Mary, the woman, who stayed at home.

'But now the world is upside down. Mary has to go to work and I have to stop at home, mind the childer, sweep and wash, bake and mend,' he sobbed. 'Thou knows, Joe, [how hard it is] for one that was used (sic) different.'

Joe agreed with all of this, and gazed at Jack sadly as he sat before the fire. He was deeply moved by his friend's tragic story, which was of course why he described the encounter in the letter that eventually made it into Friedrich Engels' hands.

Joe cursed the machines. He cursed the factory owners and the government that had let it all happen. At the end of the story Friedrich Engels posed the rhetorical question: 'Can anyone imagine a more insane state of things than that described in this letter?'

The machines had created an economy that 'unsexes the man and takes from the woman all womanliness', Engels declared. Indeed, in Lancashire, families like Jack's were by no means unusual. In the first machine age the new inventions came along and took the better-paid jobs – which were often the ones that the men had performed. In their place the factories then started to employ women and children, as physical strength was no longer necessary to production in the same way. And as women and children weren't considered equally valuable, you could get away with paying them only a third of the men's wages. Suddenly a man's wife and two children would have to get jobs in the factory just to replace his lost income. He, meanwhile, would often be left at home.

What is interesting about how Engels describes the scene

of the crying, unemployed man by the fireplace is that he doesn't focus on the material. Instead, Engels' story is first and foremost about the feeling of hopelessness that Jack experiences: he has lost his masculine pride and his direction in life. This is what Engels wants his reader to feel outraged at.

And many readers did.

Clearly Jack's pain is all too real, and it is certainly nothing to laugh at. Wounded masculinity is a grave matter. It is a force that gives rise to violence, suicide and family tragedy, one with the power to create emotional wounds that are passed on through the generations, in vicious cycles of crushed pride and hopelessness. Men too have to perform their gender roles, and men, too, suffer from them.

Developments in technology had taken from Jack everything that gave him value. His whole life he had been told that he had to work and provide for his family, or else he was not a real man. And he had believed this. He had done as he was bidden. But then the machines had taken away any chance he had of being a real man, and if he couldn't be a 'real' man, then, well, he was nothing.

At least that was what they had made him believe.

No, it wasn't strange that Jack wanted to break the machines, or that he bitterly cursed them while sitting in his damp cellar with Mary's stockings in his lap. Jack's life had been destroyed by the Industrial Revolution around him. No economist in a time machine from the future could have comforted him with the fact that the very inventions that had taken his job would eventually lead to great prosperity in society – not even had they jumped out of the time machine and whipped out some graphs, or told him that the technological achievements of the first machine age would eventually allow his great-grandchildren to earn a living as yoga instructors and management consultants. Jack wouldn't have understood.

If a technological transformation in society isn't handled in the right way, it risks leading to the destruction of many lives. That the same technology will lead to growth and riches further down the line is no comfort to those who have been sacrificed along the way. That is Jack. And it is the reason for Engels' fury.

There is, however, a question that Engels doesn't ask. And it is actually pretty basic. We hear a great deal about Jack, but what did Mary think?

We don't know.

Did Mary hate the situation – toiling away in the factory while Jack darned her stockings back at home? Or had she come to terms with it all? In the evenings, did she have the energy to smile and bat her eyelashes at her husband, to give his wounded masculinity a boost? Did she scorn him? If so, did she do it behind his back, or to his face?

Or did she simply think that their new family order was fine? With a little more money, perhaps – or if Jack could just be a little more cheerful?

We have no idea.

Engels never asked Mary anything.

———————————

The first machine age involved a huge renegotiation of gender and gender roles. And so will the second. The problem is that we so rarely consider this aspect of technology when it appears. We hold conference after conference on how robots will affect the labour market, but most of the time the topic of gender doesn't even get a look-in, despite the fact that our ideas on gender affect the entire way our labour market is structured. That women do certain things and men do others is how today's economies work. We may not want them to work in this way, but they do.

Most women today work primarily with other women, while most men work primarily with other men. In Europe, 69 per cent of all salaried women work in industries in which more than 60 per cent of the workforce are women. In Germany, 69 per cent of all men work in industries in which at least 70 per cent of their colleagues are men. In the USA, 80 per cent of all elementary- and middle-school teachers, nurses and secretaries are women. Sweden, meanwhile, is one of Europe's most gender-segregated economies: over 16 per cent of all Swedish women work in professions in which women make up 90 per cent of the workforce. And when we have children, this segregation only grows: more women take more flexible – and therefore lower-paid – jobs, while the men tend to do the opposite.

If they can, at least.

Which professions are female- and male-dominated can, of course, shift at times. Namibia and Tanzania have a much larger share of female electricians than Norway, for example. But generally speaking, women work more in the service sector while men work more in manufacturing. And this is partly why the pandemic of 2020 hit women so hard and so fast: when restaurants, hair salons and physiotherapy clinics were forced to close, many women lost their jobs. Since the 1970s, recessions have often been called 'mancessions' due to the disproportionate impact they tend to have on men's employment, but this one was different – because it started in a part of the economy where many women work.

The labour market is, quite simply, split by gender. And if we are to assume that we are in a second machine age that will upend our labour market, then its effects will be gendered as well. The only question is how.

One way of narrating recent history goes something like this: around 300 years ago we suddenly started developing machines that were physically superior to the human body, at least when it came to lifting, hammering, pulling, moving and dragging. This was the first machine age. As a result, a person's physical strength became less important to the labour market. Which meant that Jack was suddenly left darning Mary's stockings, the strength of his arms replaced by a machine that could now be operated by a mere woman. Or a child.

You can see Jack in the economic statistics of the day: in spite of all the new inventions of the nineteenth century, salaries long stagnated. For many years the new prosperity simply did not translate into better lives for normal people. Quite the opposite. When Engels wrote with revolutionary gusto that the factory owners 'grow rich on the misery of the mass of wage earners', he was simply expressing a fact. Growth in England was unparalleled, yet the people were getting poorer.

And so it continued for the first four decades of the 1800s. This period was later nicknamed 'the Engels pause', in honour of the man himself.

But then the pause came to an end. Poor Jack probably died jobless and unhappy in his dank cellar, but his grandson got a job – a better job, with a better wage. The new technology that had been introduced to such painful effect started, as much as it hurt, to create new jobs. Jack's grandson didn't need to look after house and home or darn any stockings: he could make a career and buy himself a big house in a nice suburb instead. He lived a life that Jack could never have dreamed of. When the economic growth finally started benefiting more than just the few, it didn't just solve the crisis of masculinity, but a great many other problems too.

Family after family were raised from poverty, as country after country started to enjoy the new wealth that the machines brought. Societies took it and invested it in things like public healthcare and education, which further boosted growth. And, bit by bit, something fantastic happened. Since the machines were physically stronger than humans, they freed many people from lifting and carrying. Jack's great-grandchildren didn't work with their hands, they worked in Excel! We entered what would be known as the 'knowledge economy'. What a person could offer the labour market no longer came down to their muscles, but to their brains. From 'I lift, therefore I am employed' to 'I think, therefore I am employed'. And that was how we thought things would remain. We were happy with this split. The machines would do the heavy lifting, while the humans would think. But then came the second machine age.

And threatened to upend it all again. Or so the story goes.

The thing about artificial intelligence is that it will supposedly soon be able to outthink us. This is why we are all panicking: if your brain is what counts in the economy, and the electronic brains will soon be superior to our biological ones, then what will remain for humanity to do? Besides merging ourselves with machines and becoming some sort of bio-hacked cyborg that can google in its own head?

But we have long known that neither IQ tests nor school grades can predict how economically successful a person will be. Other things will reasonably come into play. Can the machines replicate those, too – whatever they may be?

A good deal of all those 'other things' are actually precisely the things that machines have such a hard time with: emotional intelligence, the ability to build human relationships or read other people, to understand what happens between individuals when they meet, and handle that smoothly. The capacity to bring out the best in others, and to understand what is really going on in a group – in fact, pretty much all of what we condescendingly term as 'soft skills'. It is easy for male futurists to confidently assert that if machines simply get higher IQs then the whole jig is up for humankind. But the problem is that the 'knowledge economy' has always been based on many other things that the futurists have never really paid much attention to. Not least a 'relationship economy' and a 'care economy'.

For it isn't only humanity's physical strength and capacity for rational thought that make the economy go round. The labour of caring, building trust, understanding others' needs and dealing emotionally with different situations and people is an invisible part of any economy. It is also a very large aspect of almost every job. But we tend not to see the 'soft' as a skill in the same way. Because we deem it feminine.

The same applies to the labour market. The qualities that will remain once artificial intelligence eventually outdoes us in rational thought are largely those that we lazily tend to label as 'feminine'. And therefore look down on economically.

When it comes to how many jobs the robots will really

be able to take, the economists disagree. Some studies say 47 per cent, others 9. And those two figures are pretty different.

However, there is at least some consensus as to where the bottlenecks lie, and the sorts of industries in which the machines' onward march will be harder.

Here economists usually name three primary areas. The first is what we discussed in Chapter 8: robots struggle with many of the physical things we humans do without a second thought. In short, Polanyi's paradox matters to the labour market. It's easier to automate Garry Kasparov's intelligence than that of Serena Williams.

The second area in which the machines are lacking is human creativity. Who knows what technology will be capable of in decades to come, but humans are currently much better than robots at jobs that require a good dose of creative thought. If you have a hard time explaining in simple terms what exactly it is you do at work every day, your job is probably not in the danger zone for automation.

The third area in which machines struggle is in anything that requires emotional intelligence. Our human emotions give us skills that are hugely important on the labour market. Anyone who does things like looking after other people, persuading other people or communicating with other people is therefore in a pretty safe position. Most economic studies suggest we probably won't have machines as nurses, preschool teachers, psychiatrists or social workers any time soon.

However, this is not to say that there is no place for robots or AI in female-dominated industries such as care. Take elderly care, for example: the new technology has a huge potential to give many older people an entirely new sense of freedom. If we ever do get those self-driving cars that we have been promised, the elderly will be able to zip around like never before, from the allotment to the grandkids and then on to Thursday-night bingo. Despite their vision and reaction times not being what they once were.

Similarly, robots in elderly care needn't be a dystopian nightmare: lonely old folks sitting, zombie-like, in front of a couple of flashing machines. If used right, technology can give many older people both independence and dignity. Many would probably prefer a robot helping them to go to the toilet than a stranger. And though you might not want to see a robot doctor every time, it doesn't mean they wouldn't be extremely useful in a pandemic, say. The point is simply that it's hard to envisage a *fully* automated hospital in the same way as a fully automated newsagents' or train station. It is also hard to see how things like high-quality childcare can be given by anything but humans.

It is for this reason that many economic studies have lately shown that the likelihood of a job being taken by a robot is much higher in male-dominated industries than female-dominated ones. Indeed, according to a number of analyses, the more dominated an industry is by women, the smaller the risk of robots taking their roles.

Which brings us back to Jack and Mary.

Throughout history, woman's economic survival has been more dependent on her relationships to other people than man's. Not enjoying the same opportunity for economic independence as men, many women have literally lived on their ability to build, nurture and maintain social ties. Which is why women happen to be specialised in the very areas that the new machines seem to have the most trouble with.

Let's suppose this really is the second machine age, and that the machines suddenly do come thundering in and take the men's jobs, be they bankers or builders. This would create an economy in which many of the things we once dubbed 'feminine' will be in demand like never before, as we will still need people in healthcare, elderly care and childcare. Will it then be the unemployed men who make up the 'useless class' in the economy, while the women get to retain their jobs and in many ways define the new economic era through their specialisation in emotions and care, the very skills where we would still have a competitive advantage over the machines?

Jobless Jack sits in his damp basement watching YouTube videos of Jordan Peterson, while Mary goes on a Brené Brown course on 'vulnerability as a leadership skill'. Welcome to the second machine age!

This is a potential consequence of current technological developments that the male futurists have overlooked. Perhaps the economic problems of the future will be less about girls not having been encouraged to code, so much as boys not having been encouraged to care?

What is interesting is that many of the jobs robots have the most difficulty with are the very same jobs that we don't value particularly highly on the labour market. Just look at how we pay our carers: these tend to be among the least secure jobs, with the absolute worst salaries on the entire labour market.

Those who work with people earn less than those who work with numbers or engines. The question is whether this basic principle of the economy will now change. If the machines take most of the number-related jobs, and our car engines can be printed on some sort of 3D printer, will it then raise the status of working with people?

Feminists have been arguing that we should value care more for years. Firstly, because they have considered it unreasonable that a midwife should earn a quarter of what a banker does. And secondly, because the low wages in much of the care sector are one of the main reasons that women today earn less than men. Around three quarters of people working in health and social care are women, across the OECD. That's 20 million women compared with 6.3 million men. Women also tend to be in the lower-paid jobs within the sector.

Scandinavian gender-equality policies have been more ambitious than almost anywhere else in the world. Sweden invests approximately the same percentage of its gross national product into parental benefits and childcare as the USA invests into its military. But in spite of this, the gender pay gap is no smaller in Sweden than in many other parts of Europe, including countries that haven't introduced remotely as extensive gender-equality policies. The Swedish gender pay gap has also been practically unchanged for more than 30 years.

In other words, ambitious policy measures to help people combine family life with a career don't seem to be enough for women to be able to advance in their positions across all levels in society. Something else seems to be holding women back economically – something that has nothing to do with a lack of childcare or fathers willing to change nappies.

This something is about the skills we perceive as valuable and those we feel we can take for granted in the economy.

There are two possible ways out of this problem. Either

women need to start going for jobs in male-dominated industries in much greater numbers, quit hanging around the low-paid pink ghetto of the care sector and study to be engineers instead of HR specialists. Or we need to radically change how we value different professions.

The first way out may seem simple enough: teach young girls to code, build, calculate and bank. The only thing is – as we saw with the programmers and the secretaries – an industry often diminishes in status when more women enter it. The problem isn't that the men have snatched all the high-paid jobs: the problem is that certain jobs are high paid because they are filled by men.

Which leaves us with the second strategy: to try to make a radical break with how we think about men, women and economic value. This is trickier. Infinitely more. After all, we have seen how much our ideas about gender can hold us back on everything from the products we invent to the way we organise our economy. But this is also where the robots might actually be able to give us a helping hand: this could actually all happen as a side effect of the second machine age.

Since robots are bad at care, feelings and relationships, these will simply be what humans have left to specialise in. The machines would thus reverse millennia of patriarchal order – in addition to making our cars fly and giving us ladderless silk stockings. Is this what the second machine age will bring? The moment when the future literally becomes female, and the matriarchy rises up as a high-tech, relationship-based society? A world in which anyone who doesn't want to develop their emotional faculties is left behind economically, and where unemployed men who don't want to take that course with Brené Brown will simply have to take their universal basic income and spend their days sending hate mail to female politicians from dark cellars instead?

Uh, we might be getting ahead of ourselves here.

For if we go back to the economic research, we see that it isn't necessarily the case that men will be harder hit by the second machine age. Yes, there are many women in care, social services and education, and these are industries that will probably be harder to automate in the same way. But women also hold more process-driven jobs than men. They sit at the supermarket checkouts and do administration for different companies, and most analysts think this type of job will probably be automatable. Which means many of these women will then lose their jobs. A number of studies even suggest that, for this reason, it will be women more than men who will be made unemployed by the second machine age, at least in its early stages.

Still, if that does happen, these women will probably have options. The step to becoming a carer is considerably smaller for an unemployed female supermarket cashier, say, than an unemployed male trucker. This is where gender roles may suddenly become a major economic consideration – just as they were in the first machine age. In short, when the male gender role collides with an industrial revolution in full steam, it has the potential to hold back technological development and cause major social tensions. We have seen this before. Just ask Jack.

Imagine a government suddenly confronted with the political challenge of retraining 200,000 unemployed lorry drivers to become hospital orderlies. Let's suppose the machines have taken almost all the jobs in the transport sector, while there is still an ongoing need for human labour in the care sector. What would the adequate policy response be?

While the government tries to puzzle this out, a new populist party emerges. Their leader promises to protect lorry drivers' jobs at all costs, thus keeping the nation's male pride intact. This harks right back to the pain that Engels described in Jack in the 1840s: the machines took my job and now I have to become a 'woman' to survive economically, while all my life I've been taught that this is the lowest a man can sink. Having a large group of the male populace feel this way isn't exactly a recipe for peace, calm and social stability.

But perhaps it needn't be so dramatic. Most jobs probably won't be fully automated. What we call a 'job' is no homogenous thing, but a set of basically dissimilar tasks that we have decided a person with a certain title should perform between 9 am and 5 pm on weekdays. There is no natural law that says, for example, that what we call a lawyer must always do what a lawyer just so happens to do today.

Think of the tasks that various computer programs have taken over in your profession in the past few decades. There are things that we did at the office 20 years ago that we wouldn't dream of doing today. When cashpoints arrived, cashiers at banks stopped counting out notes, but their jobs remained – they simply changed. So the question should perhaps be in what way the technology will change the content of a job, rather than if it will usurp it completely.

Take radiologists, for example. This is a profession in which artificial intelligence can already compete with people. AI has proved fantastic at making correct diagnoses based on X-rays, for instance. But has this cost radiologists their jobs? No. Has it seen their salaries plummet? No, not that either.

Reading X-rays and other medical imaging is only a small part of a radiologist's job. Many radiologists often perform advanced surgery and, perhaps more importantly, every radiologist spends much of their working day communicating. Their role as specialists has a lot to do with explaining results to other doctors, which makes them a human bridge between the increasingly specialised technology and the other people in the organisation. This in no way grievous fate may await many of us in the coming years, when the second machine age eventually rolls in. We will be freed from the more robotic elements of our work and forced instead to specialise more in working with other people. Humanity combined with specialist expertise will be an increasingly sought-after asset on the labour market, while 'soft' skills will become progressively important to more jobs.

This is a less dramatic vision of what could happen. But it isn't without its gender dimensions, either. Those precise emotional and social capacities that will become prerequisites in this scenario are not compatible with the gender role that many men have been raised into. Consequently, it may be harder for these men to find their new role on the labour market. For new technology to make a difference, working methods must also be tailored around it. And here the male gender role as it currently stands might actually be a problem. Refusing to retrain as a care worker, Jack continues to sulk in front of his Jordan Peterson videos instead.

Or perhaps the exact opposite will happen. We have, if anything, seen how fluid gender roles can be. Computers went from being a low-paid job occupied by black women to a high-status field that only white men's brains were deemed capable of understanding. Might something similar happen to so-called 'soft skills' in the second machine age?

History will be rewritten. Our grandkids will be taught that 'emotional intelligence', 'intuition' and 'caring instincts' have always been inherent to human nature, at least since

Jesus washed the feet of his disciples on that Maundy Thursday. Perhaps in the future they will be writing breezy children's books encouraging girls to aim for careers in the high-paid, male-dominated care sector? You may well laugh and shake your head, but can we not agree that this is at least as plausible a scenario as people bio-hacking their bodies and uploading their brains to the cloud?

The main point is that, when trying to understand the second machine age, we must consider gender. We can't discuss technology's impact on the labour market without acknowledging that the labour market is organised by gender.

We can't forget to ask about Mary.

Namely, we face a political choice. Almost all discussion surrounding the second machine age has so far focused on how to adapt people to the developing technology. Not the technology to the people.

Will the robots take 47 per cent or 9 per cent of all jobs? This is the question we have been desperate to answer in recent years. Clearly, if our task is to adapt society to the robots and not vice versa, it is good to know what the figure will be. It gives us time to prepare. But this mode of thinking leads to a debate in which we try to predict, rather than affect, the course of technology.

A bit like trying to guess the weather for the August bank holiday.

You see, the machines aren't simply 'coming'. Someone has to pay for them, invent them, build them and sell them. If the robots are coming it's because we are creating them. And there is always a political dimension here, too.

When William Lee came to Queen Elizabeth I with his new stocking frame knitting machine in 1589, she refused to give him a patent. She didn't want to risk putting all the workers in the English stocking industry out of a job, nor did she want to create more monopolies. You may argue that this is an irrelevant thing to bring up here: yes, in the past the state shaped technological development by stymieing it just like Elizabeth I, but not any more. Today we are wiser. We have come to see that the state neither can nor should try to use strong-arm tactics to hold new technology back. The reason why we have made such technological leaps in the past 300 years is that we, unlike Elizabeth I, have not tried to steer technology by political means.

Only this isn't exactly true.

In fact, the first machine age happened in the UK largely thanks to political decisions made by the British state. Namely, it chose military intervention on the side of the machines: 14,000 armed soldiers were posted to the English countryside to stop the unemployed from attacking the new machines with sledgehammers. Many of the vandals were hanged or exiled to Australia, and so the state solved its problem by getting rid of those who stood in the way of the technological revolution.

In other words, it is simply not true that the first machine age came thundering in of its own free will: it required very tangible political interventions. At one point there were more British soldiers defending machines from violent trouble-makers in the UK than there were fighting Napoleon in Spain.

And that was no petty European war.

If the robots have a certain kind of impact on the labour market, it's because we allow them to. This is not only a question of how we regulate and finance them, but also of how we value this or that in our economy.

Your iPhone is not built by robots: it is still assembled

largely by female human hands in India and China. This not only has to do with Polanyi's paradox, i.e. that robots still struggle with their fine motor skills. It is also to do with women's hands being so cheap in the global economy.

Who will want to invent robots that can replace female hands if these hands continue to cost companies so very little? In other words, low pay and our blithe acceptance of women and people with darker skin earning very little money for very hard work can hold back technological development.

Who will want to invent a self-cleaning house when we live in a world in which women earn their living by cleaning for $8 per hour? Who will want technology to solve problems that remain invisible, since they are currently being taken care of by women for free? What we value and don't value in society affects the type of technology that tomorrow will bring. There is nothing strange about this; we simply need to be aware of it. Then we will realise that we always have a choice, and that the best way to predict the future is to create it.

There doesn't need to be a 'useless class' of billions of people roaming the streets in unemployed gangs, thieving and vandalising the flying cars of the elites. Yes, we may well end up in such a world, but it wouldn't be a consequence of the technology. It would be a consequence of the choices we have made along the way.

Even if it were possible to automate everything else, in some extreme variant of the futurists' visions, so long as there are bodies that need caring for, people who need human contact and communication, and children who need encouragement, acknowledgement and hugs, there will be things for humans to do in our economy. Then the question would just be how to finance the human jobs, and that question is eminently answerable. That's just a political choice. We can either use the wealth generated from the new technology to let a tiny elite get super rich and bio-hack their bodies, or we can use it to build an infinitely more humane society than the one we live in today. A society based on entirely different values, and a completely new analysis of what really matters to most.

Just as the first machine age eventually freed many people from back-breaking manual labour, the second machine age has the potential to free us, too; to allow us to devote ourselves more to fostering our creativity and relationships with each other. In other words, the technology should give us an opportunity to do things with our days that most people genuinely value more highly. The revolutionary potential of the second machine age lies not only in the technology as such. It lies in technology's potential to confront us with our own humanity.

It has been all too easy for us to buy into the narrative that the robots will steal all of our jobs. This narrative both captures our imagination and confirms certain things that we believe to be true of ourselves. But it is also dangerous, insofar as it blurs any alternatives and paints a picture of a single inevitable future to which we will simply have to adapt our societies and, not least, ourselves. That we have found this narrative so compelling isn't so much a matter of us overestimating the machines as us underestimating ourselves. Or, rather, the parts of ourselves that we have learned to call female, and thus look down on both existentially and economically.

We aren't used to appreciating how important feelings, relationships, empathy and human contact are to the economy. Or how central these things are to humanity as a whole. We are used to thinking of them as some sort of cherry on top – the frills that everything else may eventually lead to, as opposed to perhaps the most fundamental social infrastructure of all. Which is precisely what it is. This is what the robots may come to show us, and with this the new technology actually has the potential to make us more human, not less.

Friedrich Engels assumed that Jack was the protagonist in his story.

When it was Mary all along.

10

In which we decide not to burn the world at the stake

Princess Anne of Denmark was fifteen years old when she was married off to King James VI of Scotland in 1589. James had chosen Anne from a portrait, and the two became husband and wife in a proxy wedding without ever having met.

The North Sea lay between them, but now that September had come, the princess was to finally cross the water from the west coast of Denmark to the east coast of Scotland, meet her husband and ascend her throne.

The task of delivering the princess safely across the sea had fallen to Danish Admiral Peder Munk. Twelve stately ships set sail from Denmark that autumn, but the voyage was a disaster. Twice the ships came so close to the Scottish coast that land was literally within their sights, and twice rough winds whipped them back towards Norway.

So the story goes, at least.

Now the admiral was uneasy. These were no average autumn storms, he thought: he had never experienced anything like them in his life. Just as he was beginning to get genuinely concerned, a third storm picked up. The winds tore at the sails and tossed the fleet between the waves. A cannon was ripped from its station, rolled across the deck and crushed eight Danish sailors right before the princess's eyes. This was when the admiral made the decision to turn around. He safely sailed the princess's ship to Norway.

When the news reached King James of his young bride's trouble crossing the North Sea, he was devastated. He even made the unusual decision to try and retrieve her himself. With great effort he managed to reach Norway, where his bride was waiting. But then the weather turned yet again, and the couple had to wait almost six months before they could set sail for Scotland once more.

By this point King James had heard the odd whisper about witchcraft from the Danish crew, as the Danish court in Copenhagen had been obsessed with these things for some time. The Scottish king grew increasingly convinced that some form of witchcraft was to blame for this setback, and that someone with a flair for the black arts simply didn't want his queen to ascend the throne. The king was terrified.

Admiral Peder Munk returned to the Danish capital, where a decision had been made to get to the bottom of what had happened. Someone had to be held accountable for the princess's trouble crossing the North Sea – after all, it had almost cost the woman her life. The blame first fell on the Danish treasurer, who was accused of having neglected to correctly equip the fleet, of having skimped almost to the point of disaster for the ships out in those unforgiving autumn storms. The treasurer, however, didn't accept such accusations. He blamed it all on witches instead. Evil witches must have sent some sort of devils to climb aboard the ships and cause the storms, he argued. And people believed him. Soon the Danish state had executed 12 women for having bewitched the ships. Three of them were burned at the stake at Kronberg castle in Helsingør, and black smoke soared over the Öresund strait.

While King James hadn't been particularly fearful of the black arts before, this all changed after that voyage. He became hell-bent on taking revenge on the witches who had caused the storms. His soldiers soon found a midwife by the name of Agnes Sampson and extracted a confession from her by torture. Seventy people were prosecuted for this and other inexplicable weather phenomena, in what would become a major Scottish witch trial. Agnes Sampson was burned at the stake in February 1591, and to this day it is claimed that her spirit wanders, naked and bleeding, through the corridors of Holyrood Palace, the Edinburgh residence of the British monarchy.

King James never did get over the storms of that winter. He even went on to write a witch-hunting handbook. Literally: a guide on how to find, recognise and entrap witches. Blaming women for the weather is an age-old pursuit. That witches could cause crop failures was something that popes had been saying for years, and that witches could control the rain, or summon thunder and lightning on demand, was a belief held by many Europeans in those days.

Witches could command hailstones to fall and fields to dry out. If the weather was acting up, then the best thing, as Admiral Munk had done after his abortive North Sea mission, was to ask if anyone had happened to offend a witch lately. Was it a case of bad weather, or a wronged woman on the warpath?

The weather had been behaving very strangely in those years. Europe was going through a period that would later come to be known as the 'Little Ice Age'. This was an age of extremely harsh winters that started in 1590 – the very year that King James and his princess finally managed to make it to Scotland. From that winter on, the weather grew wetter and colder. Frost appeared out of season, hailstones clattered down from the skies and villages flooded. Mice swarmed in in their droves, and strange maggots feasted on the crops. The economic consequences were great: in a largely agrarian society the weather essentially dictates the economic outlook – and in this case it was sinking in line with the temperature.

Food was often scarce, both because the crops failed and because changes in climate meant that cod and other fish no longer migrated as far north in the seas. Suddenly it was no longer possible to fish in the same way in many parts of northern Europe. It was the witches who would come to shoulder much of the blame for nature turning on humanity in this way.

The economist Emily Oster has linked the great European witch trials to these changes in climate. Up to 1 million people, mainly women, were accused of witchcraft in Europe, and many of them were executed. Those who were murdered were primarily poor women and widows, which are of course connected: it was hard to provide for yourself without a husband. Many women were forced to rely on alms, and these were the same women society now turned on.

Life was tough and people felt small – like victims of Mother Nature's whims. Poor women unsuccessfully begging for food might perhaps swear under their breath while being shooed away. If a storm then came, or a cow died, those women would often be accused of witchcraft. This also meant their accusers wouldn't have to feel like bad Christians for shooing away a hungry woman – because she was probably in league with the devil.

Studies of modern witch-hunts have revealed similar patterns. Around the turn of the millennium, women in rural Tanzania were accused of witchcraft and killed when it rained too much or too little; the then median income in Tanzania was comparable to that of Western Europe in the early 1600s. In India, the persecution of witches has also been linked to conflicts over property. If a dead man's family doesn't like his widow, an accusation of witchcraft can be a means of getting her to relinquish her ownership of the land that she has inherited. As such, witch-hunts can be an effective way of doing away with difficult women no one wants to deal with.

In his bestselling book on witches from 1486, the German priest Heinrich Kramer wrote that 'all wickedness is but little to the wickedness of a woman'. He continued: 'What else is woman but … an inescapable punishment, a necessary evil … an evil of nature, painted with fair colours!' He claimed that woman was 'more bitter than death', weaker in both body and soul than the male, and of course more carnal. Witchcraft stemmed from woman's insatiable lust, he imagined. Her vagina just couldn't get enough. Just look at its form! It was these deeply insalubrious desires that supposedly put woman in contact with the devil and led her to ruin.

If you think the above sounds like a stretch, even for the anything but female-friendly 1500s, then you have a point. Many of the day's institutions, from the Vatican to the Spanish Inquisition, dismissed much of what Kramer had to say about witches. Nevertheless, the book was influential. It spread throughout the Continent thanks to the latest technology of the day – the printing press – and radicalised the men it reached because it played on pre-existing cultural tropes.

Historically, we have viewed woman as a deformed version of man. Man's soul and intellect were associated with the sun, the warm and the dry. Woman, on the other hand, represented the cold, the wet and the damp; when she menstruated she was considered particularly dangerous. Woman represented the most corrupting aspects of human nature, and it therefore came as no surprise that the devil would want to consort with her.

Throughout history the witch has taken on many guises, from the ugly, hook-nosed old hag to the exquisitely beautiful enchantress who lures men in only to turn them into pigs. The first woman to be accused of witchcraft in the infamous Salem witch trials was Tituba, an enslaved woman of colour, most likely an indigenous Central American.

In many ways, fear of the witch has always been a fear of women's power. But it was also a fear of women congregating and doing things together. Women who went to see other women were obviously going to a witches' sabbath to dance with the devil. What else would they be doing?

It was for this reason that Europe's great witch trials also seemed to change the nature of the devil himself. Before then he had tended to take the shape of various small demons – certainly evil and irritating, but rarely anything that couldn't be shooed away with a few well-aimed splashes of holy water. The devil was a servant you could summon to perform wicked deeds, and as humans could send for him in this way, they had some agency in the game.

But all this would change during the European witch trials in the late sixteenth and early seventeenth centuries. Suddenly it was women who were to be hunted, so men started to imagine that it was the devil who summoned the witch to him, as opposed to the other way around. The devil would brand the witch with his mark and have violent sex with her, following which she would be his maidservant and he her pimp, master and owner in one terrifying combination. So important was it to present the woman as subordinate to the man that, even when being accused of powerful black magic, women were still framed as in thrall to some masculine force. In short, the devil started playing a greater role in it all: the witches needed a male boss.

The European witch trials often targeted women who functioned as midwives, made herbal medicines or in other ways earned a living by healing animals or people. In those days, male doctors treated society's rich with so-called 'medicines' that we would generally struggle to tell from botched potions today. Witches, meanwhile, treated the poor – those who couldn't afford anything else.

Witches were long an accepted part of many societies. A reputation as a witch could even be a business strategy, albeit a risky one. If people considered you dangerous, they would be more likely to give you food if you asked them for it. They wouldn't want you to curse their cows, after all.

For other women, witchcraft was a more traditional business operation: they would relieve ailments and heal the sick for payment. The sudden elevation of witchcraft – from magic ritual and a form of medicine that had existed for generations to a demonic conspiracy that threatened society at large – was precisely what was so strange about the European witch trials. Why did people turn on the witches at that particular point in time?

This is where climate change and the Little Ice Age come in as one potential explanation. If witches could control the weather, and the weather suddenly became more dangerous, it also made the witch into more of a threat to society.

But not everyone agrees that the weather was to blame. The economist Cornelius Christian has, for example, pointed out that one period of intense witch persecution in Scotland happened to coincide with very good harvests.

Other economists also discuss the persecution of witches as some sort of unfortunate side effect of stiffening competition in the religious market. In regions where Catholics and Protestants were competing for converts, many witches were burned at the stake – a sign, perhaps, that religious leaders were trying to prove their credentials as the ones to take the hardest stance on witchcraft, not unlike how today's political parties compete for the hardest stance on crime or immigration.

There are many theories. Some blame the witch trials on Catholicism. Others Protestantism. Others on religion in general. Some believe that they were linked to periodic outbreaks of ergot poisoning, from a type of hallucinogenic fungus consumed in certain varieties of grain, while others believe they were linked to drugs more generally. The mass murder of people accused of witchcraft is most often described as an extraordinary outburst of, well, we aren't really sure. Something inexplicable. Which is of course to depoliticise everything. Witch trials were and remain a violence against (first and foremost, though not exclusively) women.

That witches would be blamed for the storms and poor harvests during Europe's Little Ice Age was entirely logical, for our notions of womanhood and nature are linked. The reason woman can be held accountable for the weather is because she is considered closer to nature than man. Until 1979, all hurricanes and tropical storms were given female names in the USA. American feminists fought hard to change this: *Can we at least have one damn piece of meteorological equality?* they thought. But these things go so much deeper than that.

For centuries we have taught ourselves to think of nature as feminine – as dark, elusive, terrifying, ominous, unpredictable and damp, but also with the ability to bring forth life from her womb. In our culture, Mother Nature is most definitely a woman. Man's task has traditionally been to take control of nature and reap its rewards, to raise himself above nature through sheer dominance of her. But when something goes wrong in this process – like a storm sweeping him off to the wrong coast, or beetles chewing up the crops – then it is often assumed that this 'female' nature must have simply gone astray. And man must take back control. With violence, if necessary. This was precisely what King James of Scotland tried to do after those ill-fated autumn storms.

By burning women, he sought to regain male control over nature. And life.

Woman has historically been seen to be more closely bound to the physical world through her body. If you can give birth, menstruate and breastfeed, you must be more animal than man, we tend to think. Just as the black or brown person has been considered more 'part of nature' than the white person, and the black or brown woman more 'part of nature' than the white woman.

If you are not a white man you must be part of nature instead, we have been taught. This means that you are not sufficiently refined, nor endowed with the same intellectual rationality as white man. Over the years this idea has been used to legitimise many of the worst forms of subordination in society. Nature is something the white man has traditionally been told he can do pretty much anything he wants with, after all. In other words, if someone compares you to nature it is rarely good news. It usually means that you – like nature – need putting in your place.

We know what it has meant for women, and people of colour, to be compared to nature throughout history, but what has this comparison meant for nature?

We perceive Mother Nature as a woman. In our patriarchal culture we generally think of her as caring, mysterious and beautiful, but also frightening and unfathomable. Her fury may be awe-inspiring, but she is something other, something set apart from the hard, masculine technology with which we attempt to dominate her. We may idolise and adore her, but the question is if we respect her or are genuinely interested in getting to know her.

At least as something other than a resource to exploit.

In the Western world we have learned to think nature exists for human domination, just as women exist because Adam needed company and could forgo a rib. To this extent, both nature and women exist largely to serve man. Within this notion lies the kernel of many of today's problems. And perhaps the most challenging of them all: the climate emergency.

The political parties and leaders who are currently doing the most to deny the climate emergency today are almost always the very same ones that want to put women back in their place. The two, in their eyes, are linked. A mastery of nature lies within the male gender role, and neither woman nor nature – and certainly not Greta Thunberg – can tell him what he can and cannot do.

In the USA, a similar proportion of men and women think climate change is real and is caused by humans, but women are more worried. They are more likely to think climate change will harm them personally and that it is a threat to plants, animals and future generations. Women also support policies like regulating CO_2 as a pollutant and setting strict CO_2 limits to a greater extent than men.

In Sweden, researchers at Chalmers University of Technology have launched the world's first academic research centre dedicated to the study of climate denialism. For them, masculinity is an obvious topic of study. Men both deny the seriousness of climate change to a greater degree than women, and feel more threatened on a very basic level – not by climate change, but by the movement that wants to stop it.

There is increasing overlap between nationalism, anti-feminism, racism and a resistance to everything that the climate movement represents. This may seem deeply illogical at first, until we consider the witches and the idea of nature as a woman.

Climate change is not only the greatest innovation problem of our day; it is also a problem that is tangled up in many of our ideas about gender. To be a real man is to dominate nature – not make compromises for its benefit. And the latter is precisely what the climate emergency appears to require of us today.

We have contrived an idea of a certain type of gas-guzzling lifestyle as 'manly', and then placed this masculine logic above all other values. So when it then turns out that this patriarchal male lifestyle is unsustainable, we find we can't give it up. Because we have placed it above all else. Even death itself.

Many of the men who deny climate change also despise the climate movement's prominent female figures with an intensity that is far from incidental or rooted in a personal distaste for teenage Swedish girls with plaits. Instead it relates to their perceptions of the climate movement as a threat to the modern, fossil-fuel-based industrial society that has been dominated by their own brand of straight white masculinity. If fossil fuels go, then masculinity goes with it, they imagine.

Which is why it all gets so existential. This has become a key political dynamic in many societies.

Jobs in the American coal-mining industry are, economically speaking, a fairly negligible part of the American economy as a whole. Yet we saw the enormous symbolic role the coal miners played in former president Donald Trump's economic policy. It is of course strange that fossil fuels in particular have become imbued with so much cultural significance. But if we have seen anything throughout this book, it's that masculinity is often thought to depend on rather random things – from suitcases without wheels to the cranking of cars.

But we have also seen how our ideas of gender can change. Perhaps in the future we will laugh at our current struggle to get many men to adopt a more environmentally friendly lifestyle, in the same way that we shake our heads at how unthinkable it was for a man to wheel his suitcase just 40 years ago.

Indeed, there is nothing to say that men cannot continue to be men in houses powered by renewable energy, or without eating bloody steaks seven days a week. At the same time, however, we should not underestimate the sheer force our ideas about gender have in the world. For men who have very little, these gender roles can feel like the last piece of certainty that they have to hold on to.

If not handled carefully, economic policy risks fuelling the already gendered political dynamic on climate change further, in ways that could prove dangerous. You can't strip a man of his well-paying job in a Scottish oil refinery, hand him an insecure gig in telesales and then scoff at him in the *Guardian* for suddenly hating Greta Thunberg. The above is a tragedy, but it is one that can be avoided. This is where policy must step in. It must ensure the creation of secure jobs that pay at least as well as those that many men will now be forced to leave for the sake of our planet.

This is eminently doable: many of the (slightly carelessly termed) 'green jobs' in the energy sector, for example, are both fairly well paid and do not require a higher education to perform. As such, the economic transition can be managed so as to avoid pitting environmentally conscious, urban, liberal women against white men from abandoned industrial regions, in some sort of turbo-charged battle of the sexes with the future of the planet at stake.

We don't have time for that.

Still, our understanding of nature itself remains bound up with our ideas of femininity and masculinity. And this affects far more than just male right-wing populists protesting against coal-mine closures and flight taxes. It marks us all. How we think about the relationship between humanity and nature reflects how we think about women and men, often without us even realising.

'Mother Nature' we say, and yes, it does have a nice ring to it. But what is a 'mother', really, in a patriarchal society? She is someone who can be expected to give her all without ever complaining, someone who has no needs of her own and lives entirely for others. Mummy dearest cleans up any traces of pollution by simply changing our nappies, and every morning when we wake up the kitchen has been cleaned and the floors mopped and we can go on flinging our toys around without a single thought to how much time it might take to pick them up. Our idea of the mother is, in essence, an idea of a woman who looks after us and loves us regardless of how we behave. This is pretty much the last thing our planet needs to be compared to right now.

We imagine that earth exists just for us in roughly the same way that a baby who is loved is convinced her mother exists just for her. To a very small baby, the mother is not a person in her own right, and she *definitely* has no needs that may differ from the child's. There is a basic economic assumption in our society that women will perform care work without pay, demands or gripes, so if nature is a woman, then she obviously has the same duty of care. She must always stand by and care for us, no matter how we behave. Otherwise she is a bad mother: BURN WITCH, BURN!

We look at photographs of earth from space, mesmerised by her perfect round beauty as she hangs there in the infinite darkness of the universe. This, unlike many other things, actually makes us want to look after her: we need to objectify the planet to be able to feel our love for her. We want her to be beautiful and vulnerable, and only then are we inclined to protect her. Or at the very least, not suffocate her further with our pollution. We want to own her, admire her and be looked after by her. But we don't want to understand her in any depth. We don't want to accept her complexity. Ideally, we want to know a little about her, in order to control and get what we want from her.

This, in short, is no healthy relationship.

We didn't persecute witches because of their magic. It wasn't the spells and the cauldrons and the potions in themselves that made us uncomfortable. You see, not all magic is created equal. Just ask any self-respecting alchemist.

For centuries alchemists attempted to produce gold and find the key to eternal youth through malodorous concoctions and mysterious symbols, but, unlike witches, alchemists generally enjoyed a high status in society. In other words, it seemed to matter whether the person mumbling mystical words over a bubbling cauldron was a witch or an alchemist. And alchemists tended to be men, while witches tended to be women.

Some of the world's most brilliant scholars were alchemists, including the father of modern physics, Isaac Newton, and the founder of modern chemistry, Robert Boyle.

Today Isaac Newton is often regarded as the first modern scientist. It was his discovery of gravity that taught us to see the world through cold, rational reason as opposed to mysticism and divine whims, we were told in school. This, however, isn't entirely correct.

In 1936, the great English economist John Maynard Keynes managed to acquire large piles of Isaac Newton's notes – papers that no one had previously studied. And when Keynes came to examine them, they gave an entirely different picture of the founder of modern physics.

Newton's papers were full of magical formulas, mystical symbols and prophecies. Here was a man who had written over a million words on alchemy in his lifetime. Newton was, as Keynes observed, 'not the first of the age of reason'; he was 'the last of the magicians'.

Alchemy's ideas of invisible spirits might even have helped Isaac Newton to envisage an uncanny, invisible force such as gravity and then try to calculate it. Still, this doesn't stop us from using his mathematical principles to send our rockets into space. The father of modern physics was a wizard – albeit a part-time one – and had he been a woman he would have been a part-time witch and would presumably have ended up at the stake. Yes, male scientists were burned, too, but not anywhere near as much as female witches.

However, this comparison doesn't quite hold up, for had Isaac Newton been a woman, he would obviously never have been able to study at that illustrious university in Cambridge, which brings us to one of the fundamental differences between wizards and witches.

In the fairy tales, wizards are well-educated, dignified men in great castles or high towers. They have, in other words, both material wealth and contacts. Whereas the witches, in spite of their magical abilities, live in ramshackle cottages with gingerbread roofs on the edges of forests. In this our fairy tales undoubtedly reflect reality: the witch, being a woman, had no access to the man's world of heavy books, formal knowledge and education. The witch had to make do with the herbs she could find in the woods and the knowledge she inherited from her mother, drawing her power from her dead ancestors, nature or animals. That was all she had access to.

Today, alchemists have to some extent been rehabilitated, with many historians viewing them as a sort of early chemist. Which makes Isaac Newton's papers more understandable, too.

Yes, the alchemists cooked up magic potions, but they also analysed metals, refined salts and produced dyes and pigments, say their defenders today. Alchemists made glass, fertilisers, perfumes and cosmetics, and they distilled and produced acids. In many ways the wildly experimenting alchemist is the archetype for today's image of the crazy male inventor with electric-shock hair and various exploding liquids on a burner before him.

But there is no such cultural archetype for women.

Or is there?

————————

'How dare you?' Greta Thunberg thundered in her already classic 2019 speech at the UN in New York. The Swedish climate activist was alluding to the world leaders' lack of action – past and present – to stop climate change.

The answer to Thunberg's question is actually pretty simple. The world's leaders generally *dare* to take the risk because some part of them believes that the technology of the future will be able to solve at least some part of the climate-change problem for them. What you choose to do and not to do about the climate emergency is directly linked to your views on technology.

American science journalist Charles C Mann has described the environmental debate of recent decades as a battle between 'wizards' and 'prophets'.

On the one hand we have the doomsday prophets. They say that if we don't respect our planet's boundaries – scale back, conserve, protect and stop consuming – earth will soon be uninhabitable.

On the other hand, we have the wizards. They instead see innovation and technology as the solution to our environmental problems: no, we can't scale back, we have to invent our way out of this crisis! Technology is what will save us, the wizard thinks, so there's no reason to sulk. It's time to start working and start inventing, for that's what humanity has always done.

The prophet sees humanity's inventiveness as the problem in itself. We insist on constantly innovating, at the cost of the planet, the animal and plant kingdoms, and ourselves. Instead we should content ourselves with living simpler lives more in harmony with nature, the prophets grumble, thinking the wizards should know better.

But for the wizards, the prophet's words on scaling back

and changing our way of life are intellectually dishonest. It is a betrayal of the world's poor and, in practice, sheer racism, the wizard thinks. The prophets are nothing but rich white Westerners who preach doom and gloom to the rest of the world, telling them that they can never experience the type of prosperity that the white West has enjoyed. No fridges or cars for you, I'm afraid! Shame on you who dream of growth and riches. The wizard thinks that the prophet's reasoning is both shameful and entirely unnecessary: humanity has always been able to invent and innovate its way out of its problems before, and much of human history has been concerned with how to manage a natural world that is constantly trying to kill us. Why should the climate emergency be any different?

The prophet in turn sniffs at the wizard's naïve faith in humanity and technology. For in practice, the prophet says, the wizard's stirring ode to innovation is nothing but a way of avoiding lifestyle change. The entire argument is deeply corrupt, and the wizard is simply providing a front for big, bad capitalist companies that depend on us continuing to consume and stuff our faces without a care in the world. Reckless capitalists are only all too happy to conceal their greed and short-sightedness in the wizard's beautiful words about technology saving us, the prophet thinks. But the only thing new inventions can do in this situation is kick the inevitable conflict between humanity and nature further down the road, the prophet thunders on. And so the debate continues.

So we have the wizards busily trying to experiment the new into existence, while the prophets warn that we are experimenting ourselves to death. Charles C Mann points out that this all boils down to values. The wizard sees growth and innovation as humanity's great blessing, while the prophet values stability and conservation. Wizards are drawn to grandiose, large-scale solutions like sending up sunlight-reflecting mirrors into the atmosphere, or constructing giant nuclear-power plants. In this sense, British Prime Minister Boris Johnson is a typical wizard when it comes to climate change; so is Elon Musk.

The prophet, in turn, is attracted to the local and the decentralised, and would love to grow their own crops and generate their own energy at home. The conflict between the wizard and the prophet is, according to Mann, not a conflict of good and evil, but of two different concepts of the good life. Is individual freedom more important than coherence? Is experimentation more important than conservation? Should we scale back, or should we invent more?

We all recognise this debate, because it is one we have been mired in for several decades. In addition, both wizards and prophets have a knack for overegging it with some fairly bizarre perspectives on Mother Nature herself. The wizard often seems to see her as an endless resource just lying there for him to exploit. Nature has no other value than as a raw material for his machines. And should Mother Nature happen to die in one of the wizard's experiments, on some level he thinks he will always be able to find himself a new planet to colonise. Once he's exhausted his current squeeze, he'll simply trade her in for a younger model, and this, as we know, is no way to treat a lady.

Meanwhile, the prophet can almost seem to get off on the fact that Mother Nature, as he sees it, is dying. He sits there like a tragic knight beside her gasping body, singing the praises of her passive beauty, which to him is made only the more beautiful by the fact that she is sick. In actual fact he was never all that committed to this relationship until he realised that she was dying. The prophet risks becoming like the mad king Théoden in J R R Tolkien's *The Lord of the Rings*, who deals with his concrete problem – an army of Orcs outside the city walls – by retreating into an idea that all hope is gone.

Most of us can probably see that the solution to the climate emergency should lie with both the wizard and the prophet: we will need to *both* invent *and* reform our way of living. In many cases these things are interconnected: only once behaviour changes in a more sustainable direction will there be a demand for more green products, and only then will the inventions in that sphere follow. This is how things normally work. In the same way, it will only be when we collectively make the decision to take the climate emergency seriously that we will be able to direct resources through the power of the state in a way that can help drive innovation in a green direction. The two are linked.

'Economic growth has not only a rate but also a direction,' as economist Mariana Mazzucato writes. But the wizards and prophets tend to ignore her.

As Charles C. Mann notes in his book about wizards and prophets: 'What's striking to me is how long these arguments have gone on without most people seeming to blend them in the middle.' We tend to be either/or, getting increasingly entrenched in our respective positions even as the clock ticks and the ice melts. The reason we have been stuck watching the duel between the wizard and prophet has to do with the view of technology that underpins their larger world view. It is the dominant view of technology in our society, which, as we have seen in this book, is deeply problematic.

We are used to envisaging technology as an unstoppable force that drives history along. The dominant narrative on

AI, beyond the gendered aspects that we have already discussed, implies that all humanity can do is adapt both ourselves and society. We invent one tool and then another, and the second is always bigger, better and more efficient than the first – innovation upon innovation in a nice, neat chain, with each 'generation' of technology leading unstoppably straight into the next. Our path to the future is unbending, and the inventions pop, oven-ready, out of the brains of different male geniuses only to push the rest of us along.

Based on the way we tend to discuss them, one might even get the impression that inventions are the active participants in history and humanity the passive.

'The car created the modern suburb,' we say.

'The washing machine liberated women.'

'AI threatens the world's lorry drivers.'

We often erroneously imagine that it is our technological inventions that do things for society and the individuals within it. As we have seen, that isn't how things work. When we consider a factor like gender, it becomes clear how technology is constantly being shaped *within* our preconceived ideas of the world, the economy and ourselves.

Many prophets may well bluster that technology and inventions won't save us from the climate threat, but in all honesty they have no idea.

The climate prophet risks becoming like Nobel-prize winning physicist Albert Michelson, who in an 1894 speech declared: 'The more important fundamental laws and facts of physical science have all been discovered.' Within a few years, of course, Einstein's theory of special relativity and quantum mechanics had both come along and changed everything.

We don't know what we don't know.

And that applies to all innovation.

In this case we know especially little about what we don't know, given how many humans we have shut out and whose ideas were never developed into inventions or innovations.

On the one hand, our societies praise innovation and entrepreneurship like never before. On the other, we have seen how the financial system has excluded women with astounding efficiency. When 97 per cent of all venture capital goes to men, something is fundamentally wrong with the entire model; with how we view risk, innovation and entrepreneurship.

When we realise just how many people we have ignored for various reasons, we also realise how much untapped human potential we are actually sitting on. We are living in a historic moment in which the groups whose experiences haven't been counted as human are raising their voices. By listening to the people we haven't listened to before, many new ideas will come. It's only logical, after all.

The way we currently describe the history of technology not only excludes women in a primary sense, it also means that our definition of technology has constantly shifted to exclude what women have done. When men knitted stockings it was a respected, technical job; when women did so it was needlework. When women churned butter it was a simple servant's task; when men did so it was a technical operation. When women programmed computers it was considered something anyone could do, but when men did so it suddenly required a very specific type of nerd brain that in all its great genius could neither shower its associated body nor be bothered to show some basic social skills.

Throughout history, innovation has been held back by

gender in all of these different ways. We have seen how suitcases could only start rolling once we changed our views on masculinity. How electric cars lost out to petrol in part because they were perceived as feminine, and how soft materials weren't counted because they were coded as female. Today's economy and its whaling logic continue to shut women out. And women's poorer economic conditions and continued responsibility for the home and children mean they cannot be a part of inventing the world in the same way. All of this has shaped the machines we built, the ideas we had and the world we thought possible. In other words, until this very moment we have been inventing with one hand tied behind our backs.

Just imagine what we could achieve if we cut that rope?

At the same time, no new 'technological solutions' will appear like a bolt from the blue. Although many wizards like to imagine that a female wizard will suddenly come up with a technology for artificial photosynthesis that can eat up all our superfluous carbon dioxide in a week, it's unlikely to happen. Technology almost never materialises in that way. Not even the wheel, as we have seen. That required a range of other devices and thousands of years for its potential to be harnessed, everything from macadam to a society capable of sharing responsibility for road maintenance.

And this time we don't have thousands of years.

The question shouldn't be if technology can or cannot save us from climate change, but about *what kind* of technology, built on what kind of assumptions, can best help us in the current emergency.

If we are to resolve the climate emergency, we have to find new ways of looking at everything, from the fashion we wear to the food on our plates. Innovation obviously isn't just about building gigantic humming machines or finding a new fuel to pump into the same old technology made from the same old blueprints. And you can't plant the deserts full of trees without a thought to how the farmers on the ground farm that land.

Another problem with the climate duel between the wizard and the prophet is that it often isn't about inventions *or* behavioural change. In fact, behavioural change can often be the innovation, or the innovation may first require a behavioural change, or the innovation may stem from the behavioural change. We have created false dichotomies.

In retrospect, it seems completely nuts that we didn't put wheels on our suitcases before the 1970s. But if you go back and look at our notions of the female and male at the time, it makes total sense. Does this mean that it was our ideas about gender that needed to change for suitcases to be able to roll? Or that the wheeled suitcase was needed for women to be encouraged to travel alone more?

It was probably a bit of both.

This is often the way with breakthroughs: they are about an ability to imagine another world and build a product for that world before it quite exists. This will of course be the key for much green innovation. In order to have the idea for the product that will make that way of being possible, affordable and popular, you must first be able to imagine another way of being.

As we have seen, our approach to nature comes right back to our most fundamental ideas on gender: that technology is made to subordinate nature, as man is made to subordinate woman. Technology is therefore given precedence over the natural world, in the same way that the qualities we perceive as 'male' are given precedence over those we have learned to regard as 'female'. All of this leads to us reducing earth to just a giant container for energy. The next technological revolution cannot be based on the same assumption.

———————

It's time to put the wizard and the prophet to one side. Let's talk about the witch instead.

Because what's the difference between a witch and a wizard, really?

You might say that wizards are men and witches are women. But that isn't the case. There are male witches, too. There *were* male witches, too. And they also got burned at the stake. No, the difference between the witch and the wizard instead relates to their relationship with nature. The wizard studies hefty books up in his tower. He takes in the knowledge they offer and learns to apply that in a world beyond the castle walls. The witch, meanwhile, is out in the forest, digging for magic herbs with her bare, dirty hands. Besides this, the witch (whether good or wicked) also performs rituals. She dances naked at the forest's edge, makes offerings in the pale moonlight, and performs some sort of rite with menstrual blood or medicinal plants or whatever it might be. In short, there is almost always a spiritual aspect to the witch.

One that you won't find in the wizard in the same way.

Although Hermione Granger in J K Rowling's Harry Potter books is called a 'witch', she is in actual fact a female wizard. There just isn't really a word for those. Which there should be, of course.

What separates the witch from the wizard is her attitude to nature. The witch is interested in convening with and understanding the plants that give her magical powers, not *just* because they give her powers, but because that connection means something to her. The wizard, however, can't really be bothered with all that. He's interested in magic for the power it brings him over the external world. Not how it connects him to himself, his body or the cosmos. He lies much closer to the vision of technology that dominates today's society. Which is why we need the witch. Not because she is a woman, but because of what she represents: a road not yet travelled.

We are technological beings just as we are beings of nature, and one of the key challenges of the coming years will be integrating the two. Our magic comes from nature, and while it can also harness and shape it, this must always be done in a sustainable way. The witch is perhaps the only model we have for this, and it's no coincidence that we tend to think of her as a woman.

The main problem with both the wizard and the prophet is that they view themselves as separate from nature. That's how masculinity has been defined, after all. You are *not* your mother. Nature is separate from you. Harming nature is harming ourselves, but this will continue if we keep viewing nature as 'female', and the 'female' as something we must subordinate to the masculine forces of technology.

Throughout human history we have gone to great lengths to create a narrative where humans are seen as a form of technology. We have done this by talking about ourselves as everything from hydraulic statues to computers. This was a way to distance ourselves from the fact that we are part of nature, which we perceive as feminine and therefore inferior. This is why bringing women back into the narrative is so crucial.

It changes everything.

The image we currently have of our own development is one of the hairy ape who slowly rises to become a bearded male who grabs hold of a sharp wooden stick, turns it into a spear and starts pointing it at his surroundings. That was how technology came to be, we think, and it's a story that still shapes our economy.

The myth of the hairy ape with his spear has led to our current dominant narrative of a violent father of invention who brings new things into the world through conflict, competition and the scaling up of ideas at the expense of everything around them. He tells us to move fast and break things and that there is no other way – that this is the price we need to pay for innovation in the economy.

If this story is true, then yes, the only way to survive on this planet will be to do what the prophet demands of us from his mountaintop: STOP! Stop growing, stop experimenting, stop inventing! For the love of God, just stop.

But if we include women's tools in the history of technology – as we have seen – its entire meaning changes. If the first tools weren't hunting tools but, say, digging sticks, it is no longer as clear that humanity's inventions must always seek to crush, dominate and exploit. If we stop ignoring women and what we have decided women are to represent, then the entire narrative we hold, about ourselves, the economy and the world, becomes something else. The ground we stand on shifts: a new way emerges.

Here is the mother of invention.

She says it is time to come home.

Notes

Chapter 1

. . . someone paid to sit at his desk, day in day out, and think about the business of suitcases: This description of how Bernard Sadow got his idea is based on Joe Sharkey, 'Reinventing the Suitcase by Adding the Wheel', *New York Times*, 4 October 2010, https://www.nytimes.com/2010/10/05/business/05road.html.

The details of the 2010 interview that Joe Sharkey conducted with Bernard Sadow were confirmed in an interview with the author on 11 August 2020. A similar description of what happened can also be found in Matt Ridley, *How Innovation Works*, 4th Estate Books, London, 2020. That, too, is based on Sharkey's 2010 interview. When Robert Shiller discussed the invention in Robert Shiller, *The New Financial Order*, Princeton University Press, New Jersey, 2003, he asked his then research assistant to conduct a telephone interview with Sadow. No transcript of the interview appears to still exist, but the account of events given in *The New Financial Order* is essentially the same as the one in Sharkey's 2010 *New York Times* article, which is therefore deemed trustworthy. In the interview with the author held on 11 August 2020, Sharkey stated that Sadow had objected to some of the content in Sharkey's 2010 *New York Times* article after publication. What these objections were Sharkey couldn't remember exactly, but they did not relate to how Sadow was cited or how the circumstances of his invention were described. As Sharkey recalled, they related to Robert Plath's invention also being mentioned.

The 30-odd hijackings that took place in the USA each year: Libby Nelson 'The US Once Had More than 130 Hijackings in 4 Years. Here's Why They Finally Stopped', *Vox*, 29 March 2016, https://www.vox.com/2016/3/29/11326472/hijacking-airplanes-egyptair.

While queuing at customs, Sadow noticed a man who presumably worked at the airport: There is some uncertainty as to where exactly Bernard Sadow was when he had his idea. The detail that he was on his way through customs at the airport when the idea struck him comes from the interview Joe Sharkey did with him for the *New York Times* in 2010. In an interview with the author on 11 August 2020, Sharkey stated that the interview transcript no longer existed as he had left the *New York Times* a long time ago, but, as he recalls, that was what Bernard Sadow had told him.

This was the future: There are other versions of how Bernard Sadow constructed – or even commissioned – his wheeled suitcase. I have chosen this one, as it is Joe Sharkey's version, which is based on a direct interview with Sadow from 2010. Many other versions of the story are not based on direct conversations with the inventor, and I therefore consider them less trustworthy.

For the human body, however, the circle is not natural: This point is made by Steven Vogel in *Why the Wheel is Round: Muscles, Technology and How We Make Things Move*, University of Chicago Press, Chicago, 2016, p. 1.

. . . long before the Mesopotamians started throwing pots on circular discs: See for example Richard W Bulliet, *The Wheel*, Columbia University Press, New York, 2016, pp. 50–59 for a summary of these theories.

It was unearthed in Slovenia, about 20 kilometres south of Ljubljana: Aleksander Gasser, 'World's Oldest Wheel Found in Slovenia', Government Communication Office of the Republic of Slovenia, March 2003. Archived version available here: https://web.archive.org/web/20160826021129/http://www.ukom.gov.si/en/media_room/background_information/culture/worlds_oldest_wheel_found_in_slovenia/.

In his application, he wrote: 'The luggage actually glides . . . any person, regardless of size, strength or age, can easily pull the luggage along without effort or strain.' Quoted from patent US3653474A, United States Patent Office.

. . . and is therefore considered the father of the wheeled suitcase: There are examples of suitcases with wheels earlier than Bernard Sadow's, as we will also see later in this chapter. It appears to be a general phenomenon that many people can have a similar idea at around the same time independently of one another. This is the case with many inventions. Who then counts as 'the inventor' can sometimes come down to luck. In the literature, however, there is some form of consensus that Bernard Sadow should be considered the inventor of the wheeled suitcase. American patents for wheeled suitcases that came before Bernard Sadow's are, for example, Arthur Browning (1969),

Grace and Malcolm McIntyre (1949), Clarence Norlin (1947), Barnett Book (1945) and Saviour Mastrontomio (1925).

Robert Shiller, a winner of the Nobel Prize for Economics: The economics prize is not a 'real' Nobel Prize in the sense that it wasn't in Alfred Nobel's will. Economics as we know it today didn't exist back then. The correct name for the prize is therefore 'The Sveriges Riksbank Prize in Economic Sciences in Memory of Alfred Nobel'.

Sadow presented his product to buyers from almost all of the USA's major department stores, and initially all of them rejected it: Robert Shiller, 2003, *The New Financial Order*, Princeton University Press, New Jersey, 2003, p. 101.

It wasn't that they thought the idea of a suitcase on wheels was a bad one. They just didn't think anyone would want to buy the product: From an interview that Shiller's research assistant conducted when working on the book *The New Financial Order*.

'Everybody I took it to threw me out,' [Sadow] would later recount. 'They thought I was crazy.' 'Everybody I took it to, threw me out – from Sterns, Macy's, A & S, all the major department stores,' Sadow said. 'They thought I was crazy, pulling a piece of luggage.'

He towed it around in his office, then called in the buyer who had originally rejected it and gave him the order to buy it: Matthew Syed, *Rebel Ideas: The Power of Diverse Thinking*, John Murray Press, London, 2019, pp. 131–2.

Then *we* could roll! Practical, no? John Allan May, 'Come What May: A Wheel of an Idea', *Christian Science Monitor,* 4 October 1951, p. 13.

In his book *Narrative Economics* [Shiller] suggests that our resistance to rolling suitcases can be explained by group pressure, which often plays a role in the scepticism surrounding newfangled ideas: See Robert Shiller, *Narrative Economics: How Stories Go Viral and Drive Major Economic Events*, Princeton University Press, Princeton/Oxford, 2019, pp. 37–8.

Having lugged heavy suitcases through airports and railway stations for years, he was astonished by his own unquestioning acceptance of the status quo. He went on to investigate this phenomenon in his book *Antifragile*: Nassim Nicholas Taleb, *Antifragile: Things that Gain from Disorder*, Penguin Books, London, 2012, pp. 187–92.

But in medicine, for example, it isn't at all uncommon for decades to pass between a discovery being made and the resulting product reaching the market: Seventeen years on average. Taleb, however, mentions more extreme examples.

. . . cried a 24-year-old Steve Jobs after seeing a pointer move across a computer screen for the first time: See, for example, Malcolm Gladwell, 'Creation Myth', *The New Yorker*, 9 May 2011.

In other words, Xerox had invented . . . the mouse: The computer mouse, an idea that Xerox had in turn got from Douglas Engelbart, an American engineer and inventor.

The emperor set load limits for wheeled carriages, and they weren't generous: That the wheel didn't immediately change the world is a point made in detail by Richard W Bulliet in *The Wheel: Inventions and Reinventions*, Columbia University Press, New York, 2016, pp. 20–24.

Still, it's hard to imagine any such economic explanation as to why the wheel only made it onto our suitcases in 1972: This point is put forward by Nassim Nicholas Taleb in *Antifragile* and is discussed in depth by Richard W Bulliet in *The Camel and the Wheel*, Columbia University Press, New York, 1990.

Passengers increasingly carried their own luggage, or used luggage trolleys: This is the basis for the invention that Bernard Sadow highlights in his patent application from 1972. His focus is on flights, which also likely reflects the fact that he is American. European discussions surrounding bags and the problems of carrying them seem to have revolved more around the railway.

You would be sweating like a pig before you even got to customs in Madrid: 'Looking at Luggage', *Tatler*, 25 January 1961, pp. 34–5.

The new wheel-strap device had its first sighting at a railway station in Coventry in 1948: 'Portable Porter Has Arrived', *Coventry Evening Telegraph*, 24 June 1948.

The company that had patented the product also just happened to hail from Coventry: In the 1940s there was a product with the same name, Portable Porter, in the USA, made by a different company: MacArthur Products Inc., Indian Orchard, Massachusetts, USA.

But this was a niche, inexpensive product for English women, and it didn't catch on: 'The Look of Luggage', *The Times*, 17 May 1956, p. 15.

His passenger, however, was unconvinced, asking: 'If I boarded a bus wearing roller-skates, would I be charged as a passenger or a pram?' *Trinity Mirror*, 19 November 1967.

[Sylvan Goldman] who owned an American grocery-store chain in the 1930s: Terry P Wilson, *The Cart that Changed the World*, University of Oklahoma Press, Norman, 1978.

'You mean with my big strong arms I can't carry a darn little basket like that?' Description by Sylvan Goldman.

Back in the twelfth century, poet Chrétien de Troyes told the story of Lancelot: Richard Bulliet, *The Wheel*, pp. 131–2.

This is the crux of Lancelot's dilemma, and what makes the dwarf's offer so diabolical: A cart of the type that the dwarf offers Lancelot to ride in was also the cart that murderers and thieves would be put in. All to truly demean them.

. . . without a man to carry their luggage, or to be expected to carry their luggage, or to be deemed insufficiently manly if he didn't: In an interview with the author held on 11 August 2020, Joe Sharkey, who was the *New York Times*'s travel correspondent at the time, recounted what a huge change this made to business travel and how suddenly it seemed to appear.

By the early 1980s Danish luggage company Cavalet had already realised that you could get around this problem by placing the wheels on the short side instead: The inventors were Helga Helene Foge and Hans Thomas Thomsen. Thanks to Roger Ekelund, who provided more information on this by email.

That was when US pilot Robert Plath created modern cabin baggage: The suitcase became known as Rollaboard, and Robert Plath founded the company Travelpro, which became dominant in the industry. All thanks to his invention.

Chapter 2

This was August 1888, and the summer holidays had just started in the Grand Duchy of Baden, a southwestern state in the relatively newly unified

German Empire: Bertha Benz's story has been recounted many times, see for example Barbara Leisner, *Bertha Benz: Eine starke Frau am Steuer des ersten Automobils* (*A Strong Woman at the Wheel of the First Car*), Katz Casimir Verlag, Gernsbach, 2014, or Angela Elis, *Mein Traum ist länger als die Nacht* (*My Dream is Longer than the Night*), Hoffmann und Campe Verlag, Hamburg, 2010. The latter makes use of fictional elements to bring the story to life. This is obviously one of the problems – that we don't know exactly what happened on the journey. I will note that in an older source like St John C Nixon, *The Invention of the Automobile (Karl Benz and Gottlieb Daimler)* (1936), new digital edition by Edizioni Savine, 2016, the journey is described differently. In Nixon's account of the journey to Pforzheim, he seems to assume that it was primarily Bertha Benz's sons who were driving, not Bertha Benz herself. This presumably reflects the values of the day. Based on what we now know about Bertha Benz's involvement in her husband's company, it seems less likely that she would, to all intents and purposes, have been a passive passenger. I have, however, tried to provide a balanced account here and describe it as a collaboration between Bertha Benz and her two teenage sons.

That morning, Bertha Benz carefully manoeuvred the horseless carriage out of the factory in which her husband had constructed it: On 2 November 1886 Karl Benz received his patent from the Imperial Patent Office for his *Fahrzeug mit Gasmotorenbetrieb* ('vehicle powered by a gas engine'). Patent Specification No. 37435.

After years of trials, the world's first automobile did, in fact, drive: This was the first car in the world to be specifically constructed as a self-powered motor vehicle. Previous practice had more or less been to motorise older horse-drawn carriages. Benz made his car with only one front wheel, which was therefore easy to make steerable.

. . . Karl Benz, whose name would eventually go down in history as one half of Mercedes-Benz, was in all honesty no great businessman: In Angela Elis's *Mein Traum ist länger als die Nacht,* he is described as someone who liked 'to invent' but not 'to have invented'.

In many spots only one cart could pass at a time, so slaves would be sent up ahead to stop any oncoming vehicles, like fleshy, privately owned traffic lights on legs: Kenneth Matthews Jr, 'The Embattled Driver in Ancient Rome', *Expedition Magazine*, vol. 2, no. 3, 1960.

And all of these debates on who they were and what they were capable of gradually worked their way into, and informed, technological development:

See Virginia Scharff, *Taking the Wheel: Women and the Coming of the Motor Age*, University of New Mexico Press, New York, 1992, pp. 22–3.

As a result, an idea soon emerged of the electric car as more 'feminine': For more on this, see for example Gijs Mom, *The Electric Vehicle: Technology and Expectations in the Automobile Age*, Johns Hopkins University Press, Baltimore, 2004, pp. 276–84 or Virginia Scharff, *Taking the Wheel*, pp. 35–50.

American car columnist Carl H Claudy wrote: 'Has there ever been an invention of more solid comfort to the feminine half of humanity than the electric carriage?' Cited in Virginia Scharff, 'Femininity and The Electric Car', *Sex/Machine: Readings in Culture, Gender, and Technology*, ed. Patrick D Hopkins, Indiana University Press, Bloomington/Indianopolis, 1998, p. 79.

The first car to ever go over 100 kilometres per hour was in fact an electric: In 1899 Belgian Camille Jenatzy drove the Belgian electric La Jamais Contente at this speed.

'Electrics . . . will appeal to anyone interested in an absolutely noiseless, odourless, clean and stylish rig that is always ready,' read the advertising copy of 1903: Advertisement for Pope-Waverley. See Virginia Scharff, *Taking the Wheel*, p. 35.

A 1909 advertisement takes a similar approach, encouraging the male consumer to buy an electric car for 'Your bride to be or your bride of many Junes past': Advertisement for Anderson Electric Car Company, cited in Virginia Scharff, *Taking the Wheel*, p. 38.

In *Taking the Wheel*, historian Virginia Scharff cites American commentators of the time who argued that 'No license should be granted to anyone under eighteen . . . and never to a woman, unless, possibly, for a car driven by electric power': Montgomery Rollins, cited in Virginia Scharff, *Taking the Wheel*, p. 42.

'In no way can a child get so much air in so little time as by the use of the automobile': Carl H Claudy, car columnist for the American *Women's Home Companion*, cited in Virginia Scharff, *Taking the Wheel*, p. 41.

Clara Ford's electric was a world away from the rattling Model T: See Virginia Scharff, *Taking the Wheel*, p. 53.

Clara Ford had no steering wheel, but instead steered the carriage from the back, using two different tillers: A so-called 'push-pull tiller'.

. . . to 'preserve her toilet immaculate, her coiffure intact', to be precise: 'To the well-bred woman The Detroit Electric has a particular appeal. In it she can preserve her toilet immaculate, her coiffure intact.' Advertisement for Detroit Electric cited in Virginia Scharff, *Taking the Wheel*, p. 38.

E P Chalfant, a member of the board for Detroit Electric, wrote rather resentfully: 'The gasoline car dealers have branded the electric as a car for the aged and infirm and for the women.' E P Chalfant wrote this in 1916. Cited in Gijs Mom, *The Electric Vehicle*, p. 279.

Another man made a similar complaint about how his friends had warned him against buying an electric car: 'It was called a lady's car,' he testified: 'It was called a lady's car; it was said it wouldn't run up hills; it was said it wouldn't go fast enough.' FM Feiker cited in Gijs Mom, *The Electric Vehicle*, p. 280.

'Having imagined effeminacy into the electric, he dismisses it from his mind and buys a gas car without a struggle.' 'The thing that is effeminate, or that has that reputation, does not find favor with the American man. Whether or not he is "red-blooded" and "virile" in the ordinary physical sense, at least his ideals are. The fact that anything from a car to a color, is the delight of the ladies is enough to change his interest to mere amused tolerance. All this, of course, is logically absurd as it applies to the electric. It is just as much a man's car as it is a woman's.' From the editorial 'The Kind of Car a Man Wants' in *Electric Vehicles* from 1916. Cited in Gijs Mom, *The Electric Vehicle*, p. 281.

Byron Carter was one of Leland's friends: There is much uncertainty surrounding this story. It is recounted in Thomas Alvin Boyd, *Charles F Kettering: A Biography*, Beard Books, Washington, 1957, p. 68. This was, however, written many decades after Byron Carter's death. He is also described here as an older man, when in fact Carter was 44 years old when he died. But there does seem to be consensus in the fact that his death was related to some sort of car cranking.

The first time he had even seen a car had been on his honeymoon, when he had chanced upon a doctor whose newfangled vehicle had broken down on the roadside: Thomas Alvin Boyd, *Charles F Kettering*, p. 54.

The *New York Times* described the innovation as 'a further item of ease and convenience for the lady': Charles Duryea, an American engineer, cited in Virginia Scharff, *Taking the Wheel*.

Until then, anyone who wanted to start their Ford without a crank had to buy an additional product: Robert Casey, *The Model T: A Centennial History*, Johns Hopkins Press, Baltimore, 2008, p. 101.

'Let *Her* drive your Ford,' read another: Advertisements cited in Virginia Scharff, *Taking the Wheel*, p. 63.

All of this was described as 'evidence of concessions to the softer sex': 'We must conclude that the feminine influence is quite largely responsible for the more obvious changes that have been made in gas car design from year to year.' 'The items of deeper and softer upholstery, easier springs, more graceful and beautiful lines, simpler control, more nearly automatic performance of the tasks of starting, tire pumping etc. are all evidence of concessions to the softer sex.' 'Every year the gas car becomes more electrical.' Excerpts from an editorial in *Electric Vehicles*, cited in Gijs Mom, *The Electric Vehicle*, p. 282.

In other words, the triumph of the petrol car was not one of price, but of other factors: Gijs Mom, *The Electric Vehicle*, p. 293.

And this was almost exclusively to do with gender: This is my interpretation of what Gijs Mom, for example, discusses as 'cultural factors', almost all of which are connected to gender and ideas thereof.

In the USA, way back in the 1800s, one such electric-car company constructed a central New York garage with a state-of-the-art, semi-automatic system that could swap car batteries in 75 seconds flat: See Alexis C Madrigal, 'The Electric Taxi Company You Could Have Called In 1900', *The Atlantic*, 15 March 2011.

Cars would drive in, have a freshly charged battery installed in a matter of minutes, and then zip out again. It was simply a different way of thinking: This was the same idea that came up again over a century later, when entrepreneur Shai Agassi in Israel argued that if the electric cars' batteries were the problem, then an infrastructure had to be built that would make it quick and easy to swap them. This attempt used robots to exchange an old battery for a newly charged one in roughly five minutes. The project took in almost $1 billion in funding but soon fell apart when pretty much everything went wrong.

Chapter 3

Abram Spanel knew immediately that it would spell trouble for his business: Nicholas de Monchaux, *Spacesuit: Fashioning Apollo*, MIT Press, Cambridge, Massachusetts, 2011, pp. 118–24.

. . . Wickham liked to pass this off as some intrepid, Victorian plant-smuggling adventure. The locals didn't even understand how valuable the trees were! Wasn't Wickham clever to trick them!? Warren Dean, *Brazil and the Struggle for Rubber: A Study in Environmental History*, Cambridge University Press, Cambridge, 1987, pp. 7–23.

The part that manufactured girdles changed its name to Playtex: Nicholas de Monchaux, *Spacesuit*, pp. 123–4.

The only question is, what type? For more on the difficulties of clothing in space, see Kassia St Clair, *The Golden Thread: How Fabric Changed History*, John Murray Press, London, 2018, pp. 223–46.

In Houston, three different suits from three different companies underwent 22 separate tests: Nicholas de Monchaux, *Spacesuit*, pp. 198–9.

Unfortunately, as Aldrin dryly remarked, it was 'the one vital breaker needed to send electrical power to the ascent engine that would lift Neil and me off the moon': Cited in Buzz Aldrin, *Magnificent Desolation: The Long Journey Home from the Moon*, Bloomsbury Publishing, London, 2009, p. 44.

Not because of any technical flaws, but because the documentation requirements for the production process were 'not being met': Nicholas de Monchaux, *Spacesuit*, pp. 209–24.

In World War II, Winston Churchill personally devoted time to inventing a gigantic trench-digger originally known as 'White Rabbit Number Six': Winston Churchill, *The Gathering Storm*, Penguin Classics, London, 2005, p. 645.

But also with 600,000 horses: Antony Beevor, *Stalingrad*, Viking, London, 1998, p. 28.

The development of the atomic bomb cost $2 billion: These figures come from Stephen Schwartz, 'The U.S. Nuclear Weapons Cost Study Project', Brookings Institute, https://www.brookings.edu/the-costs-of-the-manhattan-project/.

With the same resources, the USA could have bought planes and bombs enough to inflict just as much death: All of the bombs, mines and grenades that the USA used in World War II between 1942 and 1945 cost $31.5 billion. For sources on these figures, see Stephen Schwartz, 'The U.S. Nuclear Weapons Cost Study Project'. All tanks cost $64 billion. All calculated to the 1996 dollar value.

. . . war by its very nature destroys far more economic value than it creates through innovation: American productivity diminished. See Alexander J Field, 'World War II and the Growth of US Potential Output', Working Paper, May 2018, Department of Economics, Santa Clara University, https://www.scu.edu/business/economics/research/working-papers/field-wwii/. With regard to World War II's negative impact on innovation, see also Michelle Alexopoulos, 'Read All about It!! What Happens Following a Technology Shock?', *American Economic Review*, vol. 101, no. 4, June 2011, pp. 1144–79.

Most economic historians are in agreement here: This is absolutely not to say that technology doesn't have a role to play in war, only that the technology invented by the military is seldom the most decisive element. However, a state's ability to *use* that technology is crucial. See for example Max Boot, *War Made New: Technology, Warfare, and the Course of History – 1500 to Today*, Gotham Books, New York, 2006, in which the author describes, among other examples, the role of gunpowder in the Swedish victories at Breitenfeld and Lützen in the Thirty Years' War. These took place in the 1600s, but gunpowder had, of course, existed as a technology long before that. The key lay in its use, not its invention.

On the whole, he felt that in wartime conditions 'the advance of knowledge is slowed': 'It is a mistake to suppose that science advances rapidly in a war. Certain branches of science may receive a special stimulus, but on the whole the advance of knowledge is slowed.' Quotation taken from Presidential Address to the British Association for the Advancement of Science, September 1948. Cited in David Edgerton, *Warfare State: Britain, 1920–1970*, Cambridge University Press, Cambridge, 2006, p. 215.

With a digging stick in hand you could suddenly get underground, where there were delicious insects to sink your teeth into, not to mention yam roots: a type of sweet potato that could grow to be almost a metre long, making it almost impossible to unearth with bare hands: See Autumn Stanley, *Mothers and Daughters of Invention: Notes for a Revised History of Technology*, The Scarecrow Press, London, 1993, pp. 9–10.

There were female hunters among humans as well: recently a 9,000-year-old skeleton of a woman with hunting gear has led to some rethinking of our assumptions about gender roles in ancient tribes: 'Female hunters of the early Americas' by Randall Haas, James Watwon, Tammy Buonasera, John Southon, Jennifer C Chen, Sarah Noe, Kevin Smith, Carlos Viviano Llave, Jelmer Eerkens, Glendon Parker in *Science Advances*, 04 Nov 2020, https://advances.sciencemag.org/content/6/45/eabd0310.

Enlightenment philosopher Voltaire famously wrote: 'There have been very learned women as there have been women warriors, but there have never been women inventors.' Cited in Ann-Christin Nyberg, *Making Ideas Matter: Gender, Technology and Women's Invention*, dissertation, 2009, Luleå University of Technology, https://www.diva-portal.org/smash/get/diva2:999200/FULLTEXT01.pdf.

Voltaire even had a girlfriend who once invented a new financial product just to get him out of prison after he ran up some colossal gambling debts: Her name was Émilie du Châtelet and it was a type of modern derivative, a financial security against future income. She made a lot of money on it, and with the profits she managed to get Voltaire free.

That someone discovered that clay hardens in heat – and that she could therefore use it to store food and water – was a feat no less technological than those of bronze or iron: Kassia St Clair, *The Golden Thread*, pp. 29–34.

If a doctor was present, the midwife couldn't so much as take her own tools out of her bag: Lisa Öberg, *Barnmorskan och läkaren* (*The Midwife and the Doctor*), Ordfront, Stockholm, 1996, pp. 285–9.

Men started to take an interest in cheese: See Lena Sommestad, *Från mejerska till mejerist: En studie av mejeriyrkets maskuliniseringsprocess* (*From Dairymaid to Dairyman: A Study of the Masculinisation of the Dairy Profession*), Arkiv Förlag, Stockholm, 1992.

The other is used as a tablecloth in a summer cottage: This is based on a real example discussed in Lizzy Pook, 'Why the Art World is Finally Waking up to the Power of Female Craft Skills', *Stylist*, 2019, https://www.stylist.co.uk/life/womens-textiles-crafts-female-skills-sexism-not-seen-as-art-anni-albers-tate/233457.

That's often the way with rules. They are built for men: See for example Deborah J Merritt, 'Hypatia in the Patent Office: Women Inventors and the Law, 1865–1900', *The American Journal of Legal History*, vol. 35, no. 3, July 1991, pp. 235–306.

The company he founded, Tefal, exists to this day: Anne Cooper Funderburg, 'Making Teflon Stick', *Invention and Technology Magazine*, vol. 16, no. 1, summer 2000, https://www.inventionandtech.com/content/making-teflon-stick-1.

In other words, the head honcho was the one to assist her at the machine: Nicholas de Monchaux, *Spacesuit*, pp. 211–12.

Chapter 4

The students had three hours of lectures in the morning, followed by lunch, followed by informal seminars in the afternoon: The description of George Stibitz's lecture is based on the transcript of the lecture published in 'The Moore School Lectures: Theory and Techniques for Design of Electronic Digital Computers', *The Moore School Lectures (Charles Babbage Institute Reprint)*, ed. Martin Campbell-Kelly and Michael R Williams, MIT Press, Cambridge, Massachusetts; Tomash Publishers, Los Angeles, 1985.

'Dr Curtiss has been called away rather suddenly and I have been asked to take his place,' he said: '… and to give you my opinion of the value of automatic computers in the future and of the reason for building such machines.' Quotation from *The Moore School Lectures*, p. 4.

'Is it worthwhile to develop and build more automatic computers, and if so, why?' *The Moore School Lectures*, p. 11.

They went on listening as Stibitz noted that the computer in question had led to 'a saving of about four girl-years': *The Moore School Lectures*, p. 13.

At the end of the eighteenth century, Watt came up with a new and improved version of the steam engine: See 'James Watt (1736–1819)' in Scottish Science Hall of Fame, National Library of Scotland Digital gallery, https://digital.nls.uk/scientists/index.html.

Arial, a famed Swedish stallion of the 1950s, could produce a whopping 12.6 horsepower, for example: 'Fråga Gösta: hur många hästkrafter har en häst?' ('Ask Gösta: How Many Horsepower Does a Horse Have?'), *Allehanda. se*, 27 October 2005.

You see, not so long ago, computers were in fact women. Literally. Before a computer was a machine, it was a job: See David Allen Grier, *When Computers Were Human*, Princeton University Press, Princeton/Oxford, 2005.

As astronomer Leslie Comrie put it, the female computers were most useful 'in the years before they (or many of them) graduate to married life and become experts with the housekeeping accounts!' Leslie Comrie, 'Careers for Girls', *The Mathematical Gazette*, vol. 28, no. 28, 1944, pp. 90–95.

That was when they realised they could break up the work into smaller tasks, and bring in dedicated staff to do it instead: It is claimed that Gaspard de Prony realised that the work could be broken down in this way after reading about division of labour in Adam Smith's *The Wealth of Nations*; see for example David Allen Grier, *When Computers Were Human*, p. 36.

Many wigmakers lost their jobs: Michael Kwass, 'Big Hair: A Wig History of Consumption in Eighteenth Century France', *The American Historical Review*, vol. 111, no. 3, 2006, pp. 631–59.

. . . and a lot of them actually went on to become computers, trading in their false hair for trigonometric tables: In Grattan-Guinness, 'Work for the Hairdressers: The Production of de Prony's Logarithmic and Trigonometric Tables', *Annals of the History of Computing*, vol. 12, no. 3, summer 1990, pp. 177–85.

The computing sphere started to be filled not by the predecessors to today's hoodie-clad men (with sometimes questionable social skills), but by respectable ladies with crinolines and dreams of science: David Allen Grier, *When Computers Were Human*, pp. 112–13.

In the USA, the field was also an important employer of African Americans, Jews and people with disabilities, precisely because it was low status: 'Women probably constituted the largest number of computers, but they were joined by African Americans, Jews, the Irish, the handicapped, and the merely poor.' Quotation from David Allen Grier, *When Computers Were Human*, p. 276.

'Black plus black is black. Red plus red is red. Black plus red or red plus black – hand sheets to group two.' David Allen Grier, *When Computers Were Human*, p. 214.

That wasn't the only such term used in those years: a 'kilogirl', for example, could be used to mean something requiring 1,000 hours of calculation work: David Allen Grier, *When Computers Were Human*, p. 276.

Even indoors, in a meeting, he might whip out the mask if he suspected pollen in the air. No explanation – on it would go, and he would carry on talking like nothing had happened: Ronald Lewin, *Ultra Goes to War: The Secret Story*, Penguin Classic Military History, London, 2001; first published by Hutchinson & Co., London, 1987, p. 76.

As the secrets grew in stature, so did the complexity of the code: Michael Smith, *Station X: The Codebreakers of Bletchley Park*, Channel 4 Books, London, 1998, p. 7.

In the summer of 1939, the Poles handed over Rejewski's work to the Brits (just prior to being invaded by both Nazi Germany and the Soviet Union): Michael Smith, *Station X*, pp. 25–6.

Indeed, in battle Napoleon is said to have given the order: 'Donkeys and scholars in the middle!', which of course meant that they would be protected: Cited in Eugene Tarlé, *Bonaparte*, Knight Publications, New York, 1937, p. 66.

But those who were expected to do such morning drills were the women: Jane Abbate, *Recoding Gender: Women's Changing Participation in Computing*, MIT Press, Cambridge, Massachusetts, 2012, p. 21.

The engineers at Bletchley Park would eventually come to build the world's first electronic, programmable computer: There is a stubborn misunderstanding that the American ENIAC was the world's first electronic computer. This is due to the fact that the British Colossus, which came two years earlier, was long classified. See Jack Copeland, 'Colossus and the Rise of the Modern Computer', *Colossus: The Secrets of Bletchley Park's Codebreaking Computers*, Oxford University Press, New York, 2006, p. 101.

'I had already had the great training of teaching how to do very complicated mathematics to people who knew no mathematics at all.'¨... So the machine was really nothing but the same sort of pupil . . . . For this reason – and I say it unblushingly – I am the very best coder in the world.' Cited in Jack Copeland, 'Colossus and the Rise of the Modern Computer', p. 70.

Historian Mar Hicks has noted how the workforce building these machines was so female-dominated that the company could just as well calculate its entire staffing costs in the woman's lower hourly rate: Mar Hicks, *Programmed Inequality: How Britain Discarded Women Technologists and Lost Its Edge in Computing*, MIT Press, London, 2017, p. 21.

There was, they declared, no 'men's pay scale' in computing that the women's pay levels could be raised to meet: Mar Hicks, *Programmed Inequality*, pp. 93–4.

And if something was a 'naturally feminine attribute' then it needn't be valued economically as a formal 'skill': Harriet Bradley, 'Frames of Reference: Skill, Gender and New Technology in the Hosiery Industry', *Women Workers and the Technological Change in Europe in the Nineteenth and Twentieth Centuries*, ed. Gertjan Groot and Marlou Schrover, Taylor & Francis, London, 1995, pp. 17–33.

The idea was that if they could just get enough promising young men from the right social class to learn the basics of programming, these men could go on to fill the public sector's management roles in the field: Mar Hicks, 'When Winning Is Losing: Why the Nation that Invented the Computer Lost its Lead'. *Computer*, vol. 51, no. 10, 2018, pp. 48–57.

[Stephanie Shirley's] idea was to harness the wasted talent that had left the industry: Interview with the author dated 7 April 2020.

He is thought to have poisoned himself with cyanide: Professor Jack Copeland, expert on Alan Turing, has questioned whether his death was really suicide. The police never tested the half-eaten apple for traces of the poison. Copeland believes it is possible that Turing's death was accidental.

From antiquity until the end of the nineteenth century, the position of secretary was a high-status role for men: See for example Donald Hoke, 'The Woman and the Typewriter: A Case Study in Technological Innovation and Social Change', *Business and Economic History*, vol. 8, 1979, pp. 76–88.

But at some point in the 1920s the profession became something for women: See for example Meta Zimmeck, 'The Mysteries of the Typewriter: Technology and Gender in the British Civil Service, 1870–1914', *Women*

Workers and the Technological Change in Europe in the Nineteenth and Twentieth Centuries, ed. Gertjan Groot and Marlou Schrover, Taylor & Francis, London, 1995, pp. 52–66.

In 2018, engineer James Damore got fired from Google after writing a memo that implied that women simply weren't cut out for IT: His memo can be read here: https://gizmodo.com/exclusive-heres-the-full-10-page-anti-diversity-screed-1797564320.

Chapter 5

You fell to the floor, paralysed: The description of Aina Wifalk's illness is based on her medical records from when she was treated for polio in Lund in 1949. I am grateful to Annike Pedersen, senior archive administrator at Skåne regional archive, for her help accessing these.

But the first time the disease reached aggressive, epidemic proportions was in Sweden in the late nineteenth century: Per Axelsson, *Höstens spöke: De svenska polioepidemiernas historia (The Ghost of Autumn: the History of the Swedish Polio Epidemics),* dissertation, Umeå Universitet, Carlsson, Stockholm, 2004, p. 68.

She had just started studying in Lund, a university town not far from where her parents had rented some farmland when she was little. The year was now 1949: Many thanks to Kerstin Rännar and Margareta Machl for your huge generosity and for giving me access to the material you used when writing *Aina Wifalk och rollatorn (Aina Wifalk and the Rollator),* published by Medicinhistoriska Sällskapet Westmannia.

At the end of the 1960s, the now-41-year-old Wifalk got in touch with Gunnar Ekman, a designer at the county council's workshops: Many thanks to Margareta Machl and Kerstin Rännar for copies of Gunnar Ekman's first drawing for the rollator.

Hotels in Mallorca started serving Swedish coffee, Greek tavernas organised Swedish folk dancing, and ABBA did their very first gig for free, in exchange for a discount on a package holiday to Cyprus: See Göran Willis, *Charter till solen: När utlandssemestern blev ett folknöje (Charter to the Sun: When Holidaying Abroad Became a People's Pursuit),* Trafik-Nostalgiska Förlaget, Stockholm, 2015.

One day she noticed a book trolley at a local library in Västerås, which was used by staff to wheel the books around to the different sections: There are a few different versions of how this came about. I have relied on the version that Margareta Machl and Kerstin Rännar uncovered from their research into Aina Wifalk's life. Details from interview with the authors in Västerås, 14 January 2020.

He built one of the world's first mechanical typewriters, which allowed the pair to write letters to one another without her having to dictate her words to a servant first: See Michael H Adler, *The Writing Machine*, George Allen & Unwin, London, 1973, p. 162. In 2010 Carey Wallace wrote a novel about these events: *The Blind Contessa's New Machine*, Pamela Dorman Books, New York, 2010.

Similarly, the world's first email protocol was written by the American Vint Cerf: 'Vint Cerf on Accessibility, the Cello and Noisy Hearing Aids', *Googlers*, 4 October 2018, https://www.blog.google/inside-google/googlers/vint-cerf-accessibility-cello-and-noisy-hearing-aids/.

In 2005 Westerman sold the technology to Apple: See Sally McGrane, 'No Stress, No Press: When Fingers Fly', *New York Times*, 24 January 2002.

The global walking-aids market has been valued at $2.2 billion. This figure is expected to grow rapidly over the coming decades, as the world's population gets older and our perceptions of old age change: Nils Levsen, *Lead Markets in Age-Based Innovations: Demographic Change and Internationally Successful Innovations*, Springer Gabler, Hamburg, 2014, pp. 69–78.

Instead she sold the idea for what would be around £750 in today's money, and a royalty of 2 per cent on that particular manufacturer's sales: Elisabeth Jansson, 'Ainas idé blir exportprodukt' ('Aina's Idea Becomes Export Product'), *Metallarbetaren*, no. 35, 1981.

It is currently estimated that some 80 per cent of all female-owned businesses have an unmet need for credit: UNSGSA, 2018, *Annual Report to the Secretary-General*, p. 12, https://www.unsgsa.org/files/1715/3790/0214/_AR_2018_web.pdf. Data from: Global Banking Alliance for Women 2017, Women's World Banking/Cambridge Associates, 2017.

There isn't a single country on the planet in which women collectively don't have less money and less economic opportunity than men: However, there are a few countries in which childless women earn more than childless men.

In the 1800s, whaling was one of the grubbiest, riskiest and most violent undertakings that anyone could engage in. It was also one of the most lucrative: Nathan Heller, 'Is Venture Capital Worth the Risk?', *The New Yorker*, 20 January 2020, and Ross Baird, *The Innovation Blind Spot: Why We Back the Wrong Ideas and What to Do About It*, Benbella Books, Texas, 2017, pp. 11–14.

A new group of investors came up with the idea to go to several rich families and ask them to cough up smaller pots of money: Tom Nicholas, *VC: An American History*, Harvard University Press, New York, 2019.

In many ways this is still how venture capital works: But as Ross Baird and others point out, today we hunt 'unicorns', i.e. companies that can achieve a value of over $1 billion, not whales.

'The distribution of Swedish venture capital remains skewed between the sexes,' wrote financial newspaper *Dagens Industri* in 2020: Miriam Olsson Jeffery, 'Nya siffror: Så lite riskkapital går till kvinnor – medan miljarderna rullar till män' ('New Figures: Here's How Little Venture Capital Goes to Women – While the Billions Roll in for Men'), *DI Digital*, 9 July 2020.

Eighty-three per cent of deals made by British venture capitalists had no women at all on their founding teams, according to a 2019 report commissioned by the Treasury: The British Business Bank's 2019 report, 'UK Venture Capital and Female Founders', https://www.british-business-bank. co.uk/wp-content/uploads/2019/02/British-Business-Bank-UK-Venture-Capital-and-Female-Founders-Report.pdf.

In the rest of the European Union a very similar picture emerges: See for example Agnieszka Skonieczna and Letizia Castellano, 'Gender Smart Financing: Investing In & With Women: Opportunities for Europe', European Commission Discussion Paper 129, July 2020, https://ec.europa. eu/info/sites/info/files/economy-finance/dp129_en.pdf, p. 5.

In the USA, less than 3 per cent of venture funding goes to businesses with all-female founders . . . : See for example Kate Clark, 'US VC Investment in Female Founders Hits All-time High', *TechCrunch*, 9 December 2019, https://techcrunch.com/2019/12/09/us-vc-investment-in-female-founders-hits-all-time-high/?guccounter=1.

. . . which is quite shocking, considering that nearly 40 per cent of all businesses in the USA are owned by women: Data from the National

Association of Women Business Owners' Women Business Owner Statistics, https://www.nawbo.org/resources/women-business-owner-statistics.

Around the turn of the millennium, it used to take about three years for a tech company to return to shore (i.e. go public). Now it takes almost a decade: Leonard Sherman, '"Blitzscaling" Is Choking Innovation – and Wasting Money', *Wired*, 7 November 2019.

Google received less venture capital on its entire voyage to the stock exchange than what Swedish electric-scooter company Voi received in 2019 alone: Google took in $36 million. Voi took in $85 million in 2019. Sources: Leonard Sherman, '"Blitzscaling" Is Choking Innovation – and Wasting Money', and Steve O'Hear, 'Voi Raises Another $85M for its European E-scooter Service', *TechCrunch*, 19 November 2011.

. . . about $1.5 million more than was invested in all-female-founded companies by venture capital in the USA during the same period: See Emma Hinchliffe, 'Funding for Female Founders Increased in 2019 – but only to 2.7%', *Fortune*, 2 March 2020, https://fortune.com/2020/03/02/female-founders-funding-2019/.

Was it worth it? And could we do things differently? This argument is developed in Jennifer Brandel and Mara Zepada, 'Zebras Fix What Unicorns Break', *Medium*, 8 March 2017, https://medium.com/zebras-unite/zebrasfix-c467e55f9d96.

In 1998, 88-year-old Queen Ingrid of Denmark arrived at a lavish wedding ceremony at the Danish royal family's summer residence: It was the wedding of Princess Alexandra of Sayn-Wittgenstein-Berleburg, held at Gråsten Palace in Jutland, 1998.

Chapter 6

The technique was nothing new, nor were the colours, but the enormous demand sent prices soaring on every buying and selling site on the internet: Natalie Robehmed, 'How 20-Year-Old Kylie Jenner Built a $900 Million Fortune in Less than 3 Years', *Forbes*, 11 July 2018, https://www.forbes.com/sites/forbesdigitalcovers/2018/07/11/how-20-year-old-kylie-jenner-built-a-900-million-fortune-in-less-than-3-years/#696d992daa62.

It didn't matter that people whispered about her business largely being built on exaggerated figures and the odd lie: In 2020 *Forbes* rescinded its naming of Kylie Jenner as a 'billionaire'. See Chase Peterson-Whithorn and Madeline Berg, 'Inside Kylie Jenner's Web of Lies – And Why She is no Longer a Billionaire', *Forbes*, 1 June 2020, https://www.forbes.com/sites/chasewithorn/2020/05/29/inside-kylie-jennerss-web-of-lies-and-why-shes-no-longer-a-billionaire/#46ab247d25f7.

[Kylie Jenner] made her debut playing the role of herself in a reality-TV show about the family she happened to be born into: Her mother, Kris Jenner, was previously married to Robert Kardashian, who gained recognition as American footballer O J Simpson's defence attorney. She had four children with him – Kourtney, Kim, Khloé and Rob. She later married Olympic athlete Bruce Jenner, who came out as trans in 2017 and is now called Caitlyn Jenner. They have two daughters: Kendall and Kylie.

In February 2018, Jenner wrote on Twitter: 'Sooo does anyone else not open Snapchat anymore? Or is it just me . . . ugh this is so sad.' @KylieJenner, 21 February 2018.

Before the day's end, Snapchat's share value had caved by 6 per cent, $1.3 billion wiped from its market value: Mamta Badkar, 'Snap slips after Kylie Jenner tweet', *Financial Times*, 22 February 2018.

In 2010, renowned American investor Peter Thiel muttered in disappointment: 'We wanted flying cars, instead we got 140 characters.' Cited in George Packer, 'No Death, No Taxes: The Libertarian Futurism of a Silicon Valley Billionaire', *The New Yorker*, 21 November 2011.

. . . all while the numbers of women at major tech companies like Apple, Google, Facebook and Microsoft remained shockingly low: Apple is the only one of these companies whose workforce was 20 per cent women, and the majority of them were white.

Things like making food, planning family holidays, setting the table, arranging flowers or picking out clothes for the kids aren't counted as 'economic activities' in standard economic theory: See my previous book, Katrine Marçal, *Who Cooked Adam Smith's Dinner?* Trans. Saskia Vogel, Portobello Books, London, 2015.

A fan of shopping, she soon discovers how much cheaper it is to buy European designer goods in Europe than in China: L Zhang, 'Fashioning the Feminine Self in "Prosumer Capitalism": Women's Work and the

Transnational Reselling of Western Luxury Online', *Journal of Consumer Culture*, vol. 17, no. 2, 2017, pp. 184–204.

'Glamour labour': The term is defined in Elizabeth A Wissinger, *This Year's Model: Fashion, Media, and the Making of Glamour*, NYU Press, New York, 2015.

'The proper study of mankind is man . . . but the proper study of market is women,' wrote *Printers Ink*, the first trade magazine in the world dedicated to the burgeoning advertising industry, in 1929: Cited in Brooke Erin Duffy, *(Not) Getting Paid to Do What You Love: Gender, Social Media and Aspirational Work*, Yale University Press, New Haven/London, 2017, p. 19.

If the milk was full of liquid manure, say, or a merchant had sold them sausages filled with waste, it was in their roles as consumers that they could try to affect change: Eva Kaijser and Monica Björk, *Svenska Hem: den sanna historien om Fröken Frimans krig* (*Swedish Homes: The True Story of Miss Friman's War*), Latona Ord & Ton, Stockholm, 2014.

But it is undeniable that women in middle-class British households made use of what power they possessed as primary buyers of goods for the home: For further discussion of this, see Charlotte Sussman, *Consuming Anxieties: Consumer Protest, Gender & British Slavery, 1713–1833*, Stanford University Press, Stanford, 2000.

This was seen during the French Revolution of 1789: Here I am referring to the Women's March on Versailles, also known as the October March. This march took place on 5 October 1789, when over 6,000 people, mainly women, marched from Paris to the royal palace in Versailles. The king gave up, opened his royal stores for the starving masses and was marched back to the capital, where he was placed under house arrest at Tuileries Palace.

. . . and in Russia's February Revolution of 1917: On 8 March 1917, women demonstrated for bread on Petrograd's streets. This became the flashpoint for Russia's February Revolution, and it is also why International Women's Day is celebrated when it is.

When the modern department store was created in Paris in 1852: Le Bon Marché was founded in 1838 and revamped by Aristide Boucicaut in 1852. It is considered one of the world's first department stores and still exists to this day.

The other important innovation that came to be associated with the new department stores was fixed prices: The system of fixed prices did already exist in certain Paris stores. See Robert Tamilia, 'World's Fairs and the Department Store 1800s to 1930s', *Marketing History at the Center*, vol. 13, 2007, p. 229.

As Zola saw it, the department store arrived just as the Frenchwoman started to abandon the Church. In his eyes this was no coincidence: 'While the churches were gradually emptied by the wavering of faith, they were replaced in souls that were now empty by his emporium. Women came to him to spend their hours of idleness, the uneasy, trembling hours that they would once have spent in chapel: it was a necessary outlet for nervous passion, the revived struggle of a god against the husband, a constantly renewed cult of the body, with the divine afterlife of beauty.' Émile Zola, *The Ladies' Delight*, trans. Robin Buss, Penguin Classics, London, 2001, p. 415.

When American Harry Gordon Selfridge founded his vast department store Selfridges in London in 1906, he saw it as something of a feminist act: 'I came along just at the time when women wanted to step out on their own. They came to the store and realized some of their dreams.' Cited in Jackie Willson, *Being Gorgeous: Feminism, Sexuality and the Pleasures of the Visual*, I B Tauris, London, 2014, p. 109.

And this integration of commerce with the technology we carry around in our pockets has become a central part of how we experience the world in the early twenty-first century: Emily Hund and Lee McGuigan, 'A Shoppable Life: Performance, Selfhood, and Influence in the Social Media Storefront', *Communication, Culture and Critique*, vol. 12, no. 1, March 2019, pp. 18–35.

There are now smartphone apps capable of 'scanning' the world around you: One example of this is Slyce.

The 2010s blurred the borders between consumption and production, and we increasingly started talking about a new category of 'prosumers': See George Ritzer and Nathan Jurgenson, 'Production, Consumption, Prosumption: The Nature of Capitalism in the Age of the Digital "Prosumer"', *Journal of Consumer Culture*, vol. 10, no. 1, 2010, pp. 13–36.

Even though this hasn't been the case for any extended period of history – woman has almost always worked in the formal economy, too – this is undeniably our perception of how things stand: In Victorian England, which we otherwise tend to associate with the housewife ideal, working-class women, for example, had to work. Often 10 to 15 hours per day, in anything from farming to manufacturing shirts. Women did this work in addition to their work in the home.

Motherhood was a way of combining the glamour of celebrity with the internet's demand for intimacy: See for example Kara Van Cleaf, '"Of Woman Born" to Mommy Blogged: The Journey from the Personal as Political to the Personal as Commodity', *Women's Studies Quarterly*, vol. 43, no. 3/4, 2015, pp. 247–64.

War was raging in Europe, and in a parliamentary speech the new premier uttered the famous words: 'I have nothing to offer but blood, toil, tears and sweat.' Winston Churchill would repeat this phrase the same day in the House of Commons.

Here, Bush called on the American people to do something quite different: he told them to 'go shopping': 'Islam is Peace'. Speech by President George W Bush at the Islamic Center of Washington, DC, 17 September 2001, https://georgewbush-whitehouse.archives.gov/news/releases/2001/09/20010917-11.html.

In recent decades, a number of economists have talked about the 'feminisation' of the labour market: Guy Standing, 'Global Feminization Through Flexible Labor: A Theme Revisited', *World Development*, Elsevier, vol. 27, no. 3, 1999, pp. 583–602.

In his book *Art & Energy*, Barry Lord discusses this shift: Barry Lord, *Art & Energy: How Culture Changes*, American Alliance of Museums Press, Washington, DC, 2014.

Chapter 7

. . . tend to be suspiciously similar to the dominant technology in our societies: George Zarkadakis, *In Our Own Image: Will Artificial Intelligence Save or Destroy Us?*, Rider, London, 2015, pp. 28–47.

In the Bible we are told that God 'formed man of the dust of the ground': The Bible, Genesis 2:7.

Descartes would eventually come to formulate the very influential idea of the body as no more than 'a statue or a machine': Jessica Riskin, *The Restless*

Clock: A History of the Centuries-Long Argument over What Makes Living Things Tick, University of Chicago Press, Chicago and London, 2017, pp. 44–61.

In the early 1900s it was common to speak of the brain as some sort of telephone exchange: Matthew Cobb, *The Idea of the Brain: A History*, Profile Books, London, 2020, pp. 145–56.

. . . the human brain, he declares, works like 'a computer': L Ron Hubbard, *Dianetics: The Modern Science of Mental Health*, Hermitage House, 1950, p. 41.

'As a Scientologist, I have the technology to handle life's problems,' film star John Travolta declares on the movement's website: '... and I have used this to help others in life as well.' Cited in 'Celebrity Scientologists and Stars Who Have Left the Church', *US Weekly*, 18 June 2020, https://www.usmagazine. com/celebrity-news/pictures/celebrity-scientologists-2012107/23623-2/.

Some of the great thinkers of our time, like the physicist Stephen Hawking or cosmologist Max Tegmark, have predicted that in future we will even be able to 'upload' our consciousness to something other than the human body: Max Tegmark discussed this at the World Science Festival on 22 November 2019 in the seminar 'To Be or Not to Be Bionic: On Immortality and Superhumanism'. For Stephen Hawking's argument, see for example Meghan Neal, 'Scientists Are Convinced Mind Transfer is the Key to Immortality', *Tech By Vice*, 26 September 2013, https://www.vice.com/en_us/article/ezzj8z/ scientists-are-convinced-mind-transfer-is-the-key-to-immortality.

What is a 'black swan'? Yes, it's another metaphor, one popularised and redefined by Nassim Taleb in 2007: Nassim Nicholas Taleb, *The Black Swan: The Impact of the Highly Improbable*, Allen Lane, London, 2007, pp. xxi–xxii.

Taleb himself wrote of the risk of a future global pandemic as far back as 2007: Discussed in an interview with the author, 5 April 2020.

If they didn't follow its instructions, they could be penalised or even blocked from the platform: See for example Alex Rosenblat, *Uberland: How Algorithms Are Rewriting the Rules of Work*, University of California Press, Oakland, 2018.

In the same way, workers picking goods at Amazon's huge warehouses walked routes plotted almost entirely by algorithms: Noam Scheiber, 'Inside an Amazon Warehouse, Robots' Ways Rub Off on Humans', *New York Times*, 3 July 2019.

Your work was sliced up into different tasks, with the smartphone in your hand telling you exactly how long each should take: This is based on Åsa Plesner, *Budget ur balans: En granskning av äldreomsorgens ekonomi and arbetsmiljö* (*Budget Out of Balance: a Review of the Economics and Work Environment of Elderly Care*), Arena Idé, Stockholm, 2020, pp. 23–4.

. . . i.e. some of those who needed protecting the most from the virus – were on average coming into contact with over 16 different people in any two-week period: Johan Nilsson, '500 svenskar döda efter att ha smittats inom hemtjänsten' ('500 Swedes Dead after Home Care Infections'), *TT*, 6 May 2020.

Today many workers in the gig economy are forced to pay fines to the company they work for if they don't find a substitute: James Temperton, 'The Gig Economy is Being Fuelled by Exploitation, Not Innovation', *Wired Opinion*, 8 February 2018.

Similar systems are found in everything from start-ups to established companies owned by the French government: Parcel delivery service DPD is owned by the French state. James Temperton's article in the previous note gives an example of a DPD worker who died when they were unable to find a substitute and so went to work.

Many people clearly value the flexibility that these jobs can offer: Thor Berger, Carl Benedikt Frey, Guy Levin, Santosh Rao Danda, 'Uber Happy? Work and Well-being in the "Gig Economy"', *Economic Policy*, vol. 34, no. 99, July 2019, pp. 429–77.

Chapter 8

It is only some seven years later, when Venus comes from nowhere to reach the US Open final, that anyone really starts to believe him: Serena Williams (with Daniel Paisner), *My Life: Queen of the Court*, Simon & Schuster, New York, 2009, pp. 38–41.

. . . causing it to almost stop and drop in the right place: Nick Stockton, 'The Mind-Bending Physics of a Tennis Ball's Spin', *Wired*, 9 December 2015, https://www.wired.com/2015/09/mind-bending-physics-tennis-balls-spin/.

Sir Isaac Newton, the father of modern physics, observed this phenomenon back in the seventeenth century from his window at Trinity College,

Cambridge: James Gleick, *Isaac Newton*, HarperCollins, London, 2004, pp. 81–2.

'We can know more than we can tell,' wrote Hungarian philosopher and economist Michael Polanyi. This is what we tend to call 'Polanyi's paradox': Polanyi's paradox is discussed economically in this way in David Autor, 'Polanyi's Paradox and the Shape of Employment Growth', NBER Working Papers 20485, 2014, National Bureau of Economic Research, Inc.

Which is precisely why it has been very tricky to get machines to do something like *seeing*: Missy Cummings, 'Rethinking the Maturity of Artificial Intelligence in Safety-critical Settings', *AI Magazine*, 2020, http://hal.pratt.duke.edu/sites/hal.pratt.duke.edu/files/u39/2020-min.pdf.

Later the same year, Kasparov will become the world's youngest ever World Chess Champion: The description of Garry Kasparov's match in Hamburg is based on Garry Kasparov (with Mig Greengard), *Deep Thinking: Where Artificial Intelligence Ends . . . and Human Creativity Begins*, John Murray, London, 2017, pp. 1–5.

He isn't just playing against 32 computers: he is also walking from board to board, picking up the pieces with his very own hands: Garry Kasparov in *Deep Thinking*, p. 2.

Kai-Fu Lee, one of China's foremost investors in AI, recently stated: 'AI is great at thinking, but robots are bad at moving their fingers.' 'Algorithms can blow humans out of the water when it comes to making predictions based on data, but robots still can't perform the cleaning duties of a hotel maid. In essence, AI is great at thinking, but robots are bad at moving their fingers.' Quotation from Kai-Fu Lee, *AI Superpowers: China, Silicon Valley and the New World Order*, Houghton Mifflin Harcourt, Boston, 2018, p. 166.

Which isn't surprising, considering we're a product of 200,000-odd years of life in this unpredictable environment called earth: This famous point was made by robot researcher Hans Moravec and is called 'Moravec's paradox'. It posits that the things that we find difficult and that take many years for a human to learn, such as advanced mathematics or chess, robots find simple. The things that we people find simple, on the other hand, robots tend to find difficult. Like walking, opening a door, cycling or playing hopscotch. All of this is body intelligence: the things we learn through our bodies interacting with our surroundings through evolution. 'But as the demonstrations have mounted, it has become clear that it is comparatively easy to make computers exhibit adult-level performance in solving problems on intelligence tests or playing checkers, and difficult or impossible to give them the skills of a one-year-old, when it comes to perception and mobility.' Hans Moravec, *Mind Children: The Future of Robot and Human Intelligence*, Harvard University Press, London, 1988, p. 15. It should however be added that Hans Moravec was convinced that the machines would gradually be able to take over more or less completely. He believed that the paradox he pointed out in 1988 would eventually be overcome.

So it isn't particularly surprising that the jobs in our economy that have been automated the fastest are those in factories: Carl Benedikt Frey and Michael A Osborne, 'The Future of Employment: How Susceptible are Jobs to Computerisation?', *Technological Forecasting and Social Change*, Elsevier, vol. 114 (C), 2017, pp. 254–80.

Bats see better in the dark – does that mean in 50 years they will be our overlords? This point is made in Roger Bootle, *The AI Economy: Work, Wealth and Welfare in the Robot Age*, Nicholas Brealey Publishing, London, 2019.

Roboticist Rodney Brooks has written that AI researchers long regarded intelligence as the ability to tackle 'the things that highly educated male scientists found challenging': 'Judging by the projects chosen in the early days of AI, intelligence was thought to be best characterized as the things that highly educated male scientists found challenging.' Rodney A Brooks, *Flesh and Machines: How Robots Will Change Us*, Vintage, London, 2003, p. 36.

'Elephants don't play chess,' says Rodney Brooks: Rodney Brooks, 'Elephants Don't Play Chess', *Robotics and Autonomous Systems*, vol. 6, no. 1–2, 1990, pp. 3–15.

But then in the fifteenth century something changed: Marilyn Yalom, *The Birth of the Chess Queen: A History*, Harper Perennial, New York, 2005.

David Foster Wallace once wrote a celebrated essay on male tennis star Roger Federer: David Foster Wallace, 'Roger Federer as Religious Experience', *String Theory: David Foster Wallace on Tennis*, Library of America, New York, 2016.

. . . National Association of Black Journalists described as a 'racist, sexist caricature' that was 'unnecessarily sambo-like': 'Racist Serena Williams cartoon "nothing to do with race," paper says', CNN, 2018, https://www.kjrh.com/news/national/serena-williams-cartoon-racist.

Chapter 9

So he packed him off from the family home in what is now western Germany to spend two years in Manchester in the north of England: Friedrich Engels had just completed his military service in Berlin in October 1842.

. . . the trip to Manchester would instead lead to Engels founding modern-day communism with his friend Karl Marx: Tristram Hunt, *Marx's General: The Revolutionary Life of Friedrich Engels*, Holt Paperbacks, New York, 2009, pp. 63–4.

As the economist Joseph Schumpeter put it, capitalism isn't about producing 'more silk stockings for queens but [about] bringing them within the reach of factory girls': Joseph A Schumpeter, *Capitalism, Socialism and Democracy*, Harper Torchbooks, New York, 1976, p. 76.

Engels would come to see Irish migrants dwelling in ramshackle houses with broken windows, families in dark, damp cellars, living in stench and squalor: Friedrich Engels, *The Condition of the Working Class in England*, Oxford University Press, Oxford, 1993.

Many experts say that we are now living in a 'second machine age', an age at least as dramatic as the one that Engels bore witness to: See for example Erik Brynjolfsson and Andrew McAfee, *The Second Machine Age: Work, Progress, and Prosperity in a Time of Brilliant Technologies*, Norton & Company, New York, 2014.

This time the robots are out for the middle-class jobs too: See for example Martin Ford, *The Rise of the Robots: Technology and the Threat of Mass Unemployment*, Basic Books, New York, 2016.

Economist Carl Benedikt Frey, has described how the rural English high society of Jane Austen's novels sat in their southern counties proposing to each other over their floral teacups: Carl Benedikt Frey, *The Technology Trap: Capital, Labor, and Power in the Age of Automation*, Princeton University Press, Princeton/Oxford, 2019, p. 11.

Economists were quick to point out that the American states that voted for Donald Trump in 2016 were also the states in which the most jobs had been replaced by machines: Carl Benedikt Frey, Thor Berger and Chinchih Chen, 'Political Machinery: Did Robots Swing the 2016 US Presidential Election?', *Oxford Review of Economic Policy*, vol. 34, no. 3, 2018, pp. 418–42.

This group consists of all the people who the robots have put out of jobs along the way: Yuval Noah Harari, *Homo Deus: A Brief History of Tomorrow*, Vintage, London, 2016, pp. 369–81.

In recent years this has become one of the major issues discussed at tech conferences on the future, tickets for which will set you back a neat $10,000: Tickets to a TED conference cost $10,000, but it is also possible to find them for $5,000.

Which is why a large number of well-known tech billionaires have recently started to embrace the idea of universal basic income: Of whom Mark Zuckerberg and Elon Musk are the most famous.

Here young Engels tells a story that was previously recounted to him in a letter. It goes something like this: The following passage is based on Friedrich Engels, *The Condition of the Working Class in England*, pp. 154–7.

In the USA, 80 per cent of all elementary- and middle-school teachers, nurses and secretaries are women: 'Men Still Pick "Blue" Jobs and Women "Pink" Jobs', *The Economist*, 16 February 2019.

Namibia and Tanzania have a much larger share of female electricians than Norway: Smita Das and Aphichoke Kotikula, *Gender-based Employment Segregation: Understanding Causes and Policy Interventions*, 2019, International Bank for Reconstruction and Development/World Bank.

But generally speaking, women work more in the service sector while men work more in manufacturing: Women dominate the services sector in every region in the world (except in South Asia) and men dominate industry throughout the world.

When Engels wrote with revolutionary gusto that the factory owners 'grow rich on the misery of the mass of wage earners', he was simply expressing a fact: See Robert Allen, 'Engels' Pause: Technical Change, Capital Accumulation, and Inequality in the British Industrial Revolution', *Explorations in Economic History*, vol. 46, no. 4, 2009, pp. 418–35.

But we have long known that neither IQ tests nor school grades can predict how economically successful a person will be: Jay L Zagorsky, 'Do You Have to be Smart to be Rich? The Impact of IQ on Wealth, Income and Financial Distress', *Intelligence*, vol. 35, no. 5, 2007, pp. 489–501.

Other things will reasonably come into play: See for example K Richardson and S H Norgate, 'Does IQ Really Predict Job Performance?', *Applied Developmental Science*, vol. 19, no. 3, 2015, pp. 153–69.

Some studies say 47 per cent: Carl Benedikt Frey and Michael A Osborne, *The Future of Employment: How Susceptible are Jobs to Computerisation?*, Oxford Martin School, Oxford, 2013.

. . . others 9: Melanie Arntz, Terry Gregory and Ulrich Zierahn, 'The Risk of Automation for Jobs in OECD Countries: A Comparative Analysis', *OECD Social, Employment and Migration Working Papers*, no. 189, 2016, OECD Publishing, Paris.

And those two figures are pretty different: These figures relate to the US labour market.

However, there is at least some consensus as to where the bottlenecks lie, and the sorts of industries in which the machines' onward march will be harder: Frey and Osborne (2013) discuss three types of bottlenecks: the ability to perform physical tasks in an unstructured environment; cognitive intelligence, i.e. creativity and an ability for complex reasoning; and social intelligence. Ljubica Nedelkoska and Glenda Quintini, 'Automation, Skills Use and Training', *OECD Social, Employment and Migration Working Papers*, no. 202, 2018, OECD Publishing, Paris, discusses very similar bottlenecks.

Most economic studies suggest we probably won't have machines as nurses, preschool teachers, psychiatrists or social workers any time soon: Michael Webb, 'The Impact of Artificial Intelligence on the Labor Market', paper, Stanford University, 6 November 2019, shows that female-dominated industries therefore generally run a much smaller risk of automation.

It is for this reason that many economic studies have lately shown that the likelihood of a job being taken by a robot is much higher in male-dominated industries than female-dominated ones: Michael Webb, 'The Impact of Artificial Intelligence on the Labor Market'. Webb (2019) splits up the risk of automation into three categories: jobs that are automated by robots; jobs that are taken over by new software; and jobs that are taken over by AI. In all of these categories, the risk/possibility was much smaller in female-dominated industries.

The only thing is – as we saw with the programmers and the secretaries – an industry often diminishes in status when more women enter it: Paula

Asaf Levanon and Paul Allison England, 'Occupational Feminization and Pay: Assessing Causal Dynamics Using 1950–2000 U.S. Census Data', *Social Forces*, vol. 88, no. 2, December 2009, pp. 865–91.

Which means many of these women will then lose their jobs. A number of studies even suggest that, for this reason, it will be women more than men who will be made unemployed by the second machine age: Ariane Hegewisch, Chandra Childers and Heidi Hartmann, *Women, Automation and the Future of Work*, Institute For Women's Policy Research, 2019, https://www.researchgate.net/profile/Ariane_Hegewisch/publication/333517425_Women_Automation_and_the_Future_of_Work/links/5cf15aca4585153c3daa1709/Women-Automation-and-the-Future-of-Work.pdf.

Take radiologists, for example. This is a profession in which artificial intelligence can already compete with people: See for example Sara Reardon, 'Rise of Robot Radiologists', *Nature*, 18 December 2019, https://www.nature.com/articles/d41586-019-03847-z.

But has this cost radiologists their jobs? No. Has it seen their salaries plummet? No, not that either: I consider US figures relevant here as salaries in American healthcare are 'market-steered' in a way they are not in Europe. See Michael Walter, 'Radiologists Earn $419K per Year, up 4% from 2018', *Radiology Business*, 11 April 2019.

When William Lee came to Queen Elizabeth I with his new stocking frame knitting machine in 1589, she refused to give him a patent: Economists like to tell this story. See for example World Bank Group, 'The Changing Nature of Work', *World Development Report 2019*, p. 18.

. . . and so the state solved its problem by getting rid of those who stood in the way of the technological revolution: This point about state intervention is made by Carl Benedikt Frey in *The Technology Trap: Capital, Labor, and Power in the Age of Automation*, Princeton University Press, Oxford, 2019.

At one point there were more British soldiers defending machines from violent troublemakers in the UK than there were fighting Napoleon in Spain: See Eric J Hobsbawm, 'The Machine Breakers', *Past & Present*, no. 1, 1952, pp. 57–70.

Chapter 10

The North Sea lay between them: See for example Cynthia Barnett, *Rain: A Natural and Cultural History*, Crown Publishing, New York, 2015, pp. 46–8.

King James . . . went on to write a witch-hunting handbook: The book was called *Daemonologie* and it was published in 1597.

That witches could cause crop failures was something that popes had been saying for years: As stated in 1484 in *Summis desiderantes affectibus*, published by Pope Innocent VII.

Suddenly it was no longer possible to fish in the same way in many parts of northern Europe: See for example Brian Fagan, *The Little Ice Age*, Basic Books, New York, 2000.

The economist Emily Oster has linked the great European witch trials to these changes in climate: Emily F Oster, 'Witchcraft, Weather and Economic Growth in Renaissance Europe', *Journal of Economic Perspectives*, vol. 18, no. 1, 2004, pp. 215–28.

This also meant their accusers wouldn't have to feel like bad Christians for shooing away a hungry woman – because she was probably in league with the devil: John Swain, 'Witchcraft, Economy and Society in the Forest of Pendle', *The Lancashire Witches: Histories and Stories*, ed. Robert Poole, Manchester University Press, Manchester, 2002, pp. 73–88.

Around the turn of the millennium, women in rural Tanzania were accused of witchcraft and killed when it rained too much or too little: Edward Miguel, 'Poverty and Witch Killings', *Review of Economic Studies*, vol. 72, no. 4, 1153–1172, 2005, http://emiguel.econ.berkeley.edu/assets/assets/miguel_research/44/_Paper__Poverty_and_Witch_Killing.pdf

. . . the then median income in Tanzania was comparable to that of Western Europe in the early 1600s: This point is made by Chelsea Follett, 'How Economic Prosperity Spared Witches', *USA Today*, 28 October 2017.

If a dead man's family doesn't like his widow, an accusation of witchcraft can be a means of getting her to relinquish her ownership of the land that she has inherited: Soma Chaudhuri, 'Women as Easy Scapegoats: Witchcraft Accusations and Women as Targets in Tea Plantations of India', *Violence Against Women*, vol. 18, no. 10, 1213–1234, 2012.

As such, witch-hunts can be an effective way of doing away with difficult women no one wants to deal with: Outspoken widows, or women who have become pregnant outside wedlock, for instance. A similar mechanism can be seen in parts of Ghana in the 1990s, where women were accused of witchcraft because society needed someone on whom to blame illness or accidents. They then took outspoken women, who often lived outside the village, and branded them as witches. Kati Whitaker, 'Ghana Witch Camps: Widows' Lives in Exile', *BBC News*, 1 September 2012.

In his bestselling book on witches from 1486, the German priest Heinrich Kramer wrote that 'all wickedness is but little to the wickedness of a woman': He wrote the book with Jakob Sprenger.

He claimed that woman was 'more bitter than death', weaker in both body and soul than the male, and of course more carnal: See Walter Stephens, *Demon Lovers: Witchcraft, Sex, and the Crisis of Beliefs*, University of Chicago Press, Chicago, 2002, pp. 36–7.

Many of the day's institutions, from the Vatican to the Spanish Inquisition, dismissed much of what Kramer had to say about witches: In 1538 the Spanish Inquisition cautioned against believing everything that was in the book.

In short, the devil started playing a greater role in it all: the witches needed a male boss: Silvia Federici, *Caliban and the Witch: Women, the Body and Primitive Accumulation*, Autonomedia, pp. 186–7, New York, 2004.

The economist Cornelius Christian has, for example, pointed out that one period of intense witch persecution in Scotland happened to coincide with very good harvests: Cornelius Christian, 'Elites, Weather Shocks, and Witchcraft Trials in Scotland', Working Papers 1704, Brock University, Department of Economics, 2017.

Other economists also discuss the persecution of witches as some sort of unfortunate side effect of stiffening competition in the religious market: Peter T Leeson and Jacob W Russ, 'Witch Trials', *The Economic Journal*, vol. 128, no. 613, 2018, pp. 2066–2105.

. . . for our notions of womanhood and nature are linked: The best-known feminist work on this subject is probably Carolyn Merchant, *The Death of Nature: Women, Ecology, and the Scientific Revolution*, HarperCollins, New York, 1983.

If fossil fuels go, then masculinity goes with it, they imagine: The term 'petro masculinity' encapsulates this. See for example Cara Daggett, 'Petro-masculinity: Fossil Fuels and Authoritarian Desire', *Millennium*, vol. 47, no. 1, 2018, pp. 25–44.

This is eminently doable: many of the (slightly carelessly termed) 'green jobs' in the energy sector, for example, are both fairly well paid and do not require a higher education to perform: Mark Muro, Adie Tomer, Ranjitha Shivaram and Joseph Kane, 'Advancing Inclusion Through Clean Energy Jobs', *Metropolitan Policy Program*, Brookings, April 2019.

In 1936, the great English economist John Maynard Keynes managed to acquire large piles of Isaac Newton's notes – papers that no one had previously studied: Daniel Kuehn, 'Keynes, Newton and the Royal Society: the Events of 1942 and 1943', Notes Rec. 6725–36, 2013.

Newton was, as Keynes observed, 'not the first of the age of reason'; he was 'the last of the magicians': John Maynard Keynes as cited in Richard Davenport-Hines, *Universal Man: The Lives of John Maynard Keynes*, Basic Books, New York, 2015, p. 138.

Today, alchemists have to some extent been rehabilitated: Richard Conniff, 'Alchemy May Not Have Been the Pseudoscience We All Thought It Was', *Smithsonian Magazine*, February 2014, https://www.smithsonianmag.com/history/alchemy-may-not-been-pseudoscience-we-thought-it-was-180949430/.

'How dare you?' Greta Thunberg thundered in her already classic 2019 speech at the UN in New York: Greta Thunberg, 25 September 2019 at the UN in New York.

American science journalist Charles C Mann has described the environmental debate of recent decades as a battle between 'wizards' and 'prophets': Charles C Mann, *The Wizard and the Prophet: Science and the Future of Our Planet*, Picador, New York, 2018.

The conflict between the wizard and the prophet is, according to Mann, not a conflict of good and evil, but of two different concepts of the good life: Charles C Mann, *The Wizard and the Prophet*, p. 8.

'The more important fundamental laws and facts of physical science have all been discovered.' Albert A Michelson, in an 1894 speech at Ryerson Physics Lab, University of Chicago.

Bibliography

Abbate, Jane, *Recoding Gender: Women's Changing Participation in Computing*, MIT Press, Cambridge, Massachusetts, 2012

Adler, Michael H, *The Writing Machine*, George Allen & Unwin, London, 1973

Aldrin, Buzz, *Magnificent Desolation: The Long Journey Home from the Moon*, Bloomsbury Publishing, London, 2009

Alexopoulos, Michelle, 'Read All about It!! What Happens Following a Technology Shock?', *American Economic Review*, vol. 101, no. 4, June 2011

Allan May, John, 'Come What May: A Wheel of an Idea', *Christian Science Monitor*, 4 October 1951

Allehanda.se, 'Fråga Gösta: hur många hästkrafter har en häst?' ('Ask Gösta: How Many Horsepower Does a Horse Have?'), 27 October 2005

Allen, Robert, 'Engels' Pause: Technical Change, Capital Accumulation, and Inequality in the British Industrial Revolution', *Explorations in Economic History*, vol. 46, no. 4, 2009

Arntz, Melanie, Gregory, Terry and Zierahn, Ulrich, 'The Risk of Automation for Jobs in OECD Countries: A Comparative Analysis', *OECD Social, Employment and Migration Working Papers*, no. 189, OECD Publishing, Paris, 2016

Asaf Levanon, Paula and England, Paul Allison, 'Occupational Feminization and Pay: Assessing Causal Dynamics Using 1950–2000 U.S. Census Data', *Social Forces*, vol. 88, no. 2, December 2009

Autor, David, 'Polanyi's Paradox and the Shape of Employment Growth', NBER Working Papers 20485, National Bureau of Economic Research, Inc., 2014

Axelsson, Per, *Höstens spöke: De svenska polioepidemiernas historia* (*The Ghost of Autumn: the History of the Swedish Polio Epidemics*), dissertation, Umeå University, Carlsson, Stockholm, 2004

Badkar, Mamta, 'Snap slips after Kylie Jenner tweet', *Financial Times*, 22 February 2018

Baird, Ross, *The Innovation Blind Spot: Why We Back the Wrong Ideas and What To Do About It*, Benbella Books, Texas, 2017

Barnett, Cynthia, *Rain: A Natural and Cultural History*, Crown Publishing, New York, 2015

Beevor, Antony, *Stalingrad*, Viking, London, 1998

Berger, Thor, Frey, Carl Benedikt, Levin, Guy and Rao Danda, Santosh, 'Uber Happy? Work and Well-being in the "Gig Economy"', *Economic Policy*, vol. 34, no. 99, July 2019

The Bible, Genesis

Boot, Max, *War Made New: Technology, Warfare, and the Course of History – 1500 to Today*, Gotham Books, New York, 2006

Bootle, Roger, *The AI Economy: Work, Wealth and Welfare in the Robot Age*, Nicholas Brealey Publishing, London, 2019

Boyd, Thomas Alvin, *Charles F Kettering: A Biography*, Beard Books, Washington, 1957

Bradley, Harriet, 'Frames of Reference: Skill, Gender and

New Technology in the Hosiery Industry', *Women Workers and the Technological Change in Europe in the Nineteenth and Twentieth Centuries*, ed. Gertjan Groot and Marlou Schrover, Taylor & Francis, London, 1995

Brandel, Jennifer and Zepada, Mara, 'Zebras Fix What Unicorns Break', *Medium*, 8 March 2017, www.medium.com

British Business Bank, 'UK Venture Capital and Female Founders', report, 2019

Brooks, Rodney, 'Elephants Don't Play Chess', *Robotics and Autonomous Systems*, vol. 6, no. 1–2, 1990

—, *Flesh and Machines: How Robots Will Change Us* (Vintage, London, 2003)

Brynjolfsson, Erik and McAfee, Andrew, *The Second Machine Age: Work, Progress, and Prosperity in a Time of Brilliant Technologies*, Norton & Company, New York, 2014

Bulliet, Richard W, *The Camel and the Wheel*, Columbia University Press, New York, 1990

—, *The Wheel: Inventions and Reinventions*, Columbia University Press, New York, 2016

Campbell-Kelly, Martin and Williams, Michael R (ed.), 'The Moore School Lectures: Theory and Techniques for Design of Electronic Digital Computers', *The Moore School Lectures (Charles Babbage Institute Reprint)*, MIT Press, Cambridge, Massachusetts; Tomash Publishers, Los Angeles, 1985

Casey, Robert, *The Model T: A Centennial History*, Johns Hopkins Press, Baltimore, 2008

Chaudhuri, S, 'Women as Easy Scapegoats: Witchcraft Accusations and Women as Targets in Tea Plantations of India', *Violence Against Women*, vol. 18, no. 10, 1213–1234, 2012

Christian, Cornelius, 'Elites, Weather Shocks, and Witchcraft Trials in Scotland', Working Papers 1704, Brock University, Department of Economics, 2017

Churchill, Winston, *The Gathering Storm*, Penguin Classics, London, 2005

Clark, Kate, 'US VC Investment in Female Founders Hits All-time High', *TechCrunch*, 9 December 2019

Cobb, Matthew, *The Idea of the Brain: A History*, Profile Books, London, 2020

Comrie, Leslie, 'Careers for Girls', *The Mathematical Gazette*, vol. 28, no. 28, 1944

Conniff, Richard, 'Alchemy May Not Have Been the Pseudoscience We All Thought It Was', *Smithsonian Magazine*, February 2014

Copeland, Jack, 'Colossus and the Rise of the Modern Computer', *Colossus: The Secrets of Bletchley Park's Codebreaking Computers*, Oxford University Press, New York, 2006

Cummings, Missy, 'Rethinking the Maturity of Artificial Intelligence in Safety-critical Settings', *AI Magazine*, 2020, http://hal.pratt.duke.edu/sites/hal.pratt.duke.edu/files/u39/2020-min.pdf

Daggett, Cara, 'Petro-masculinity: Fossil Fuels and Authoritarian Desire', *Millennium*, vol. 47, no. 1, 2018

Das, Smita and Kotikula, Aphichoke, *Gender-based Employment Segregation: Understanding Causes and Policy Interventions*, International Bank for Reconstruction and Development/The World Bank, 2019

Davenport-Hines, Richard, *Universal Man: The Lives of John Maynard Keynes*, Basic Books, New York, 2015

Dean, Warren, *Brazil and the Struggle for Rubber: A Study in Environmental History*, Cambridge University Press, Cambridge, 1987

283

Duffy, Brooke Erin, *(Not) Getting Paid to Do What You Love: Gender, Social Media and Aspirational Work*, Yale University Press, New Haven/London, 2017

The Economist, 'Men Still Pick "Blue" Jobs and Women "Pink" Jobs', 16 February 2019

Edgerton, David, *Warfare State: Britain, 1920–1970*, Cambridge University Press, Cambridge, 2006

Elis, Angela, *Mein Traum ist länger als die Nacht (My Dream is Longer than the Night)*, Hoffmann und Campe Verlag, Hamburg, 2010

Engels, Friedrich, *The Condition of the Working Class in England*, Oxford University Press, Oxford, 1993

Fagan, Brian, *The Little Ice Age* (Basic Books, New York, 2000)

Federici, Silvia, *Caliban and the Witch: Women, the Body and Primitive Accumulation*, Autonomedia, New York, 2004

Field, Alexander J, 'World War II and the Growth of US Potential Output', working paper, Department of Economics, Santa Clara University, May 2018

Follett, Chelsea, 'How Economic Prosperity Spared Witches', *USA Today*, 28 October 2017

Ford, Martin, *The Rise of the Robots: Technology and the Threat of Mass Unemployment*, Basic Books, New York, 2016

Frey, Carl Benedikt and Osborne, Michael, *The Future of Employment: How Susceptible are Jobs to Computerisation?*, Oxford Martin School, Oxford, 2013

Frey, Carl Benedikt, Berger, Thor and Chen, Chinchih, 'Political Machinery: Did Robots Swing the 2016 US Presidential Election?', *Oxford Review of Economic Policy*, vol. 34, no. 3, 2018

Frey, Carl Benedikt, *The Technology Trap: Capital, Labor, and Power in the Age of Automation*, Princeton University Press, Oxford, 2019

Funderburg, Anne Cooper, 'Making Teflon Stick', *Invention and Technology Magazine*, vol. 16, no. 1, summer 2000

Gasser, Aleksander, 'World's Oldest Wheel Found in Slovenia', Government Communication Office of the Republic of Slovenia, March 2003, www.ukom.gov.si

Gladwell, Malcolm, 'Creation Myth', *The New Yorker*, 9 May 2011

Gleick, James, *Isaac Newton*, HarperCollins, London, 2004

Googlers, 'Vint Cerf on Accessibility, the Cello and Noisy Hearing Aids', 4 October 2018, www.blog.google/inside-google/googlers

Grattan-Guinness, I, 'Work for the Hairdressers: The Production of de Prony's Logarithmic and Trigonometric Tables', *Annals of the History of Computing*, vol. 12, no. 3, summer 1990

Grier, David Allen, *When Computers Were Human*, Princeton University Press, Princeton/Oxford, 2005

Harari, Yuval Noah, *Homo Deus: A Brief History of Tomorrow*, Vintage, London, 2016

Hegewisch, Ariane, Childers, Chandra and Hartmann, Heidi, *Women, Automation and the Future of Work*, Institute For Women's Policy Research, 2019

Heller, Nathan, 'Is Venture Capital Worth the Risk?', *The New Yorker*, 20 January 2020

Hicks, Mar, *Programmed Inequality: How Britain Discarded Women Technologists and Lost Its Edge in Computing*, MIT Press, London, 2017

—, 'When Winning Is Losing: Why the Nation that Invented the Computer Lost its Lead', *Computer*, vol. 51, no. 10, 2018

Hinchliffe, Emma, 'Funding for Female Founders Increased in 2019 – but only to 2.7%', *Fortune*, 2 March 2020

285

Hobsbawm, E J, 'The Machine Breakers', *Past & Present*, no. 1, 1952

Hoke, Donald, 'The Woman and the Typewriter: A Case Study in Technological Innovation and Social Change', *Business and Economic History*, vol. 8, 1979

Hubbard, L Ron, *Dianetics: The Modern Science Of Mental Health*, Hermitage House, 1950

Hund, Emily and McGuigan, Lee, 'A Shoppable Life: Performance, Selfhood, and Influence in the Social Media Storefront', *Communication, Culture and Critique*, vol. 12, no. 1, March 2019

Hunt, Tristram, *Marx's General: The Revolutionary Life of Friedrich Engels*, Holt Paperbacks, New York, 2009

Jansson, Elisabeth, 'Ainas idé blir exportprodukt' ('Aina's Idea Becomes Export Product'), *Metallarbetaren*, no. 35, 1981

Kaijser, Eva and Björk, Monica, *Svenska Hem: den sanna historien om Fröken Frimans krig* (*Swedish Homes: The True Story of Miss Friman's War*), Latona Ord & Ton, Stockholm, 2014

Kasparov, Garry (with Mig Greengard), *Deep Thinking: Where Artificial Intelligence Ends ... and Human Creativity Begins*, John Murray Press, London, 2017

Kuehn, Daniel, 'Keynes, Newton and the Royal Society: the Events of 1942 and 1943', Notes Rec. 6725–36, 2013

Kwass, Michael, 'Big Hair: A Wig History of Consumption in Eighteenth Century France', *The American Historical Review*, vol. 111, no. 3, 2006

Lee, Kai-Fu, *AI Superpowers: China, Silicon Valley and the New World Order*, Houghton Mifflin Harcourt, Boston, 2018

Leeson, Peter T and Russ, Jacob W, 'Witch Trials', *The Economic Journal*, vol. 128, no. 613, 2018

Leisner, Barbara, *Bertha Benz: Eine starke Frau am Steuer des ersten Automobils* (*Bertha Benz: A Strong Woman at the Wheel of the First Car*), Katz Casimir Verlag, Gernsbach, 2014

Levsen, Nils, *Lead Markets in Age-Based Innovations: Demographic Change and Internationally Successful Innovations*, Springer Gabler, Hamburg, 2014

Lewin, Ronald, *Ultra Goes to War: The Secret Story*, Penguin Classic Military History, London, 2001, first published by Hutchinson & Co., London, 1987

Lord, Barry, *Art & Energy: How Culture Changes*, American Alliance of Museums Press, Washington, DC, 2014

Madrigal, Alexis C, 'The Electric Taxi Company You Could Have Called In 1900', *The Atlantic*, 15 March 2011

Mann, Charles C, *The Wizard and the Prophet: Science and the Future of Our Planet*, Picador, New York, 2018

Marçal, Katrine, *Who Cooked Adam Smith's Dinner?*, trans. Saskia Vogel, Portobello Books, London, 2015

Matthews, Kenneth Jr, 'The Embattled Driver in Ancient Rome', *Expedition Magazine*, vol. 2, no. 3, 1960

McGrane, Sally, 'No Stress, No Press: When Fingers Fly', *New York Times*, 24 January 2002

Merchant, Carolyn, *The Death of Nature: Women, Ecology, and the Scientific Revolution*, HarperCollins, New York, 1983

Merritt, Deborah J, 'Hypatia in the Patent Office: Women Inventors and the Law, 1865–1900', *The American Journal of Legal History*, vol. 35, no. 3, July 1991

Miguel, Edward, 'Poverty and Witch Killings', *Review of Economic Studies*, vol. 72, no. 4, 1153–1172, 2005

Mom, Gijs, *The Electric Vehicle: Technology and Expectations in the Automobile Age*, Johns Hopkins University Press, Baltimore, 2004 de Monchaux, Nicholas, *Spacesuit: Fashioning Apollo*, MIT Press, Cambridge, Massachusetts, 2011

Moravec, Hans, *Mind Children: The Future of Robot and Human Intelligence*, Harvard University Press, London, 1998

Muro, Mark, Tomer, Adie, Shivaram, Ranjitha and Kane, Joseph, 'Advancing Inclusion Through Clean Energy Jobs', *Metropolitan Policy Program*, Brookings, April 2019

Neal, Meghan, 'Scientists Are Convinced Mind Transfer is the Key to Immortality', *Tech By Vice*, 26 September 2013

Nedelkoska, Ljubica and Quintini, Glenda, 'Automation, Skills Use and Training', *OECD Social, Employment and Migration Working Papers*, no. 202, 2018, OECD Publishing, Paris

Nelson, Libby, 'The US Once Had More than 130 Hijackings in 4 Years. Here's Why They Finally Stopped', *Vox*, 29 March 2016

Nicholas, Tom, *VC: An American History*, Harvard University Press, New York, 2019

Nilsson, Johan, '500 svenskar döda efter att ha smittats inom hemtjänsten' ('500 Swedes Dead after Home Care Infections'), *TT*, 6 May 2020

Nixon, St John C, *The Invention of the Automobile: Karl Benz and Gottlieb Daimler* (1936), new digital edition by Edizioni Savine, 2016

Nyberg, Ann-Christin, *Making Ideas Matter: Gender, Technology and Women's Invention*, dissertation, Luleå Tekniska Universitet, 2009

Öberg, Lisa, *Barnmorskan och läkaren* (*The Midwife and the Doctor*), Ordfront, Stockholm, 1996

O'Hear, Steve, 'Voi Raises Another $85M for its European E-scooter Service', *TechCrunch*, 19 November 2011

Olsson Jeffery, Miriam, 'Nya siffror: Så lite riskkapital går till kvinnor – medan miljarderna rullar till män' ('New Figures: Here's How Little Venture Capital Goes to Women – While the Billions Roll in for Men'), *DI Digital*, 9 July 2020

Oster, Emily F, 'Witchcraft, Weather and Economic Growth in Renaissance Europe', *Journal of Economic Perspectives*, vol. 18, no. 1, 2004

Packer, George, 'No Death, No Taxes: The Libertarian Futurism of a Silicon Valley Billionaire', *The New Yorker*, 21 November 2011

Peterson-Whithorn, Chase and Berg, Madeline, 'Inside Kylie Jenner's Web of Lies – and Why She is no Longer a Billionaire', *Forbes*, 1 June 2020

Plesner, Åsa, *Budget ur balans: En granskning av äldreomsorgens ekonomi and arbetsmiljö* (*Budget Out of Balance: a Review of the Economics and Work Environment of Elderly Care*), Arena Idé, Stockholm, 2020

Pook, Lizzy, 'Why the Art World is Finally Waking Up to the Power of Female Craft Skills', *Stylist*, 2019, www.stylist.co.uk

Reardon, Sara, 'Rise of Robot Radiologists', *Nature*, 18 December 2019

Richardson, Ken and Norgate, Sarah H, 'Does IQ Really Predict Job Performance?', *Applied Developmental Science*, vol. 19, no. 3, 2015

Ridley, Matt, *How Innovation Works*, 4th Estate Books, London, 2020

Riskin, Jessica, *The Restless Clock: A History of the Centuries-Long Argument Over What Makes Living Things Tick*, University of Chicago Press, Chicago and London, 2017

Ritzer, George and Jurgenson, Nathan, 'Production,

Consumption, Prosumption: The Nature of Capitalism in the Age of the Digital "Prosumer'", *Journal of Consumer Culture*, vol. 10, no. 1, 2010

Robehmed, Natalie, 'How 20-Year-Old Kylie Jenner Built a $900 Million Fortune in Less than 3 Years', *Forbes*, 11 July 2018

Rosenblat, Alex, *Uberland: How Algorithms Are Rewriting the Rules of Work*, University of California Press, Oakland, 2018

Scharff, Virginia, *Taking the Wheel: Women and the Coming of the Motor Age*, University of New Mexico Press, New York, 1992

—, 'Femininity and the Electric Car', *Sex/Machine: Readings in Culture, Gender, and Technology*, ed. Patrick D Hopkins, Indiana University Press, Bloomington/Indianapolis, 1998

Scheiber, Noam, 'Inside an Amazon Warehouse, Robots' Ways Rub Off on Humans', *New York Times*, 3 July 2019

Schumpeter, Joseph A, *Capitalism, Socialism and Democracy*, Harper Torchbooks, New York, 1976

Schwartz, Stephen, 'The U.S. Nuclear Weapons Cost Study Project', Brookings Institute, 1 August 1998, www.brookings.edu

Sharkey, Joe, 'Reinventing the Suitcase by Adding the Wheel', *New York Times*, 4 October 2010

Sherman, Leonard, '"Blitzscaling" Is Choking Innovation – and Wasting Money', *Wired*, 7 November 2019

Shiller, Robert, *The New Financial Order*, Princeton University Press, New Jersey, 2003

—, *Narrative Economics: How Stories Go Viral and Drive Major Economic Events*, Princeton University Press, Princeton/Oxford, 2019

Skonieczna, Agnieszka and Castellano, Letizia, 'Gender Smart Financing: Investing In & With Women: Opportunities for Europe', European Commission Discussion Paper 129, July 2020

Smith, Michael, *Station X: The Codebreakers of Bletchley Park*, Channel 4 Books, London, 1998

Sommestad, Lena, *Från mejerska till mejerist: En studie av mejeriyrkets maskuliniseringsprocess* (*From Dairymaid to Dairyman: A Study of the Masculinisation of the Dairy Profession*), Arkiv Förlag, Stockholm, 1992

Standing, Guy, 'Global Feminization Through Flexible Labor: A Theme Revisited', *World Development*, vol. 27, no. 3, Elsevier, 1999

Stanley, Autumn, *Mothers and Daughters of Invention: Notes for a Revised History of Technology*, Scarecrow Press, London, 1993

St Clair, Kassia, *The Golden Thread: How Fabric Changed History*, John Murray Press, London, 2018

Stephens, Walter, *Demon Lovers: Witchcraft, Sex, and the Crisis of Beliefs*, University of Chicago Press, Chicago, 2002

Stockton, Nick, 'The Mind-Bending Physics of a Tennis Ball's Spin', *Wired*, 9 December 2015

Sussman, Charlotte, *Consuming Anxieties: Consumer Protest, Gender & British Slavery, 1713–1833*, Stanford University Press, Stanford, 2000

Swain, John, 'Witchcraft, Economy and Society in the Forest of Pendle', *The Lancashire Witches: Histories and Stories*, ed. Robert Poole, Manchester University Press, Manchester, 2002

Syed, Matthew, *Rebel Ideas: The Power of Diverse Thinking*, John Murray Press, London, 2019

Taleb, Nassim Nicholas, *The Black Swan: The Impact of the Highly Improbable* (Allen Lane, London, 2007)

—, *Antifragile: Things that Gain from Disorder*, Penguin Books, London, 2012

Tamilia, Robert, 'World's Fairs and the Department Store 1800s to 1930s', *Marketing History at the Center*, vol. 13, 2007

Tarlé, Eugene, *Bonaparte*, Knight Publications, New York, 1937

Tatler, 'Looking at Luggage', 25 January 1961

Temperton, James, 'The Gig Economy is Being Fuelled by Exploitation, Not Innovation', *Wired Opinion*, 8 February 2018

The Times, 'The Look of Luggage', 17 May 1956

UNSGSA, 2018, *Annual Report to the Secretary-General*, www.unsgsa.org

Van Cleaf, Kara, '"Of Woman Born" to Mommy Blogged: The Journey from the Personal as Political to the Personal as Commodity', *Women's Studies Quarterly,* vol. 43, no. 3/4, 2015

Vogel, Steven, *Why the Wheel is Round: Muscles, Technology and How We Make Things Move*, University of Chicago Press, Chicago, 2016

Wallace, David Foster, 'Roger Federer as Religious Experience', *String Theory: David Foster Wallace on Tennis*, Library of America, New York, 2016

Walter, Michael, 'Radiologists Earn $419K per Year, up 4% from 2018', *Radiology Business*, 11 April 2019

Webb, Michael, 'The Impact of Artificial Intelligence on the Labor Market', paper, Stanford University, 6 November 2019

Whitaker, Kati, 'Ghana Witch Camps: Widows' Lives in Exile', *BBC News*, 1 September 2012

Williams, Serena (with Daniel Paisner), *My Life: Queen of the Court*, Simon & Schuster, New York, 2009

Willis, Göran, *Charter till solen: När utlandssemestern blev ett folknöje* (*Charter to the Sun: When Holidaying Abroad Became a People's Pursuit*), Trafik-Nostalgiska Förlaget, Stockholm, 2015

Willson, Jackie, *Being Gorgeous: Feminism, Sexuality and the Pleasures of the Visual*, I B Tauris, London, 2014

Wilson, Terry P, *The Cart that Changed the World*, University of Oklahoma Press, Norman, 1978

Wissinger, Elizabeth A, *This Year's Model: Fashion, Media, and the Making of Glamour*, NYU Press, New York, 2015

World Bank Group, 'The Changing Nature of Work', World Development Report 2019

Yalom, Marilyn, *The Birth of the Chess Queen: A History*, Harper Perennial, New York, 2005

Zagorsky, Jay L, 'Do You Have to be Smart to be Rich? The Impact of IQ on Wealth, Income and Financial Distress', *Intelligence*, vol. 35, no. 5, 2007

Zarkadakis, George, *In Our Own Image: Will Artificial Intelligence Save or Destroy Us?*, Rider, London, 2015

Zhang, L, 'Fashioning the Feminine Self in "Prosumer Capitalism": Women's Work and the Transnational Reselling of Western Luxury Online', *Journal of Consumer Culture*, vol. 17, no. 2, 2017

Zimmeck, Meta, 'The Mysteries of the Typewriter: Technology and Gender in the British Civil Service, 1870–1914', *Women Workers and the Technological Change in Europe in the Nineteenth and Twentieth Centuries*, ed. Gertjan Groot and Marlou Schrover, Taylor & Francis, London, 1995

Zola, Émile, *Au Bonheur des Dames (The Ladies' Delight)*, trans. Robin Buss, Penguin Classics, London, 2001

Acknowledgements

First of all, I would like to thank my translator, Alex Fleming, for doing the difficult work of finding my voice in English. Translation must be a very hard task as it is, I can only assume it's even more difficult with an author like me who speaks fluent English as well as Swedish and therefore has opinions about everything.

I would like to thank my agent Tracy Bohan at Wylie Agency for being incredibly good at her job: it's a joy to watch. I'd also like to thank Caroline Criado-Perez for introducing me to Tracy.

I'd like to thank Arabella Pike at William Collins for believing in the project at an early stage and Grace Pengelly for all her hard work making the book a whole lot better.

I would like to thank Emma Ulvaeus, Simon Brouwers and Olle Grundin at Mondial in Stockholm for everything they did for the book. Torbjörn Nilsson has (as always) worked behind the scenes as an unofficial editor and been incredibly important to the project.

I am grateful to Kerstin Rännar and Margareta Machl for all your help in Västerås and for sharing your research material on Aina Wifalk with me. Thanks to Alexander Rath and Annika Pedersen at Skåne regional archive and to Sara Lagergren at the Swedish Labour movement's archive and Library. I would like to thank Juan Salinas for patiently

294

explaining car engines to me when I needed to know about cranks and Cecily Motley for helping me find a title for the book in English. I would also like to thank Mats Persson.

Joe Sharkey generously agreed to answer my questions on travel and rolling suitcases and my father, Waldemar Kielos, put in a heroic effort reading material on midwifery when I couldn't get it over to the UK during the chaos of the pandemic. Thanks to Elise Kielos for legal assistance and a special thanks to my mother Maria Kielos.

I would also like to thank everyone I work with at Dagens Nyheter, especially Pia Skagermark, Björn Wiman and Peter Wolodarski.

Finally: thank you to my family, who mean everything to me.

Index